Informatik – Fachberichte

Band 117: J. Röhrich, Parallele Systeme. XI, 152 Seiten. 1986.

Band 118: GWAI-85. 9th German Workshop on Artificial Intelligence. Dassel/Solling, September 1985. Edited by H. Stoyan. X, 471 pages. 1986.

Band 119: Graphik in Dokumenten. GI-Fachgespräch, Bremen, März 1986. Herausgegeben von F. Nake. X, 154 Seiten. 1986.

Band 120: Kognitive Aspekte der Mensch-Computer-Interaktion. Herausgegeben von G. Dirlich, C. Freksa, U. Schwatlo und K. Wimmer. VIII, 190 Seiten. 1986.

Band 121: K. Echtle, Fehlermaskierung durch verteilte Systeme. X, 232 Seiten. 1986.

Band 122: Ch. Habel, Prinzipien der Referentialität. Untersuchungen zur propositionalen Repräsentation von Wissen. X, 308 Seiten. 1986.

Band 123: Arbeit und Informationstechnik. GI-Fachtagung. Proceedings, 1986. Herausgegeben von K. T. Schröder. IX, 435 Seiten. 1986.

Band 124: GWAI-86 und 2. Österreichische Artificial-Intelligence-Tagung. Ottenstein/Niederösterreich, September 1986. Herausgegeben von C.-R. Rollinger und W. Horn. X, 360 Seiten. 1986.

Band 125: Mustererkennung 1986. 8. DAGM-Symposium, Paderborn, September/Oktober 1986. Herausgegeben von G. Hartmann. XII, 294 Seiten, 1986.

Band 126: GI-16. Jahrestagung. Informatik-Anwendungen – Trends und Perspektiven. Berlin, Oktober 1986. Herausgegeben von G. Hommel und S. Schindler. XVII, 703 Seiten. 1986.

Band 127: GI-17. Jahrestagung. Informatik-Anwendungen – Trends und Perspektiven. Berlin, Oktober 1986. Herausgegeben von G. Hommel und S. Schindler. XVII, 685 Seiten. 1986.

Band 128: W. Benn, Dynamische nicht-normalisierte Relationen und symbolische Bildbeschreibung. XIV, 153 Seiten. 1986.

Band 129: Informatik-Grundbildung in Schule und Beruf. GI-Fachtagung, Kaiserslautern, September/Oktober 1986. Herausgegeben von E. v. Puttkamer. XII, 486 Seiten. 1986.

Band 130: Kommunikation in Verteilten Systemen. GI/NTG-Fachtagung, Aachen, Februar 1987. Herausgegeben von N. Gerner und O. Spaniol. XII, 812 Seiten. 1987.

Band 131: W. Scherl, Bildanalyse allgemeiner Dokumente. XI, 205 Seiten. 1987.

Band 132: R. Studer, Konzepte für eine verteilte wissensbasierte Softwareproduktionsumgebung. XI, 272 Seiten. 1987.

Band 133: B. Freisleben, Mechanismen zur Synchronisation paralleler Prozesse. VIII, 357 Seiten. 1987.

Band 134: Organisation und Betrieb der verteilten Datenverarbeitung. 7. GI-Fachgespräch, München, März 1987. Herausgegeben von F. Peischl. VIII, 219 Seiten. 1987.

Band 135: A. Meier, Erweiterung relationaler Datenbanksysteme für technische Anwendungen. IV, 141 Seiten. 1987.

Band 136: Datenbanksysteme in Büro, Technik und Wissenschaft. GI-Fachtagung, Darmstadt, April 1987. Proceedings. Herausgegeben von H.-J. Schek und G. Schlageter. XII, 491 Seiten. 1987.

Band 137: D. Lienert, Die Konfigurierung modular aufgebauter Datenbanksysteme. IX, 214 Seiten. 1987.

Band 138: R. Männer, Entwurf und Realisierung eines Multiprozessors. Das System „Heidelberger POLYP". XI, 217 Seiten. 1987.

Band 139: M. Marhöfer, Fehlerdiagnose für Schaltnetze aus Modulen mit partiell injektiven Pfadfunktionen. XIII, 172 Seiten. 1987.

Band 140: H.-J. Wunderlich, Probabilistische Verfahren für den Test hochintegrierter Schaltungen. XII, 133 Seiten. 1987.

Band 141: E. G. Schukat-Talamazzini, Generierung von Worthypothesen in kontinuierlicher Sprache. XI, 142 Seiten. 1987.

Band 142: H.-J. Novak, Textgenerierung aus visuellen Daten: Beschreibungen von Straßenszenen. XII, 143 Seiten. 1987.

Band 143: R. R. Wagner, R. Traunmüller, H. C. Mayr (Hrsg.), Informationsbedarfsermittlung und -analyse für den Entwurf von Informationssystemen. Fachtagung EMISA, Linz, Juli 1987. VIII, 257 Seiten. 1987.

Band 144: H. Oberquelle, Sprachkonzepte für benutzergerechte Systeme. XI, 315 Seiten. 1987.

Band 145: K. Rothermel, Kommunikationskonzepte für verteilte transaktionsorientierte Systeme. XI, 224 Seiten. 1987.

Band 146: W. Damm, Entwurf und Verifikation mikroprogrammierter Rechnerarchitekturen. VIII, 327 Seiten. 1987.

Band 147: F. Belli, W. Görke (Hrsg.), Fehlertolerierende Rechensysteme / Fault-Tolerant Computing Systems. 3. Internationale GI/ITG/GMA-Fachtagung, Bremerhaven, September 1987. Proceedings. XI, 389 Seiten. 1987.

Band 148: F. Puppe, Diagnostisches Problemlösen mit Expertensystemen. IX, 257 Seiten. 1987.

Band 149: E. Paulus (Hrsg.), Mustererkennung 1987. 9. DAGM-Symposium, Braunschweig, Sept./Okt. 1987. Proceedings. XVII, 324 Seiten. 1987.

Band 150: J. Halin (Hrsg.), Simulationstechnik. 4. Symposium, Zürich, September 1987. Proceedings. XIV, 690 Seiten. 1987.

Band 151: E. Buchberger, J. Retti (Hrsg.), 3. Österreichische Artificial-Intelligence-Tagung. Wien, September 1987. Proceedings. VIII, 181 Seiten. 1987.

Band 152: K. Morik (Ed.), GWAI-87. 11th German Workshop on Artificial Intelligence. Geseke, Sept./Okt. 1987. Proceedings. XI, 405 Seiten. 1987.

Band 153: D. Meyer-Ebrecht (Hrsg.), ASST'87. 6. Aachener Symposium für Signaltheorie. Aachen, September 1987. Proceedings. XII, 390 Seiten. 1987.

Band 154: U. Herzog, M. Paterok (Hrsg.), Messung, Modellierung und Bewertung von Rechensystemen. 4. GI/ITG-Fachtagung, Erlangen, Sept./Okt. 1987. Proceedings. XI, 388 Seiten. 1987.

Band 155: W. Brauer, W. Wahlster (Hrsg.), Wissensbasierte Systeme. 2. Internationaler GI-Kongreß, München, Oktober 1987. XIV, 432 Seiten. 1987.

Band 156: M. Paul (Hrsg.), GI – 17. Jahrestagung. Computerintegrierter Arbeitsplatz im Büro. München, Oktober 1987. Proceedings. XIII, 934 Seiten. 1987.

Band 157: U. Mahn, Attributierte Grammatiken und Attributierungsalgorithmen. IX, 272 Seiten. 1988.

Band 158: G. Cyranek, A. Kachru, H. Kaiser (Hrsg.), Informatik und „Dritte Welt". X, 302 Seiten. 1988.

Band 159: Th. Christaller, H.-W. Hein, M. M. Richter (Hrsg.), Künstliche Intelligenz. Frühjahrsschulen, Dassel, 1985 und 1986. VII, 342 Seiten. 1988.

Band 160: H. Mächer, Fehlertolerante dezentrale Prozeßautomatisierung. XVI, 243 Seiten. 1987.

Band 161: P. Peinl, Synchronisation in zentralisierten Datenbanksystemen. XII, 227 Seiten. 1987.

Band 162: H. Stoyan (Hrsg.), Begründungsverwaltung. Proceedings, 1986. VII, 153 Seiten. 1988.

Informatik-Fachberichte 211

Herausgeber: W. Brauer
im Auftrag der Gesellschaft für Informatik (GI)

H. W. Meuer (Hrsg.)

SUPERCOMPUTER '89

Anwendungen, Architekturen, Trends
Seminar, Mannheim, 8.–10. Juni 1989
Proceedings

Springer-Verlag Berlin Heidelberg GmbH

Herausgeber

Hans W. Meuer
Universität Mannheim, Rechenzentrum
L15, 16, D-6800 Mannheim 1

Seminar SUPERCOMPUTER '89

Veranstalter:

Leitung:

H. W. Meuer, Mannheim
H.-M. Wacker, Oberpfaffenhofen

CR Subject Classification (1987): C.1.2, C.2.1, C.4, C.5.1, D.1.3, D.3.4, D.4.4, F.2.1, G.4, I.3.5, I.3.7, J.2, J.4, K.6.2

ISBN 978-3-540-51310-0 ISBN 978-3-642-74844-8 (eBook)
DOI: 10.1007/978-3-642-74844-8

UNIX ist ein eingetragenes Warenzeichen von AT & T.

2145/3140-543210 - Gedruckt auf säurefreiem Papier

Vorwort

Jährlich im Juni trifft sich in Mannheim die deutschsprachige Supercomputergemeinde zum Seminar "SUPERCOMPUTER - Anwendung, Architekturen und Trends". In diesem Jahr findet die vom Verein zur Förderung der wissenschaftlichen Weiterbildung an der Universität Mannheim e.V. veranstaltete Seminarreihe zum vierten Mal statt.

Die Situation auf dem Gebiet der Höchstleistungsrechner, mit weltweit ca. 400 installierten Systemen im Frühjahr 1989, läßt sich wie folgt charakterisieren:

- Nach Hitachi mit der S-820 Serie, die eine Spitzenleistung von 3 GFLOPS mit dem Modell-80 erreicht, hat kürzlich auch Fujitsu seine 2. Generation von Supercomputern, die VP-2000 Serie, angekündigt. Zwar wurde der Schritt zu MP-Systemen noch nicht vollzogen, jedoch ist evident, daß sich das jetzige Konzept der Dual-Skalar-Architektur mit einer annähernd 2 x 30 MFLOPS Skalarleistung und einer Spitzenleistung von 4 GFLOPS der Vektoreinheit zu einem MP-System erweitern läßt. Während die neue Hitachi-Serie bereits im Einsatz ist, werden die neuen Fujitsu-Supercomputer ab Ende 1989 in Japan und ab Mitte 1990 in Europa installiert werden.

- Bei Cray Research ist die Situation dadurch gekennzeichnet, daß der Firmengründer, Seymour Cray, bereits von der CRAY 4 spricht, die es 1992 auf eine Spitzenleistung von 128 GFLOPS bei 64 Prozessoren bringen soll, während überraschenderweise die CRAY 3 noch nicht angekündigt wurde. Möglicherweise wird die Ankündigung verzögert, um die sehr leistungsfähige CRAY YMP-Serie nicht mit Konkurrenz aus dem eigenen Hause zu belasten.

- Parallelrechner (im engeren Sinne) kennzeichnen die 3.Generation von Supercomputern nach Vektorrechnern (1.Generation) und MP-Vektorrechnern mit gemeinsamem Speicherkonzept (2.Generation). Allerdings ist noch kein Durchbruch mit solchen MIMD-Rechnern in der Praxis gelungen. Dieses ehrgeizige Ziel verfolgt die SUPRENUM GmbH mit ihrem Konzept hoher Parallelität und mittlerer Granularität sowie einer (konzeptionell) sehr flexiblen Kommunikationsstruktur. Das SUPRENUM-Konzept steht vor der Bewährungsprobe.

- Im vergangenen Jahr wurde ein skaliertes Amdahl-Gesetz, das sogenannte Gesetz von J. Gustafson, als Allheilmittel gegen die "Amdahl'sche Schranke", ins Feld geführt. Einer kritischen Analyse hält dieses Gesetz allerdings nicht stand.

- Zu den klassischen Supercomputer-Anwendungen sind eine ganze Reihe von Innovationen hinzugekommen, wie beispielsweise Drug Design und betriebswirtschaftliche Anwendungen. Diese Expansion dürfte für den über 30prozentigen Zuwachs neuer Supercomputerinstallationen seit einem Jahr mitverantwortlich sein.

Das diesjährige Seminar arbeitet alle diese Entwicklungen auf und versammelt wiederum Supercomputer-Anwender, -Betreiber, und -Hersteller zu einem fruchtbaren Dialog und Erfahrungsaustausch. Darüber hinaus sollen gerade denjenigen wertvolle Informationen geliefert werden, die in absehbarer Zeit einen Supercomputer einsetzen wollen bzw. als Entscheidungsträger und Planer für Informationsverarbeitung zuständig sind.

Neben den "Aktuellen Informationen" sind die Schwerpunkte des diesjährigen Seminars :

- Visualisierung / Mensch-Maschine-Schnittstelle
- Architekturen
- Streitgespräch über "Parallel Versus Vector Processing"
- Innovative Anwendungen

Alle Beiträge hierzu werden mit diesem Band schriftlich vorgelegt.

Abschließend möchte ich mich bei allen Referenten dieses Seminars bedanken. Ohne meine beiden wissenschaftlichen Hilfskräfte, Peter Vogel und Dirk Wenzel, hätte der Seminarband allerdings nicht in dieser einheitlichen Form rechtzeitig zum Seminar erscheinen können. Mit Hilfe des optischen Zeichenerkennungsprogramms AutoREAD® von I.S.T.C. Paris haben sie sich der mühsamen, aber erfolgreichen Vereinheitlichung der mit den verschiedensten Textsystemen erstellten Vorlagen unterzogen, wofür ich mich besonders herzlich bedanke.

Mannheim, im April 1989 Hans W. Meuer

Inhaltsverzeichnis

Innovative Anwendungen

Global Simulations on Vector and Parallel Supercomputers

Enrico Clementi

IBM Corporation, Data Systems Division
Dept. 48B/MS 428, Neighborhood Road
Kingston, NY 12401
USA

In the last forty years the computational community has witnessed the birth and evolution of computers, minicomputers, personal computers and supercomputers. However, all the available indications point to the expectation that we are only at the beginning of a new socio-economic era, where computing machines and signal processing machines will play a most determinant role. Ages are often classified in terms of some characteristic of its production tools; thus the *stone*, the *bronze*, the *iron* ages. As we know, "tools" enhance the dimension and the power of man; in the past the *physical* dimension, but today the *intellectual* and *mental* dimension. Clearly our age is the *computer* age (also referred to as the "information society"). A basic goal in science is to achieve universal understanding, thereby providing quantitative models for any specific event, as well as for all events in general. Engineering attempts to put this understanding to work in practical applications and realizations of ever increasing complexity and boldness. These goals and attempts have been with mankind since the beginning of our evolution but today seem to be more and more at hand. A turning point on the learning curve is the ability to perform "global simulations", which can be accomplished only if supercomputers are *extensively* available.

For some time we have been advocating the "*global simulation*" approach to computer simulations in science and engineering. The main idea is borrowed from history, exactly from the events leading England to the first industrial revolution, when *human-size* "assembly lines" were introduced, thus enormously increasing productivity per unit worker. In an "assembly line" one starts with simple raw materials and, step by step, without interruption, one transforms the raw materials into a more and more finished and complex product. Today we use *robot-size assembly lines* and this is sometimes referred to as the *second industrial revolution*; of course the basic concept remains the same. In the "global simulation model" we start with the most "simple" assumption that molecules are built up of point charge nuclei and electrons. With *quantum mechanics* we can then "assemble" simple molecules, or larger ones. With *statistical mechanics* we can consider many molecules at a given pressure and temperature, and consider trajectories involving time; finally for even larger systems we can use micro-dynamics and *fluid dynamics* where viscosity, transport coefficient, convection, turbulence, etc., can be analyzed. Of course all of this is well known at the theoretical level, but the novel aspect we have been stressing is *how to achieve this at the operational level* in such a way that the entire process is self-consistent for computer simulations.

Briefly stated, in the *global simulation* model we decompose a given problem into n *subproblems* each one corresponding to a submodel 1, ..., i, ...n. The operational rules are that the input needed in the submodel "i" is fully obtained as the output from submodel "i–1" and that the input for submodel "1" must be "very simple", in a computational sense. Thus the global simulation approach is an "*assembly line*" designed to increase our productivity in generating *information*.

Let us now consider in some detail the relationships between "*global simulation modelling*" and *productivity*; as it is known, the latter correlates both to *goods* and to *information*. The main evolution of productivity in human history is sketched in Fig.1. As any natural process, it follows an S–type "growth curve", and it is likely we are far from the saturation limit, assuming no catastrophic event.

The productivity of information *trails* the main phases of the productivity of goods; it is therefore not surprising that whereas production via assembly–lines has revolutionized industrial output since the early 1800s, the "global simulation" method is being intoduced *only* now. We recall that two conditions (market demand and the "tool", the automated loom) were essential for initiating a "revolution" in the textile and smelting industry. Equivalently, the need and the demand of inter–disciplinarity in information, essential to avoid expensive errors in our highly technical (and thus risk–prone) society, had to wait for the appropriate tool – the supercomputer – before we could set up an "*assembly–line" for information* namely *the "global simulation" approach*.

The advances in material sciences, brain research, networking, signal processing, cybernetics, and artificial intelligence are sufficiently reliable pointers for confidently predecting intelligent robots for productivity of goods and "intelligent" supercomputers for productivity of information (see Fig.1). Again, "*intelligent robots*" are expected to occur before "*intelligent supercomputers*"; we recall that intelligent robots are essentially at hand. An intelligent supercomputer, in our context, is an engine of one to a few gigaflops sustained performance, (thus with much higher peak performance, up to about a few hundred gigaflops) and with the attributes to "hear", "talk", and – within the limit of expert systems – "understand" some extremely rudimental language, and to "see", "display" and "understand" a few two–dimensional patterns, like digits and logical–mathematical symbols. We recall that pattern and voice recognition and artificial intelligence are most definitely capable – today – of these tasks, which could notably increase the user friendliness of computer systems and thus enhance the user's productivity. An ICAP/3090 (see IBM System Journal, December, 1988) could become the low entry point of intelligent supercomputer; the SSI could be one of the first intelligent supercomputer, even if it will start only as a very, very fast computer. Indeed we recall that an ICAP/3090 with 24 nodes (four clusters of IBM–3090/600) would exhibit a peak performance of about 3 gigaflops; the same architecture and software with a faster cycle time would yield a notable performance increase. In the 11 years between today and the end of this century we can expect up to three "new" generations with a performance increase of up to a factor of three each time; thus one would expect to reach a peak performance of the order of 0.X teraflops. Thus, our forecast of an "intelligent" supercomputer within this century is not unreasonable.

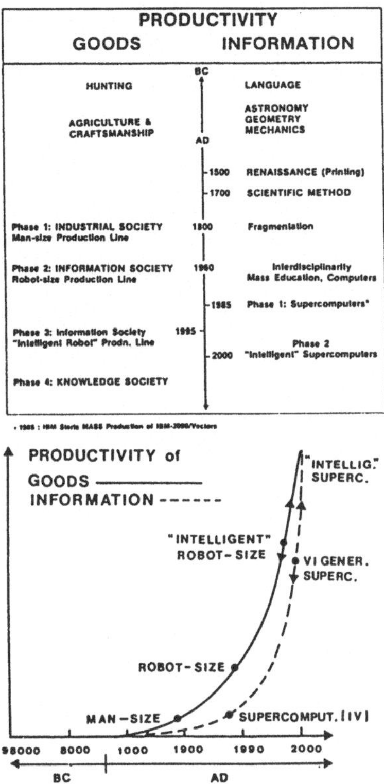

Figure 1. Sketch of some aspects of Productivity's evolution. "Landmark dates" for productivity of goods *and* information are drawn onto the time axis.

In Fig. 2 we provide the speed–up obtained with an ICAP/3090 parallel supercomputer consisting of three IBM–3090/400s and two IBM–3090/200s yielding a total of 16 nodes. The computations at the top refer to a quantum chemistry code we used to obtain the wave function for an 87–atom fragment of DNA with 408 electrons. At the top of Fig. 2 we show the CPU–intensive operation (integrals generation), and at the bottom we present the I/O–intensive operation (the self–consistent field, which reads an integral file of 0.67 GByte 13 times).The elapsed time for the integral generation is 18.92 minutes and the elapsed time for the SCF part is 28.01 minutes. This total of 46.93 minutes can be reduced substantially (to about 20 minutes) by keeping the integral in the extended storage which, for four IBM–3090/400s or four IBM–3090/600s, is up to 8 GBytes.

Unfortunatelly, few people realize the enormous impact such tools will have on our society and our way of life ! Increasing the productivity of information via the "global simulation approach" could bring about conditions such that, for the first time in human history, we could have "productivity of information" preceding rather than trailing the "productivity of goods". This reversal, if properly exploited, could bring about the upgrading from "information" society into "knowledge" society. At the same time one should not underestimate the difficulty and cost for this type of initiative.

A (CPU Intensive)

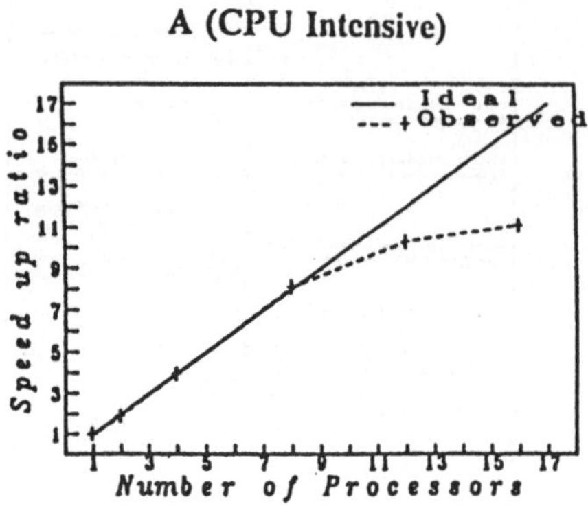

B (I/O Intensive)

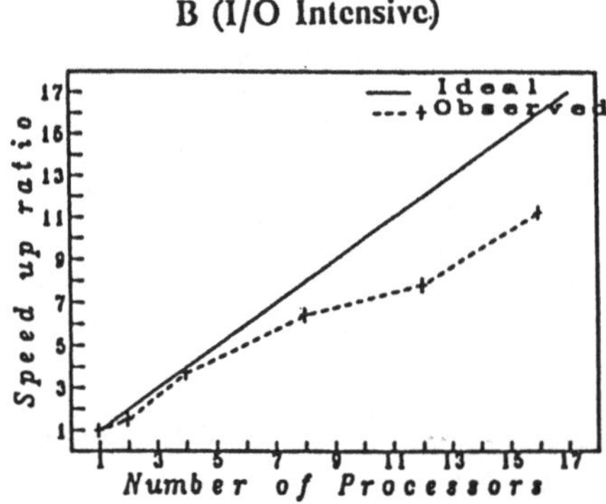

Figure 2. (TOP) *Operation*: Computes and writes file(s) of 0.67 GByte on 1 to 16 3380 Disk(s); (BOTTOM) *Operation*: Reads and processes 13 times the file(s) (see TOP) generating the Fock-matrix.

Summarizing, there have been two main industrial revolutions (productivity of goods), the man-size assembly line and the robot-size assembly line, and we are now moving toward the intelligent-robot-size assembly line, the third stage. In a similar way we have the global simulation approach on the IV generation supercomputers; but we expect to have much more powerful computers of the SSI family (VI generation computers) and finally intelligent supercomputers, the knowledge-engine based designs which have been referred to as V generation computers. (Note that it is not too surprising to expect the VI generation computers to appear before the "V generation": the latter are based on very far reaching and novel concepts and this takes much time, more than "speeding up" today's supercomputer.)

The three stages in the productivity of goods and of information bring about necessarily three stages in the evolution of the computer's applications. *The first stage* can be called "Computerization of simulation", and it corresponds simply to replacing "hand" computation with computer computation. In the early 1920s Richardson - the father of modern meteorology - envisioned a system of hundreds of humans properly positioned in a large and specially built room with the task of hand computing the numerical equation governing weather changes. Well, *the first stage* is to use a supercomputer for the task envisioned by Richardson ! In chemistry, programs like GaussianXX, HONDO, KGNMOL, CHARMm, etc., are other examples. Codes like NEKTON and FIDAP are equivalent examples in fluid dynamics. But this first stage is rapidly coming to an end.

The *second stage* is due to the realization that we can have "global simulations", as explained above. This stage can be called "*Modelling within a simulation environment*" and above we mentioned the "environment of mechanics" - from quantum, to statistical, to fluid dynamics as an example. But most modern and comlex undertakings, from space-stations to human genome, to sea-oil-exploration etc., are additional examples.

The second stage is like evolving from mechanization (man-size assembly lines) into robot assembly lines. Each industy has its own "environment", thus each industry should have its own specifically tailored modelling. This is done today only in the space industry and a few more where large "libraries" of programs are collected, updated and maintained, and this type of work is realized to be a major activity, not simply a service. The concept however has not broadly penetrated the computational field. MOTECC-89 is a first attempt in "Modelling within a simulation environment".

It is foreseen that the second stage will bring about necessarily the *third one*, namely modelling within a given environment but with models which have artificial intelligence both to improve the use of the model and to have *dynamical* feedback, error corrections, etc. This third stage can be called "intelligent simulation" or - more kindly - "*knowledge based simulation*". It is equivalent to an assembly line with "intelligent robots" rather than simple robots. Scientific Engineering is the initial field to fill the impact of this evolution. But business, banks and other commercial activities will soon follow on this pattern.

Our plan for MOTECC-89 is to reach the second stage in 1989 and we look forward to MOTECC-90 where we shall reach the third stage.

In Fig.3 we illustrate this evolution for computer applications, indicating its historical basis first in the productivity of goods and then of information via computers and, finally, its implications for computer applications. A *posteriori* this evolution in computer applications is very obvious, but let us recall that most of today's applications are still at the *computerization level.*

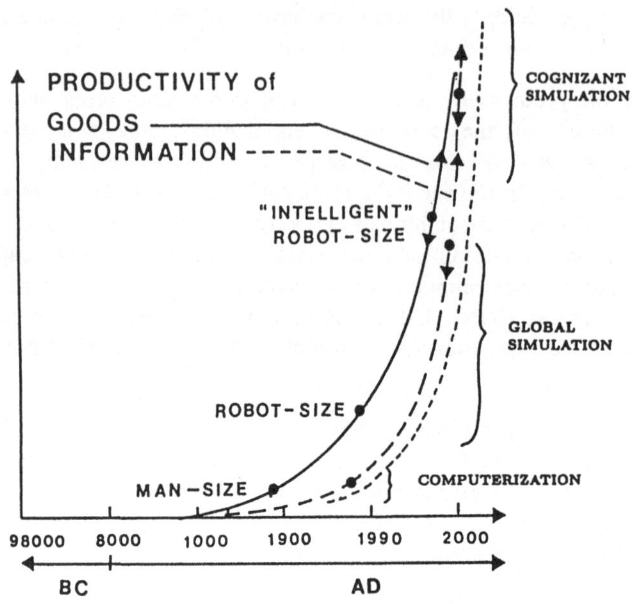

Figure 3. Evolution of computer applications

Let us discuss in some detail what MOTECC-89 will contain. This ensemble of application packages has been previously discussed [1] and is schematically shown in Fig.4.

The assembly line starts with quantum mechanics. At the atomic level we consider three types of packages: the ATOMIC SCF program [2], a Dirac-Fock program [3], and a correlation program [4]. The ATOMIC SCF can use spherical Slater or spherical Gaussian basis sets, and the latter can be either contracted or uncontracted. A third type basis set is Cartesian-Gaussian. The Dirac-Fock program is a recent one and has been written for Gaussian basis sets, particularly for the geometrical basis sets with the same number of basis functions for the large and small components connected by "kinetic balance" [5]. The data thus far obtained for closed and open shell [3] atoms from Z = 2 to Z = 86 indicate excellent agreement with other numerical computations [6].

For correlated functions we are considering both an *ab initio* and empirical approach. The latter consits of a Coulomb hole generated by the introduction of an operator $e^{-\eta_{ij} r_{12}^2}$ where r_{12} is the inter-electronic distance and η_{ij} is an empirical parameter which varies for various symmetry species (s and p orbitals, for example).

This empirical approach yields tables of pair correlation energies which can be used, for example, in predicting atomic ionization potentials or atomic electron affinities [4]. A ful configuration interaction program developed over the past year at Okkaido University will eventually be added, thus making possible the computation of correlated wave functions for atoms.

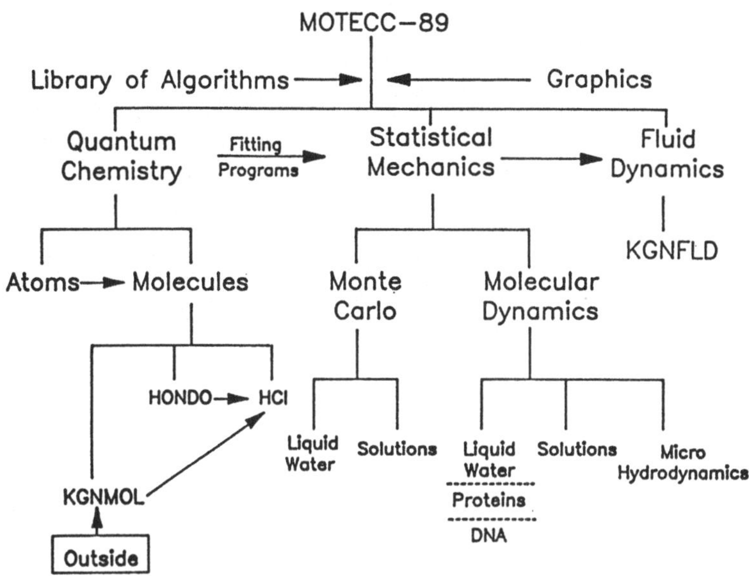

Figure 4. Library of application programs in MOTECC–89

The quantum mechanical molecular packages are essntially: KGNHYCOIN, KGNMOL, and HONDO. The first one is for very high accuracy functions of Hylleraas-type Configuration Interaction [7],[8],[9]. It has been used [10],[11] for H_2, H_3^+ and HeH^+ and can be used for any geometry. The basis set is of Gaussian type. This package should be used only for systems with few electrons, since it is extremely heavy computationally. KGNMOL [12] (previously IBMOL) and HONDO [13] are known molecular programs. The former is especially designed for computation of energy surfaces resulting from the interaction of two molecules. It has an SCF package (open and closed shells) and it can (1) estimate the correlation correction using the atomic table of empirical pair correlation energies, (2) compute the dispersion interaction energy following K. Szalewicz and B. Jeziorski [14], and (3) compute the MP2 energy following HONDO. The HONDO package [13] contains SCF, MP2, MP4, MCSCF, CI, gradient, geometry optimization programs, and special features like packages to compute hyperpolarizability. Both programs have been deposited with QCPE (Quantum Chemistry Program Exchange, University of Indiana, Bloomington, Indiana).

As we know, the operational "link" between quantum mechanics and statistical mechanics is provided by *ab initio* interaction potentials. MOTECC–89 has a standard package to obtain intermolecular potentials (pair–wise) from an optimal fit of the *ab initio* interaction energies as obtained, for example, from KGNMOL or HONDO. These potentials have different degrees of reliability; one factor influencing reliability is the number of *ab initio* computations which are performed to obtain the pair potentials. Clearly, the number of *ab initio* energies must be equal to the number of parameters (in the potential) times a factor which is about equal to ten. For the systems considered [15]–[19] (water, selected ions, amino acid residues, and those fragments needed to built up nucleic acids and membranes) the number of *ab initio* computations needed is extremely high and by now is over the 10.000 mark. The second factor is the quality of the *ab initio* computation. Historically we started with small basis sets (7s, 3p for Li $\rightarrow$ Ne); we then added superposition corrections and extended basis set to double-ζ plus polarization and, finally, we added correlation corrections either by computing dispersion correction or by MP2 corrections. For very accurate potentials we have also used extensive CI calculations, like in the case of the water–water interaction. For water, we have also 3– and 4–body interaction potentials which are, however, very expensive in terms of computer time if included in M.C. or M.D. simulations. For this reason we have recently changed the form of the 2–body potential, the so–called MCY potential, and we have introduced explicitly a polarization term which depends on the field of the surrounding molecules. Therefore, this potential automatically includes part of the many–body corrections [20].

These interaction potentials can be used either in Monte Carlo or Molecular Dynamics techniques. Both types of package are part of MOTECC. The integrators for M.D. include the Verlet algorithm and the Gear–predictor–corrector; corrections for the finite box size, as Ewalds sums are also included. Finally, special packages for the computation of free–energy are available, both at the Monte Carlo and the Molecular Dynamics levels.

A possible link between the size of the system we can study with M.D. (or M.C.) and those we can study with fluid dynamics is provided by microdynamics. Here we use M.D., but for a non–equilibrium system, with flow and/or temperature differential, etc. With Newton equations and the molecular dynamics of open systems we can study the flow of fluids in pipes, with or without obstruction [21]–[24], with different types of boundaries, with different densities [25], with or without temperature differentials between different size of boundaries [26]. A program which allows this type of numerical experimentation is included in MOTECC–89.

Fluid dynamics is basic to the understanding of chemical processes such as stirring in a reaction vessel, or the overall thermodynamic cycle of a chemical factory. MOTECC–89 incorporates a fluid flow program based on the p–version of finite elements [27].

The p–version of finite elements was originally developed for adaptive computations; the approach is to increase the order of the polynomials in a region where greater accuracy is required, as opposed to the traditional h–version that uses a finer grid where higher accuracy is required. However, an additional benefit of the p–version is that it gives rise to nested matrices, which allows the use of a novel multilevel iteration scheme for rapid solution of the matrix equations. In addition to the multilevel solution method, a direct solution technique is also available in the fluid flow program.

Two extensions are considered: one is the use of cellular automata for fluid flow computations where a grid of cells with very simple sampling rules can simulate two–dimensional fluid flow. The problem with the use of this approach for the three–dimensional problems are discussed in the extended theoretical documentation which is part of MOTECC–89. A second line of extension is the use of a finite element approach to compute Hartree–Fock functions for atoms.

Thus we have come full circle, starting with nuclei and electrons and concluding again with nuclei and electrons.

Today, computational output necessarily includes graphics. Indeed, often the amount of data to be presented is extremely large and therefore requires a graphic form of expression. Graphics can also provide information which is very difficult to express in any other form - this is especially true in animation, namely time-dependent graphics. Another use would be on-line graphics, where the user interacts with the system and uses graphics as the major language. MOTECC-89 has graphic interfacing with quantum chemistry, molecular dynamics, microdynamics and fluid dynamics. More details can be obtained in Ref.28.

References

[1] E. Clementi, S. Chin, G. Corongiu, J.H. Detrich, M. Dupuis, D. Folsom, G.C. Lie, D. Logan and V. Sonnad in *Biological and Artificial Intelligence Systems*, E. Clementi and S. Chin, Eds., ESCOM Science Publishers, The Netherlands, 319 (1988)

[2] B. Roos, C. Salez, A. Veillard and E. Clementi, IBM Technical Report RJ578 (1968)

[3] A.K. Mohanty and E. Clementi, Chem. Phys. Lett. (submitted 1989)

[4] S. Chakravorty and E. Clementi, Phys. Rev. A. (to appear March, 1989)

[5] E. Clementi and G. Corongiu, Chem.Phys. Lett., **90**, 359 (1982)

[6] I.P. Grant, B.J. McKenzie, P.H. Norrington, D.F. Mayers, N.C. Pyper, Comp. Phys. Comm., **21**, 207 (1980), J.P. Desclaux, At. Data Nucl. Data Tables, **12**, 311 (1973)

[7] A. Largo-Cabrerizo and E. Clementi, J. Comp. Chem., **8**, 1191 (1987)

[8] A. Largo-Cabrerizo, C. Urdaneta, G.C. Lie and E. Clementi, Int. J. Quant. Chem.: Quantum Chem. Symp. , **21**, 677 (1987)

[9] D. Frye, G.C. Lie and E. Clementi, IBM-Kingston Tech. Rep. KGN-180 (1989).

[10] C. Urdaneta, A. Largo-Cabrerizo, J. Lievvin, G.C. Lie and E. Clementi, J. Chem. Phys., **88**, 2091 (1988).

[11] D. Frye, G.C. Lie and E. Clementi, IBM-Kingston Tech. Rep. KGN-176 (1989).

[12] R. Gomperts and E. Clementi, IBM Research Report KGN-118 (1987); Q.C.P.E. Program Number 538.

[13] M. Dupuis, J.D. Watts, H.O. Villar, G.J.B. Hurst, IBM Research Report KGN-169 (1988); Q.C.P.E. Program Number 544; M. Dupuis and P. Mougenot, this volume.

[14] K. Szalewicz and B. Jeziorski, MOL. Phys., **38**, 191 (1979).

[15] O. Matsuoka, E. Clementi and M. Yoshimine, J. Chem. Phys., **64**, 1351 (1976).

[16] E. Clementi, F. Cavallone and R. Scordamaglia, J Am. Chem. Soc., **99**, 5531 (1977).

[17] E. K. Sagarik, G. Corogiu and E. Clementi (to be published); R. Scordamaglia, F. Cavallone and E. Clementi, J Am. Chem. Soc., **99**, 5545 (1977).

[18] E. J.A. Sordo, M. Probst, S. Chin, G. Corongiu and E. Clementi, in *Structure & Dynamics of Nucleic Acids, Proteins & Membranes*, E. Clementi and S. Chin, Eds., Plenum Publishers, New York, 89 (1986); J.A. Sordo, S. Chin and E. Clementi, J Am. Chem. Soc., **109**, 1702 (1987).

[19] E. M. Aida, G. Corongiu and E. Clementi, (to be published).

[20] E. U. Nieser, G. Corongiu and E. Clementi, Int. J. Quant. Chem. (to be submitted).

[21] E. L. Hannon, G.C. Lie and E. Clementi, Phys. Lett. A., **119**, 174 (1986).

[22] E. D.C. Rapaport and E. Clementi, Phys. Rev. Lett., **57**, 695 (1986).

[23] E. L. Hannon, G.C. Lie and E. Clementi, J. Sci. Computing, **1**, 145 (1986).

[24] E. L. Hannon, G.C. Lie and E. Clementi, J. Stat. Phys., **51**, 965 (1988).

[25] E. D.K. Bhattacharya and G.C. Lie, Phys. Rev. Lett., **62**, 897 (1989).

[26] E. D.K. Bhattacharya, G.C. Lie and E. Clementi, in *Proceedings of the 4th Intl. Conf. on Supercomputing*, L.P. Kartashev and S.I. Kartashev, Eds., International Supercomputing Institute, Inc., St. Petersburg, Florida (in press, 1989).

[27] E. V. Sonnad, S. Hassanzadeh and S. Foresti, in *Proceedings of the 4th Intl. Conf. on Supercomputing*, L.P. Kartashev and S.I. Kartashev, Eds., International Supercomputing Institute, Inc., St. Petersburg, Florida (in press, 1989).

[28] E. S. Chin, D.P. Vercauteren, D. Vanderveken, R. Scateni and E. Clementi, in *Proceedings of the 4th Intl. Conf. on Supercomputing*, L.P. Kartashev and S.I. Kartashev, Eds., International Supercomputing Institute, Inc., St. Petersburg, Florida (in press, 1989).

Distributed Supercomputing for Graphics Applications: A Case Study on an Implementation of the Radiosity Approach

Jose Encarnacao, Georg Köberle, Ning Zhang*)

ZGDV (Computer Graphics Center)
Wilhelminenstr. 7
D-6100 Darmstadt
Federal Republic of Germany

Abstract

Besides the ray tracing technique, the radiosity method is another major approach for global illumination modeling in the field of computer graphics. Since this method needs a huge amount of storage space (both memory and disk) and a long pre-computation cycle, it is not suitable to implement it on conventional workstations, so therefore that supercomputers are necessary for such kind of graphics applications.

However, some problems appeared due to the integration of supercomputers and workstations in a distributive computing environment, especially for graphics application.
The major problems are

- unavailability of standard higher-level mechanism for building distributed application
- transparent access to supercomputers without remote login or file transfer sessions
- computation balance to make the best use of the performance of supercomputers and workstations
- data transfer/storage strategy between supercomputers and workstations
- conflict between interaction and response time for graphics application

In this paper we suggest our solutions to the above mentioned problems based on the remote procedure call (RPC) and the client/server model, for the radiosity package implementation. After the introduction of the radiosity method, we concentrate on the principle, strategy and solution of the integration between supercomputers and workstations. We also convey some general issues related to distributed computing and present our experience of the implementation, such as the application protocol definition, error recovery, code debugging etc. The radiosity package has been implemented at ZGDV in Darmstadt in a network environment including a Multiflow TRACE 7/300 supercomputer and a lot of VAX and SUN workstations.

*) Permanent address: Institute of Artificial Intelligence, Zhejiang University, Hangzhou, P.R.China

1. Introduction

The mode of computing has changed quickly since the last decade. The performance of computer systems has also been improved greatly by the latest technology. Distributed computing based on network technology has been recognized as advantageous, compared to the traditional batch job oriented or time sharing based computing environments. In addition workstations play a major role in such kind of distributed environment. However, for the purpose of computing intensive applications, such as complex graphics applications, conventional workstations have their inherent limitations of storage capability, calculation speed etc. Therefore, supercomputers are necessary for such kinds of applications.

Network technology, which makes resource sharing possible, plays a key role in a distributed computing environment. However, in a network environment including supercomputers and workstations for graphics applications, the integration approach of supercomputers and workstations will determine the style of users' access to supercomputers from workstations. Although there are many methods for this purpose, the interactivity is one of the most important things for graphics applications, and it should make best use of the abilities of supercomputers and workstations.

The problem of interconnection between supercomputers and workstations is also very critical for graphics applications. Current commercially available network systems, such as Ethernet, Token Ring etc. have their limitations as far as transmission speed, throughput etc. are concerned. But some typical graphics applications (such as the radiosity algorithm) generate huge amount of data for visualization. The problem now is how to balance the computation performed on a supercomputer and a workstation and how to avoid the transfer of a huge amount of data via network which influences the effectiveness and efficiency of such interconnection.

This paper gives our solution and experience of implementing the radiosity package in a distributed environment including supercomputers and workstations. In section 2, we give an introduction of the radiosity method and point out the necessity of supercomputing for the implementation. In section 3, we discuss the load sharing method for distributed computation and the basic requirement for the method. In section 4, based on the RPC (remote procedure call) and the client/server model, we present our strategy and solution of load sharing for the radiosity package implementation.

2. The Radiosity Method

In the field of computer image synthesis, there are two major kind of methods nowadays used for global illumination modeling. The first one is well known as the ray tracing technique [1]. The other one is called the radiosity method.

The radiosity method was first developed within the field of radiative heat transfer for calculating heat exchange between surface in an enclosure environment, such as a spacecraft. The method was delivered in 1981. In 1984, D. Greenberg and his students of Cornell University, USA, presented the first attempt to use the radiosity method in computer graphics [2].

The primary motivation in using this new method in realistic image synthesis is to simulate the interreflection effects (such as complex soft shadows, color–bleeding, etc.) between surfaces in an environment. These effeets cannot be obtained by the conventional ray tracing method. By investigating the radiosity method, a correct result for the ambient part in the illumination model, which is omitted or considered as a constant by the conventional ray tracing method, can be obtained.

The theoretical foundation of the radiosity method relies on the principle of the conservation of energy. Therefore, an environment which can be processed by the radiosity method should be an enclosed one, i.e. there is no energy exchange with other objects which are not included in the environment. An external light source is assumed as a virtual surface with light emission. For image synthesis purpose, one assumption is that the light energy residing in the environment does not change into other kinds of energy, and vice versa. Another important assumption is that each surface in the environment is an ideal Lambertian surface, i.e. at any given point on the surface, there is an equal emission intensity in all directions. It should be pointed out that the energy arriving at one point of a surface may come from any direction with any distribution. To solve this problem with point sample methods such as ray tracing is very difficult. That is the reason why the radiosity method was developed.

Based on the above mentioned assumptions, we can say that the total energy leaving a surface (i.e. the radiosity of a surface which is used to generate the final images) includes two parts. The first part is the emission energy by the surface itself. The second part is the light reflected by the surface and depends on the reflective property of the surface material and the sum of the whole light arriving from other light sources and reflecting surfaces in the environment.

Omitting the deduction, we get a series of simultaneous equations in the form of

$$\begin{bmatrix} 1-\rho_1 F_{11} & -\rho_1 F_{21} & \cdots & -\rho_1 F_{n1} \\ -\rho_2 F_{12} & 1-\rho_2 F_{22} & \cdots & -\rho_2 F_{n2} \\ \cdots & \cdots & \cdots & \cdots \\ -\rho_n F_{1n} & -\rho_n F_{2n} & \cdots & 1-\rho_n F_{nn} \end{bmatrix} \begin{bmatrix} b_1 \\ b_2 \\ \cdot\cdot \\ b_n \end{bmatrix} = \begin{bmatrix} e_1 \\ e_2 \\ \cdot\cdot \\ e_n \end{bmatrix}$$

In the above equations, n is the number of surfaces in the environment. b_i is the radiosity, ρ_i is the reflective factor and e_i, is the emission of surface i. F_{ij} is called the form–factor in radiosity, and is the factor for describing the fraction of energy leaving surface i and arriving at surface j.

To get a more accurate image of an environment, each surface should be discretized (or subdivided) into a lot of small patches. All the surfaces in the above mentioned equations should be replaced by these smaller patches. Since the number of patches may be very large, the equation group becomes very large ($n*n$ degree). But it is very fortunate that this equation group can be solved efficiently through a Gauss–Seidel iterative technique. If all b_i are known, we can get an image by a simple, fast Z–buffer algorithm. e_i and ρ_i are constant to a given environment at a specific moment. Thus, we have to know F_{ij} , the form–factors.

The form–factor calculation is the most intensive part of the radiosity approach as far as computation is concerned. It needs $O(n*n)$ memory space and has $O(n*n)$ time complexity. The form–factors describe the direct energy exchange between two discrete surface patches. The calculation of the form–factor between each pair of patches is some like solving a hidden surface problem and furthermore the calculation uses a special version of Sutherland–Hodgman clipping algorithm [3], [4].

If the radiosity gradient changes too much between two adjacent patches, (for example sharp shadow areas), these patches should be subdivided. But this results in more calculation time and memory consumption. To solve this problem with less computation cost, a two–level adaptive subdivision approach is used, i.e. subdividing these patches into smaller patches called elements which only receive energy. The patches act as light sources and they also receive energy. (Some details will be described in the following paragraphs).

The radiosity algorithm consists of five major parts. The first part is to build the description file of an enclosure environment and to create the internal data structure for each surface in the enclosure for further processing. This internal data structure is actually an octree. First an octree in which each leaf node is called a patch is created. Then for each patch it creates a sub octree in which each leaf node is called an element. This part is neither time nor space consuming. The environment is created by a solid modeling software and then is subdivided by a post–processing program.

The second step is to calculate the form–factor between each pair of patches and elements in the enclosure. This is the most time and space consuming part. In fact, this part is a loop for each element in the enclosure environment:

```
for (each element in the environment) do
    for (each patch in the environment) do
        calculate the form-factor
            between the patch and the element
```

The form–factor calculation uses a special version of a 3D Sutherland–Hodgman clipping and a Z–buffer algorithm. If there are m patches and n elements in the enclosure (generally, m is much less than n), one needs $O(m*m + m*n)$ memory space to store the form–factors; the time complexity is also $O(m*m + m*n)$.

The third part is to get the color intensity of each patch or element. First we have to solve a $m*m$ degree linear equation group (which is diagonally dominant and can be solved by the Gauss–Seidel iteration method) for the color intensity for each patch. For the RGB color model, the equations should be solved three times, but for spectral color model, it should be solved for each sampled spectrum. The current algorithm implementation uses the RGB model, so it needs less space and is less time consuming.

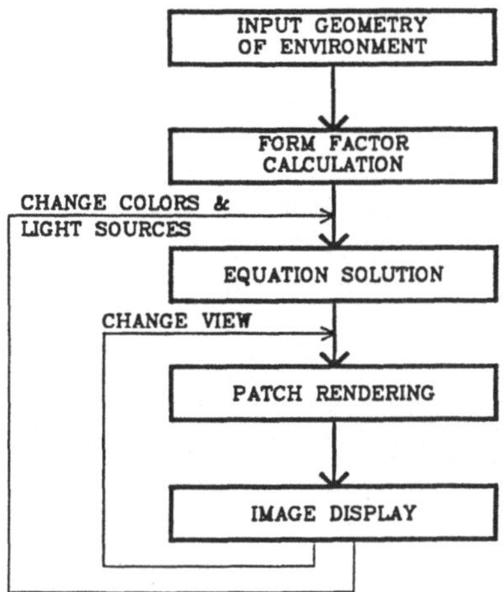

Figure 1: The Flow Diagram of the Radiosity Method

After the color intensity of each patch is known, then the color intensity of each element needs to be derived. At this moment, each patch acts as a light source and the intensity of each element is determined by these patch lighting and the pre-calculated form-factors between each pair of an element and a patch. Following the prosess described before, the transformation from the intensity of patches and elements to that of vertices of patches and elements in the octree are performed. Then these vertices are connected into a lot of polygons according the vertex connectivity.

The final step is to display these polygon with Gouraud shading by a Z-buffer algorithm. It includes coordinate projection and polygon scan-conversion.

The wireframe modeling of the environment can be done on the local workstation. This include the selection of the eye position. The color selection can also be done on the local workstation. Many high performance workstations have the capability of Gouraud shading and Z-buffer. So the display part can be performed on local workstation.

The radiosity method differs very much from ray tracing. Ray tracing is view-dependent and based on point sample.This means that the image should be re-calculated if the view point is changed and no object space coherence is used. The radiosity method calculate the color intensity for each surface and the form-factors are constants in a static environment. It couples with the benefits of object space coherence and view-independence. Its computational cost does not heavily depend on the number of light sources and the image resolution. It allows for rapid image sequences to be generated for a static environment with the current workstation technology.

Besides the above mentioned advantages, the radiosity method can get correct diffuse interreflection including color-bleeding and complex soft shadow effects. The method has the ability to change colors and lighting without heavy computation. Finally it is also a good pre-process for ray tracing methods.

The radiosity method also has some disadvantages. It needs a huge amount of memory space and a long computation cycle for form-factors. It is not suitable to simulate the environment including much specular highlights, specular reflections, refractions and sharp shadows, i.e. these effects can be more easily obtained by a ray tracing algorithm. Therefore the combination of the radiosity method and ray tracing algorithm is efficient and has been done by some researchers in Cornell University [5] and Zhejiang University [6].

Figure 2: A Picture Generated by the Radiosity Method

As pointed out before, the most heavy computation is necessary for the calculation of form-factor. It needs a huge amount of storage space (both disk and memory) and spends very long time. For example, to generate the picture shown in Figure 2, it spends 11 CPU hours on VAX-11/750 (with FPU) and produces 4 MB data for form-factors. Therefore, supercomputers are necessary for such kind of graphics applications.

3.The Load Sharing Concept

The most important advantage of a distributed computing environment is the posibility for various resources which are shared between different computers [8]. The network includes the computational resource, such as high-performance processors, the input/output resource, such as mass storage, printers, graphics workstations, and the software resource such as special-purpose programs.

In a distributed computing environment including supercomputers and workstations, different computing equipments play different roles. Supercomputers with their "number-crunching" power are mainly used as servers for calculation intensive applications. On the other hand, workstations with good human-machine interface perform less computation sensitive tasks, including graphics displaying. Thus, workstations very often act as the front-end of supercomputers.

Traditional batch job oriented or time sharing based computation are widely used in the computing environment including supercomputers. There are two methods for an application to take advantage of supercomputers. One is to implement the application totally on supercomputers and often this is referenced as the host-terminal based computing. This method does not take any advantage of network technology in a distributed environment. The other one is to separate an application into different tasks and run the most heavy computation parts on supercomputers. Based on this method, a user should prepare some data files on the local workstation, transfer them to the supercomputer and run the computation intensive task there, and then take back the results which are normally stored in some files. This method makes use of the capabilities of a workstation and is much better than the host-terminal computing. However, there are still some shortcomings. First, each user should be granted an account on each system. The user should understand the operation, command language etc. of each system involved. Second, the user should take a lot of time for executing remote login and file transfer sessions to access remote facilities and these sessions are all done manually. Finally, very often a user does only access some specific services rather than the whole facilities provided by the remote system because the user can do most tasks on the local workstation.

Thus, the transparent access of remote facility should be provided in a distributed computation environment. Although many systems have provided tools to simplify the remote access, for example, rsh (remote execute), rcp (remote copy) and rdist (remote distribution) etc. which make the network access easier in the 4BSD UNIX systems. But these tools are not sufficient by the means of transparent access, especially in a heterogeneous environment including many different architectures. Figure 3 shows the load sharing concept based on the principle of transparent access and resource sharing, where an application could be viewed virtually as the combination of many interactive parts and computation intensive parts.

In order to take advantage of resource sharing as far as an application is concerned, the first step is to separate the original algorithm into several tasks. A supercomputer can provide very powerful "number crunching" capability and a workstation has the sufficient performance in man-machine interaction. So the separation should focus on the reformulation of interaction part and computation part in a computation sensitive application. Such kind of separation is very similar to the concept used in UIMS (user interface management systems) and sometimes it is not very easy because of complex semantics and contexts.

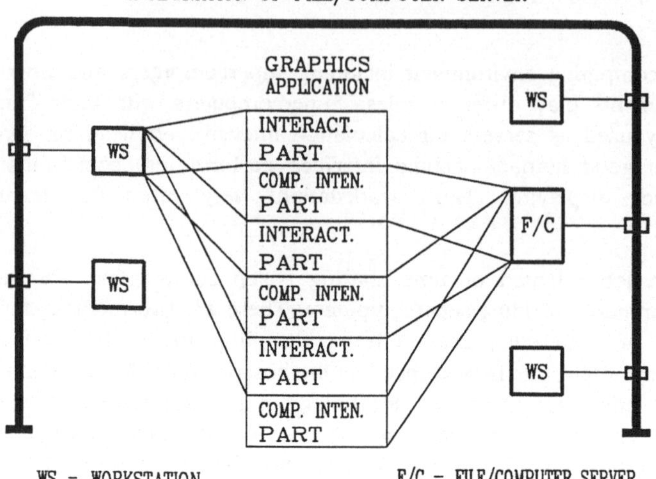

Figure 3: The Load Sharing Concept

Another problem for load sharing is the network traffic. Nowadays, the comercially available network systems, such as Ethernet, Token Ring have their inherent limitation in throughput, transmission speed etc. Their performances would be degraded if the network traffic becomes heavy. But generally, a graphics application generates a huge amount data during computation. It makes no sense to transfer these large data files via network, even through transparent access facilities, such as NFS (network file system) because the response time is critical for interactive graphics applications. By this means, it also makes no sense to run many heavy tasks on the supercomputer in parallel.

4. Implementation

4.1 RPC and Client/Server Model

Currently, the available protocols for network communication are all in different forms. There is no single standard shared by all of them. This causes the heterogeneity among systems in a distributed computing environment. The other serious problem is that there is no high level protocol for building distributed application. Almost all vendors' network implementation only provide some low level service, such as TCP/IP, UDP/IP for Ethernet etc. ISO transport standard is also too low a focus. Only a few higher level facilities, such as TELNET, FTP etc. are available to an ordinary user. The absence of high level protocol makes a distributed application heavily dependent on the actual protocol used. This also leads to the problem of software portability and makes the programmer rather focus on the low level protocols than on the application itself. Furthermore, the building of a distributed application based on low level protocols is beyond the capabilities of most programmers.

There are two basic mechanisms for communication of different programs running on different computers. One is the message passing approach which consists of passing messages asynchronously among the cooperative processes and makes both sending and receiving processes proceed concurrently. But the messages usually appear to the program as a stream of bytes. The other very attractive approach is the remote procedure call (RPC) facility [9], which also provides a mechanism on user-level for network communication. It has a very similar syntax and semantics to local procedure call and makes programmers free of considering the data encoding (byte order, floating point format) and transport protocol (TCP/IP, UDP/IP etc.). These characters make RPC itself as an ideal vehicle for network communication in a heterogeneous environment. Together with RPC, XDR. (eXternal Data Representation) [10] is used for data format conversion.

In our environment, there are two kinds of byte order and floating point formats. One is the VAX format, another is the IEEE format, which is used by Multiflow TRACE and SUN workstations. According to an experiment for testing XDR conversion, conversion of floating point format is more expensive than swapping of byte order and takes about 50% of CPU time, comparing to 7% for byte order swapping, in this specific case. This is the other reason why the form-factor data files (all floating point numbers) are not transferred via network.

The RPC facility is generally based on the client(caller)/server(callee) model, which is the most common approach used in building distributed applications. Figure 4 shows the basic diagram of a remote procedure call session. First, a client should contact with the local transport mechanism for telling the remote transport mechanism which program has to be run and getting the server's port number back. When the client makes a remote procedure call, the local RPC facility translates the procedure number and call parameters to the network standard format (i.e. XDR). The remote RPC facility conversely converts these arguments to the server's format. Then the server executes the specific request according to the procedure number, and sends the results back to the client. Note that the parameters and results transferred may be structured data, including the data in form of byte stream.

4.2 Algorithm Reformulation

Porting a software package to take advantage of load sharing concept and make the best use of the performance of supercomputers and workstations, we should do the following:

- Algorithm Analysis: This means we should know the distribution of calculation intensity, for example, which part of a algorithm takes most of the CPU time, which part needs a lot of storage space, how many parameters are passed from one part to another etc.

- Algorithm Reformulation: Based on algorithm analysis, we should divide the original algorithm into several parts and determine which parts will run on supercomputers and which parts on workstations. For the parts to be run on supercomputers, although almost all supercomputer vendors provide powerful compilers to take advantage of their hardware architectures, such as optimization, vectorization etc., the algorithm itself should be adjusted manually to get further improvement of performance.

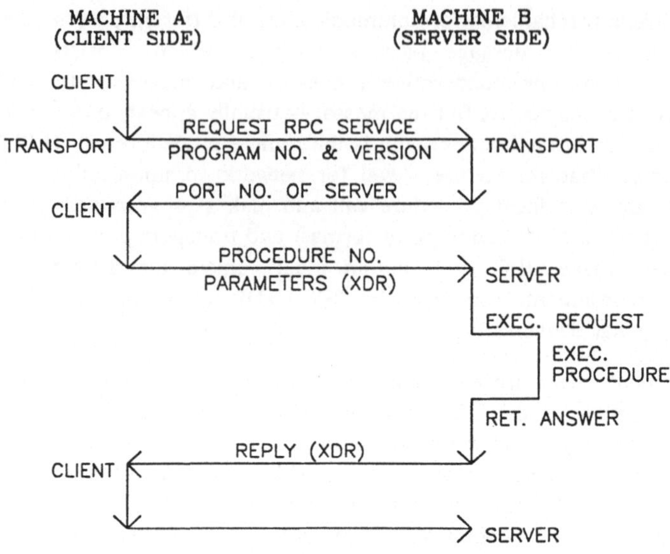

Figure 4: RPC and Client/Server Model

We separated the radiosity package into five tasks (as shown in Figure 1 and 5) with file interface first. This gives us a good comprehension about the data flow and network traffic and also helps us to decide which task should be run on a supercomputer, which on a workstation, based on the criteria described before. As described in section 2, the best scheme obviously is to run the form-factor calculation and equation solution part on supercomputer, others on workstation. The server has only two functions, one is for form-factor calculation, the other for equation solution. For a given environment, the form-factor calculation part should be called by the client first then a flag will be returned to tell the client whether the calculation succeeded. The equation solution part returns the color intensities of all patches, if the call is successfull. We keep a huge amount of form-factor data files resided at the supercomputer side, and eliminate the heavy network traffic.

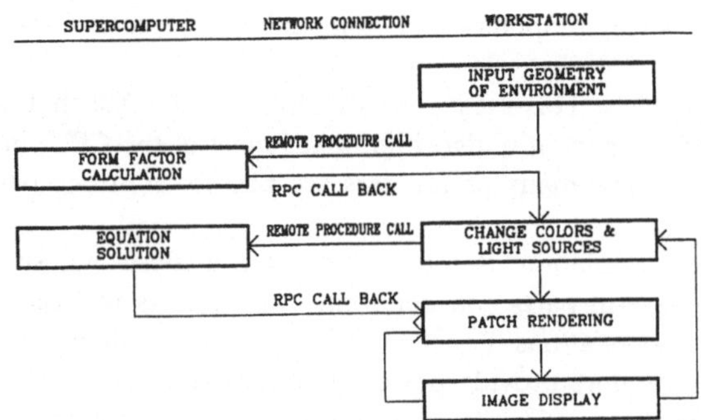

Figure 5: The Structure of the Radiosity Package Based on Load Sharing

4.3 Callback Mechanism

It should be pointed out that the conventional client/server model which simulates the local procedure call semantics is still not enough for distributed application construction. The reason is that it lacks of callback mechanism which provides the possibility of parallel computation among the machines running the clients and servers. Based on the conventional model, the client is blocked if a remote procedure call is issued and the client has to wait until the server finishes the computation task. Because it is very common that the application running on supercomputers still cannot get real time response, a callback mechanism should be provided.

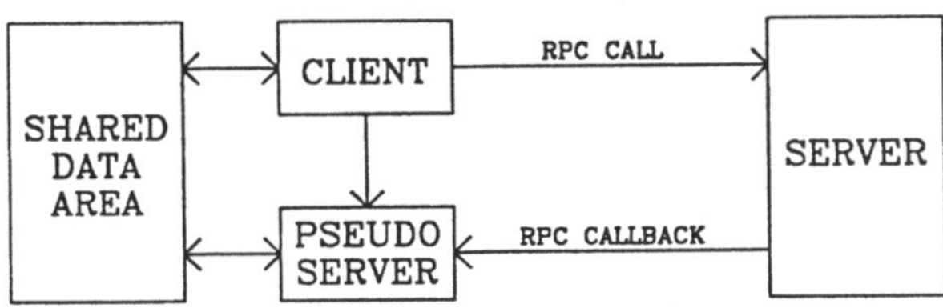

Figure 6: The Callback Mechanism

Unfortunately, even with RPC, which has the synchronous nature, to implement a callback mechanism is still difficult, to some extent because of the lack of light weight process facility which permits a single program to define multiple threads of control. We implement a special version of callback mechanism based on a shared memory method to avoid the user's idle waiting on the client side and make the task execution parallelly on both sides. The callback mechanism is shown in Figure 6. After a remote procedure call is set, the client generates a sub-process which acts as a pseudo-server to response the callback of the remote server (which acts as a pseudo-client) and modifies the shared data structures according to the results sent by the server. The client will check the shared data structures if the call is successful. For the radiosity package implementation, the shared data include a flag to indicate whether a remote procedure call is successful or not, in addition a data area to store the color intensity of each patch.

4.4 Result

A prototype implementation of the radiosity package based on the load sharing concept is running now in a network environment including a Multiflow TRACE-7/300 and a lot of VAX and SUN workstations. The RPC facility is SUN's implementation [11] which supports TCP/IP and UDP/IP protocols.

As a result, the time for form-factor calculation of the same picture shown in Figure 2 has been reduced to 20 CPU minutes on Multiflow TRACE-7/300, compared to 11 CPU hours on VAX-11/750. After form-factor calculation has finished, the image generation is nearly in real time. The user does only interact with the local workstation and, does no remote login or file transfer session, so that he/she gets the advantage of supercomputers.

During the implementation, there are several other problems which are common for building distributive application:

- user-level protocol description: When the interactive operations of a computing intensive application are very complicate, it is very difficult to maintain the coexistence among the tasks running on different machines. The user-level protocol, its syntax and semantics become very complex. Unfortunately, there are no efficient tools to describe these protocols and create a fast-prototype for a distributed application.

- code debugging: Because a distributed application may involve several different machines, some tools are needed to debug a program running on a remote computer. A remote debugging tool itself is a special kind of distributed application and is also very difficult to be implemented.

- error recovery: In a distributed application, an error may occur at any time and any place. Besides the hardware failures, most errors are caused by software. For the reliability of a distributed application, at least each cooperative program should inform each other sensibly for various errors and probe the possibility of remote failure.

5. Summary

In this paper, based on the experience of implementing a typical graphics application (the Radiosity package) in a distributed environment, which includes supercomputers and workstations, we suggest some solutions of the problems mentioned above. These can be summerized as follows:

- Before the standard remote computing protocol is not available, RPC (the remote procedure call) is a good approach for the interconnection between workstations and supercomputers.

- The original computational methods or algorithms in the host-terminal environment should be revised or adjusted to make best use of both resources of the supercomputer and the workstation. Sometimes these revisions are difficult.

- The transfer of a huge amount of data between the supercomputer and the workstation should be avoided to reduce both network traffic and graphics response time should be avoided.

- By transparent access of server running on the supercomputer, the user does only see the local workstation which has very high-performance virtually. A significant amount of time for remote login and file transfer is saved.

- User-level protocol description language is necessary for complex applications which have complicate RPC semantics. The callback mechanism, light weight process etc. are also very important for building distributive applications. In addition other development tools, such as remote debug tools, should also be provided.

- Error recovery facility is the most weak part in a distributed application. This is due to many other problems of heterogeneity, such as file name format, command semantics, etc. A remote computing program should be aware of the possible error conditions and inform sensibly the cooperative programs.

Distributive computing has been recognized as a very effective approach for resource sharing. The load sharing concept, which is based on the transparent access and resource sharing, is very suitable for computation intensive applications, especially graphics applications, to take advantage of supercomputers and workstations in a distributed environment. Although there are still some difficulties with distributed application construction, the current trend toward inter-connection among heterogeneous systems will make distributive computing easier.

Acknowledgments

Many thanks to Annelore Buhmann, Hans Joseph and Jaromir Likavec for their help in preparing this paper.

References

[1] Whitted, T., An Improved Illumination Model for Shaded Display, Communication of ACM, Vol.23, No.6, June 1980, pp. 343–349

[2] Goral, C.M., Torrance, K.E., Greenberg, D.P. and Battaile B., Modeling the Interaction of Light between Diffuse Surfaces, Computer Graphics, Vol.18, No.3, July 1984, pp.213–222

[3] Cohen, M.F. and Greenberg, D.P., The Hemi-cube: A Radiosity Solution for Complex Environments, Computer Graphics, Vol.19, No.3, July 1985, pp.31–40

[4] Cohen, M.F., Greenberg, D.P., Immel, D.S. and Brock, P.J. , An Efficient Radiosity Approach for Realistic Image Synthesis, IEEE Computer Graphics and Applications, Vol.6, No.3, March 1986, pp.26–35

[5] Rogers, D.F., Procedural Elements for Computer Graphics, McGraw–Hill Book Company, 1985

[6] Wallace, J.R., Cohen, M.F. and Greenberg, D.P., A two–pass Solution to the Rendering Equation: A Synthesis of Ray tracing and Radiosity Methods, Computer Graphics, Vol.21, No.3, July 1987, pp.311–320

[7] Shao, M.Z., Peng, Q.S. and Liang Y.D., A New Radiosity Approach by Procedure Refinements for Realistic Image Synthesis, Computer Graphics, Vol.22., No.3, July 1988, pp.93–101

[8] Lampson. B.W., Paul, M. and Siegert H.J., Distributed System: Architecture and Implementation Springer-Verlag, 1981

[9] Birrel, A.D. and Nelson, B.J., Implementing of Remote Procedure Call, ACM Transaction on Computer Systems, Vol.2, No.1, Feb. 1984, pp.39-59

[10] Sun Microsystems, External Data Representation Reference Manual, Sun Microsystems, Jan. 1985

[11] Sun Microsystems, Remote Procedure Call Protocol Specification, Sun Microsystems, Jan. 1985

Mensch–Maschine–Schnittstelle

Werner Schneider

Zentrum für das Studium von Mensch und Computer
Universität Uppsala und UDAC
Rechenzentrum
Box 2103
S–750 02 Uppsala
Schweden

Es ist das Ziel dieses Vortrages, die durch ungeeignet konstruierte Mensch-Computer-Schnittstellen hervorgerufenen kognitiven Probleme darzustellen und zu analysieren sowie Lösungsansätze aufzuzeigen. Die dabei vorzustellenden Beispiele von Lösungen im Rahmen spezifischer Arbeitsplätze und Arbeitsaufgaben – ganz besonders auch solcher auf dem Gebiete der Anwendung von Supercomputern – eignen sich jedoch nicht für eine 'statisch-monochrome' Darstellung in der Form einer schwarz-weiß gedruckten Veröffentlichung und müssen deshalb weggelassen werden.

"Super, Mikro, Megamini – Minisuper, Gigapico und so fort – Gateways, Fiber, LAN und WAN – Robotvision, PACS, Expertsystem – E-Mail, Fax, und Teletex – Laservision, CD-ROM und Bildschirmtext ! Weg von Büchern, Ordnern, Mappen, weg von Bleistift, Gummi und Papier, weg von Werkzeug, weg vom Schweiß ! Nur nicht menschlich handeln, menschlich denken, 'Human Factors' sind zu unbequem. "Automatisiert, computerisiert und robotorisiert wird's bequemer und doch besser, produktiver, effektiver, rationell !". Das ist der Lockruf der Computersirenen, und eine immer größer werdende Schar von Verunsicherten begibt sich auf die ungewisse Fahrt in Richtung der Göttinnen auf den Inseln der digital-elektronischen Welt. Ausdrücke wie "da muß man halt mitmachen", "besser jetzt gleich umstellen" oder "wenn die Firma XY so ein Gerät hat, müssen wir auch eines haben" sind typisch, und der Bedarf an externen Beratern nimmt rasch zu. So ist es denn auf dem Gebiet der Computeranwendungen mehr die Nachfrage als das Können, was Leute zu Experten macht.

"Das mag ja ein Problem sein für gewisse Teile der Wirtschaft und des öffentlichen Bereichs," wird ein typischer Supercomputer-Anwender einwenden, "denn für die an der Front von Wissenschaft und Forschung Tätigen ist im Gegenteil die Verfügbarkeit der letzten Errungenschaften auf Gebieten wie Elektronik, formale Sprachen und KI eine Vorraussetzung für den Fortschritt in der Arbeit." Als Spezialisten plagt ihn im Unterschied zu der Mehrzahl der Beschäftigten nicht zunehmend die Unruhe bezüglich der Erhaltung des Arbeitsplatzes, auch nicht die Frage, inwiefern die verbleibende Arbeit nach Art und Inhalt noch "menschlich" ist, d.h. ob sie noch menschliche Fähigkeiten und Berufskompetenz erfordert oder nur noch "Knopfdrücken nach Schema". Getragen von der Idee, das Neueste vom Neuen mit den neuesten von neuen Hilfsmitteln zu finden oder zu erfinden, nimmt der Supercomputer-Anwender praktisch alles auf sich, was die Technik von ihm verlangt. Dabei merkt er nicht, daß auch er schlechter arbeitet, **weil bei der heutigen Art des Arbeitens mit Computern genuin menschliche Fähigkeiten und Teile der Berufskompetenz überhaupt nicht zum Zuge kommen können**, die auch für seine Tätigkeit von großer Bedeutung sind.

Was sind denn genuin menschliche Fähigkeiten und was ist menschliche Kompetenz? Und wenn es sie gibt, ist sie nicht hinfällig geworden im Zeitalter des Computers und der künstlichen Intelligenz? Obwohl sich schon viele einem solchen **Pessimismus** hingeben - darin bestärkt durch die vielen Forscher, die behaupten, es sei nur eine Frage der Zeit, bis der Computer den Menschen voll ersetzen könne - ist die **Wirklichkeit** eine ganz andere. Ohne diese Frage hier im Detail erörten zu können, sei nur festgestellt, daß dieser Typ von **Mißverständnis** bezüglich menschlicher Kompetenz und menschlicher Fähigkeiten stark darauf beruht, daß man in der kognitiven Forschung den Computer immer mehr als Metapher für die Konzeptualisierung menschlicher Informationsverarbeitung braucht. Das führt zu der Vorstellung, der Mensch sei eine aktive, analytische Denkmaschine, die man dann wiederum mit existierenden oder geplanten Computersystemen vergleichen könne, vor allem natürlich in bezug auf die Begrenzungen beim Menschen. Daß der Mensch nicht nur eine solche Denk- oder gar Rechenmaschine ist, sondern außerdem ein **äußerst komplexes Wahrnehmungssystem**, daran denkt man vorerst überhaupt nicht. Und trotzdem ist es wohl gerade die Kombination dieser beiden "Modi" die den Menschen, soweit wir es voraussehen können, in vielem **noch lange allen Maschinen überlegen sein läßt**.

Das **menschliche Wahrnehmungssystem** ist z.B. hoch spezialisiert bezüglich der Verarbeitung von **räumlicher Information**, es besitzt aber auch eine enorme Fähigkeit zum Erkennen und zur Analyse von **Ähnlichkeiten** . Das gilt nicht nur für das, was wir mit unseren Sinnen direkt wahrnehmen können (z.B.eine Form und Gestalt eines gewissen Objekts), wir haben außerdem die Fähigkeiten, **dynamische Modelle** von Situationen und Situationsabfolgen zu bilden und so **Ähnlichkeiten aus der Sicht der Steuerung und Regelung** zu erkennen und zu analysieren. Berücksichtigt man diese Eigenschaften, erhält man bezüglich eines Vergleiches zwischen Mensch und Computer ganz andere Resultate als die, mit welchen uns die Computerpropaganda und die opportunistische technische Journalistik füttern: Wohl kann der Mensch kaum eine, der Computer jedoch Milliarden Additionen pro Sekunde ausführen, der Mensch ist im **'direkten' Erkennen** von Bildern und Ähnlichkeiten aber **schneller als der schnellste Supercomputer** und wird es wegen seiner grundsätzlichen 'Konstruktionsbegebenheiten' auch bleiben.

"Der Computer vergißt nichts !" wird weiter oft behauptet, obwohl das gar nicht stimmt. Wer hat nicht etwa schon von den Folgen von 'Viren', 'trojanischen Pferden' usw. gehört oder solche gar schon 'erlebt' ? Auch ein 'ganz blöder' Programmfehler kann ja bekanntlich schon dazu führen, daß Teile des Datenspeichers gelöscht werden. Noch schlimmer als das Löschen von Daten und Programmen ist deren mögliche Verfälschung, wovon der Computer kaum etwas merkt, ja oft nicht merken kann. Es gibt aber Sachen, die der - sogenannte vergeßliche - Mensch überhaupt nicht vergessen kann, z.B. die erste Liebe, den ersten Flug. Dazu umfaßt die **Erinnerung** ganze Filmabschnitte - mit anderen Worten Pixelmengen - die heute mit modernsten Speichertechniken erst so langsam in Angriff genommen werden können. Ganz abgesehen davon, daß Menschen schon über Ähnlichkeiten von Details direkt zu jener Stelle des Films assoziieren, wo diese Details vorkommen; etwas, das in der 'Computerwelt' noch sehr lange nicht möglich sein wird. Auch das unmittelbare Erkennen von nicht normierten Schriftzeichen und damit gebildeten Worten stellt für den Menschen kaum ein Problem dar. Für den Computer ist das aber heute noch eine praktisch unlösbare Aufgabe und für die Spezialfälle, für die es eine Lösung gibt, handelt es sich um Investitionen, deren Größenordnung den Menschen als billige Arbeitskraft erscheinen läßt.

Auch der Feststellung einiger Forscher, der Mensch habe eine beschränkte **Lesegeschwindigkeit** von rund 50 Bit/s, ist mit Vorsicht zu begegnen. Es handelt sich hierbei um die Gechwindigkeit beim Lesen von **Text** . Die Aufnahme von **Bildern** erfordert jedoch vom Menschen eine Eingabegeschwindigkeit, die um Potenzen höher liegt, und die von der der Allgemeinheit zugänglichen Technik noch lange nicht geleistet werden wird. Es ließen sich noch viele solche Vergleiche anführen. Hier genügt es jedoch festzustellen, daß **eine optimale Anwendung der Computertechnik nur dann erreicht werden kann, wenn auch der Mensch sein Bestes geben kann.**

In erster Linie ist dazu die richtige Gestaltung der Arbeitsverteilung zwischen Mensch und Computer von größter Bedeutung; d.h. beide werden für das eingesetzt, wozu sie besonders befähigt sind. "Das ist ja nun wirklich der Fall an meinem Arbeitsplatz !" wird der Supercomputer-Anwender ausrufen. Und er hat wohl meist auch recht damit.

Es stellen sich jedoch noch zwei weitere, auch für den Supercomputer-Anwender große Probleme: Wie steht es mit der **Zusammenarbeit** zwischen menschlicher und elektronischer Arbeitskraft und wie mit der **Kommunikation** ? Leider müssen wir feststellen, daß in dieser Beziehung die Technik so unterentwickelt ist, daß trotz an sich richtiger Arbeitsverteilung der Mensch weit davon entfernt ist, sein Bestes geben zu können. Im Gegenteil: Die **menschliche Produktivität** wird oft um Faktoren **gesenkt**. Warum?

So weit die kurze Geschichte der Computer reicht, hat man immer nur von Ein- und Ausgabe gesprochen: Man gibt 'ihm' etwas ein, 'er' tut damit etwas - oft unerhört vieles -, und dann gibt er wieder etwas aus, alles ausgerichtet auf Leistung; d. h. auf Zeichen oder Bildpunkte pro Sekunde. Was, wann, wie und wo einzugeben ist und was, wann, wie und wo herauskommt, wird von den Möglichkeiten und Begrenzungen der Technik und den Software-Konstrukteuren bestimmt. Die Folge dieses **einseitigen Verhältnisses zugunsten des Computers** und der computergestützten Roboter sind nun aber **entscheidende Einbußen** bezüglich der Produktivität des Anwenders, von denen im folgenden einige aufgezeigt werden sollen.

Die leider auch heute noch **verbreitetste** Form von Ein- und Ausgabegeräten ist das **alphanumerische Bildschirmgerät** mit 24 Zeilen x 80 Zeichen. Es 'entstammt' den Stanzformularen der Lochkartenzeit und wurde ja auch beim Übergang vom Kartenlochen zum 'On-line-Lochen' spezifiziert. Die **hauptsächlichen Begrenzungen** sind: beschränkte Bildfläche, beschränkte Zeichenmenge, keine Graphik. Die im wesentlichen zur verbesserten Präsentation von Resultaten verwendeten graphischen Farbbildschirme der PC-Welt, die für ein sogenanntes 'anwenderfreundliches' Arbeiten benutzten Schirme der Mac-Welt sowie die moderne Fenstertechnik stellen in diesem Zusammenhang wohl große Fortschritte dar. Sie können die Situation jedoch **nur im Rahmen der vorhandenen Bildfläche** verbessern, die immer noch sehr begrenzt ist. Das führt zu einer mehrfachen Aufteilung des Arbeitsprozesses. **Mit anderen Worten, der Computer zwingt den Menschen zu sequentiellem Arbeiten.**

Im **manuellen Arbeitsmilieu** ist das gesamte **Blickfeld** das 'Menu' und alles, was sich innerhalb der Reichweite befindet, direkt **greifbar**. Dokumente, Mappen, Kartotheken, die Agenda, technische Werkzeuge können also direkt erkannt und gleichzeitig ergriffen werden. Der **Computer** mit seinem Bildschirm ist aber **entweder/oder** Agenda, Bibliothek, ein Buch, ein Bestellblock usw. Wir müssen zuerst erkennen, was er gerade ist, und ihm dann mitteilen, was er im Moment sein soll. Dies geschieht **über mühsame Menu-Hierarchien** und außerdem über **formalsprachliche Codes**, was genau das ist, wozu sich der Mensch nicht eignet. Auch wenn man wie z. B. viele Naturwissenschaftler, Techniker und Computerspezialisten ein Virtuose im Hantieren von formalen Sprachen ist, zeigt es sich, daß man wesentlich besser arbeitet, wenn die Interaktion mit dem Computer nicht auf formalsprachlichen Codes und strikt einzuhaltenden Kommandosequenzen aufbaut.

Um die obengenannten einzigartigen **perzeptiven Fähigkeiten des Menschen** zum Zuge kommen zu lassen, muß also alles das direkt - in Bild und Ton - erfaßbar sein, was aus der Situation heraus notwendig ist. Vieles ist in dieser Beziehung im Werden und einiges ist auch schon realisiert und z.T. kommerziell ausgewertet worden - u.a. auch an den Instituten des Verfassers. Dazu braucht es z.B. **Digitalisierungsplatten, hochauflösende graphische Farbbildschirme,** mehr als einen einzigen Bildschirm zum Zwecke des Erreichens einer genügend großen Bildfläche, weiterhin Bildschirme mit **Touchfunktionen** liegend positioniert, um ein Ermüden des Zeigearms zu vermeiden. Als Weiterentwicklung ließe sich denken, daß die Pultplatte mit mehreren kleineren und größeren, flachen Bildschirmen versehen wäre, für spezifische Arbeitsaufgaben ergänzt durch Ton und Sprache generierende und erkennende Geräte.

Blättern in Büchern und Heften, **Überschauen** von mehreren **nebeneinanderliegenden Dokumentseiten** sowie - davon ausgehend - Schreiben, Rechnen, Zeichnen u.a. ist die normale manuelle Tätigkeit an vielen Arbeitsplätzen. Außerdem ist beim **gewöhnlichen Bildschirm** ein richtiges **Hin-und-her-blättern nicht möglich** und fast alle Teilarbeitsmomente müssen der Reihe nach ausgeführt werden. Das führt nicht nur zu - u.a. in vom Verfasser geleiteten Projekten gemessenen - **großen Zeitverlusten**, sondern auch dazu, daß gewisse menschliche Intelligenzleistungen gar nicht mehr stattfinden können, da beispielsweise das Assoziieren ein gleichzeitiges - oder mindestens 'genügend' gleichzeitiges - Vorliegen des zu Assoziierenden voraussetzt.

Besonders problematisch ist außerdem, daß beim konventionellen Bildschirm eine **längere Befehlseingabe** automatisch das **Löschen der Resultate** zur Folge hat. Man stelle sich vor, bei jeder Planung eines nächsten Arbeitsschrittes würde zuerst die Pultoberfläche geleert ! Die **moderne Fenstertechnik** kann auch diese Situation **nur im Rahman der vorhandenen Bildfläche** verbessern. Ein von der Resultatanzeige - in der Form von Text und/oder Bild - getrennter

Befehlsdialog ist deshalb auf alle Fälle eine der Grundbedingungen für ein effektives Arbeiten mit dem Computer. Bei einigen Anwendungen kann das sogar mit einem konventionellen Bildschirm realisiert werden.

Eine weitere wesentliche Problematik bezüglich der Zusammenarbeit zwischen Mensch und Computer ergibt sich dadurch, daß die Computersysteme in der Regel so konstruiert sind, daß der menschliche Anwender sich **keine dynamischen Modelle** von seinem elektronischen 'Partner' machen kann. Im Unterschied zu einer zwischenmenschlichen Situation kann der menschliche Operator das **Verhalten seines Partners nicht antizipieren** und mit ihm auf Basis gegenseitigen Anpassens kooperieren. Es ist deshalb von **größter Wichtigkeit**, die Anwendungssysteme so zu konstruieren , daß sie für den Anwender auch in **unvorhergesehenen Situationen transparent und steuerbar sind.**

Abschließend sei noch das Problem der Kommunikation zwischen Mensch und Computer angesprochen. Der Computer verlangt **formalsprachlichen Umgang**, obwohl gerade diese Ausdrucksweise uns Menschen aus verschiedenen Gründen ganz und gar nicht liegt. Unter anderem baut sie auf schwer aus der Erinnerung generierbaren formalen Ausdrücken auf - also nicht auf Erkennen ! Sie verlangt zusätzlich auch **ein striktes Einhalten von Regeln** und oft langen **sequentiellen Abfolgen**. Außerdem muß diese Art von Kommunikation **schriftlich** geschehen. Genügend leistungsfähige 'voice input-' und 'voice output'-Systeme werden noch für einige Jahre nicht zu einem für die Mehrzahl der Arbeitsplätze erschwinglichen Preis erhältlich sein. Außerdem eignet sich ein formalsprachlicher Dialog kaum für eine mündliche Eingabe, da die meisten Ausdrücke dieser Art nur schwer aussprechbar und in einer durch den Computer synthetisierten 'Stimmausgabe' - wenn überhaupt - kaum verständlich sind.

"Aber", werden einige einwenden, "natürlich-sprachliche Kommunikation mit dem Computer ist unterwegs, und dann sind diese Probleme doch gelöst !" Sicher hat man diesbezüglich schon große Fortschritte gemacht, besonders in Forschungslaboratorien. Bis jedoch eine echt natürlich-sprachliche Kommunikation zwischen Mensch und Computer stattfinden kann, braucht es noch viel mehr als man oft zugeben will. Es sei nur daran erinnert, daß dazu eine gemeinsame Art der Wahrnehmung notwendig ist, und daß gerade diesbezüglich Computer und computergestützte Roboter noch ganz am Anfang sind. Im Rahmen der Computerprojekte der sogenannten 5. Generation hat man mit diesen Aufgaben begonnen. Es handelt sich also nicht nur um linguistische Probleme, wenngleich auch diese noch lange nicht gelöst sind.

Interessant ist, daß eine **natürlich-sprachliche Kommunikation** (mündlich oder schriftlich) **nur einen Teil der Schwierigkeiten beseitigt**. Erstens beruht ein großer Teil der Effektivität eines Arbeitsteams auf nicht verbaler Kommunikation (z.B. auf Zeigen), und zweitens kommuniziert der Mensch mit sich selbst nur selten verbalsprachlich. Wenn wir ein Dokument hervorholen, sagen wir bekanntlich nicht: Aufstehen - zum Büchergestell gehen - Kopf bewegen bis Dokument erblickt - kontrollieren, ob Abstand zum Greifen richtig und Hand leer - wenn ja, greifen usw. Wir tun es einfach ! Noch wichtiger, wir erinnern uns bei Büchern und Dokumenten selten an den genauen Titel, den Namen des Verfassers, das Druckjahr usw. Das verlangt aber z.B. unser Office-Computer-System. Wohl findet man mit diesem - oft in Blitzesschnelle - alle

Dokumente, in denen das Wort "Grippe" (und sogar Synonyme davon) vorkommt, ein spezifisches Dokument zu finden, dauert jedoch um so länger.

Ohne eine wesentlich verbesserte Mensch-Computer-Interaktion kommen spezifisch menschliche Fähigkeiten und Kompetenzen nicht nur nicht zum Zuge, sie verkümmern langsam aber sicher. Wollen wir z. B. von den einzigartigen Kapazitäten unseres perzeptiven Systems das räumliche Vorstellungsvermögen benutzen, muß das konzeptionelle Modell vom Büchergestell bewahrt werden, so daß uns einzelne Dokumente nur durch ein 'sie-Sehen' mit nachfolgendem 'Darauf-Zeigen' unmittelbar zugänglich sind. Zusammen mit einer - noch nicht erfundenen - effektiven Methode des Blätterns könnten dann die **Vorteile von 'elektronischen' Dokumenten** ganz zum Durchbruch kommen; d.h. kein mühsames Umschreiben dank Wort -und Textverarbeitung, schnelles Suchen nach Schlüsselwörtern und mit linguistischen Methoden im freien Text, elektronisches Vervielfältigen und Vermitteln über (fast) beliebig lange Distanzen. Und sollte man trotzdem einmal etwas ausdrucken, sind natürlich nur noch 'Schöndrucker' zugelassen.

An der Entwicklung von **menschenwürdigen Interfaces** zum Computer hängt es zum großen Teil, ob wir unsere beruflichen Kompetenzen und Fähigkeiten zum Wohle aller erweitern werden, oder ob sie verkümmern. Wir sind optimistisch ! In Schweden und einigen anderen Ländern sind heute schon mehrere Forschungs- und Entwicklungsteams an der Arbeit, um mit den hier besprochenen Problemen fertig zu werden. Einige der vielen, bereits erzielten Resultate zeigen klar, daß eine 'menschlichere' Zukunft möglich ist.

Die neuen Supercomputer von CRAY

Robert Übelmesser

Cray Research GmbH
Kistlerhofstraße 168
D-8000 München 70

1. Kundenbasis

Cray Research ist weltweit der Marktführer bei Supercomputern mit über 240 installierten Systemen. In Deutschland werden derzeit 14 Cray Rechner eingesetzt. Viele der installierten und die meisten der neu bestellten Cray Rechner sind Multiprozessor Systeme, so daß heute über 700 Cray CPUs bei Kunden installiert sind. Etwa 35 % der Cray Kunden sind im industriellen Bereich und 65 % im wissenschaftlichen Bereich sowie bei Regierungseinrichtungen angesiedelt. Bild 1 gibt einen Überblick über die Neuinstallationen von Cray Systemen in den letzten Jahren.

2 . Produktstrategie

Jährlich investiert Cray Research etwa 15 % des Umsatzes in Forschung und Entwicklung. Davon werden etwa 50 % in Hardware Produktentwicklung investiert und 50 % in Software Entwicklung. Bild 2 zeigt die F & E Investitionen von Cray in den letzten Jahren. Zusätzlich werden Aufwendungen für die Entwicklung, Portierung und Optimierung von Anwendungssoftware getätigt. Es ist das erklärte Firmenziel von Cray mit dem Top Modell den jeweils leistungsfähigsten Rechner für technisch-wissenschaftliche Anwendungen anzubieten. Systeme im mittleren Leistungsbereich der Cray Produktpalette zeigen jeweils ein hervorragendes Preis- /Leistungsverhältnis durch die hohe Durchsatzleistung der angebotenen Multiprozessor Systeme und die Qualität und Quantität der verfügbaren System- und Anwendungssoftware. Ein günstiges Einstiegsmodell wird angeboten, um den Einsatz von Supercomputern in entwicklungsfähigen Regionen oder neuen Anwendungsgebieten aufzubauen, die längerfristig das Potential für echte Supercomputer Anforderungen erwarten lassen.

3. System Architektur

Ziel der Cray Systemarchitektur ist es, ein äußerst leistungsfähiges, aber doch ausgewogenes Gesamtsystem anzubieten. Die Systemarchitektur muß ferner sehr flexibel und anpassungsfähig sein, um auch bei den fortschreitenden Änderungen im Anwendungs- und Einsatzprofil weiter eine hohe Leistung abzugeben. Außerdem muß es die Systemarchitektur erlauben, dem Benutzer und dem Betreiber das Leistungspotential des Rechners vom Betriebssystem und vom Compiler automatisch ohne hohen Optimierungs- und Verwaltungsaufwand zur Verfügung zu stellen. Um ein leistungsfähiges Gesamtsystem anbieten zu können, bieten Cray Rechner nicht nur eine hohe CPU Leistung. Cray Rechner enthalten speziell entwickelte Prozessoren zur Unterstützung der Ein-/Ausgabe; Cray war Pionier in der Einführung von Erweiterungsspeichern in Halbleiter Technologie für Supercomputer, und Cray hat selbst das leistungsfähigste am Markt verfügbare

Magnetplatten-System für technisch wissenschaftliche Anwendungen entwickelt. Bild 3 zeigt die Systemarchitektur der Cray Rechner im Überblick.
Große Leistungsverbesserungen für ein breites Spektrum von Anwendungen sind nur durch den Einsatz von Multiprozessor Systemen möglich. Cray Research hat deshalb bereits 1982 den ersten Multiprozessor-Vektorrechner auf den Markt gebracht. Hardware und Software der Cray Rechner wurden seither kontinuierlich verbessert, um die Parallelverarbeitung noch flexibler, benutzerfreundlicher und leistungsfähiger zu machen.
Die Flexibilität der Cray Systemarchitektur ist durch die Ausbaufähigkeit aller Teilkomponenten, nämlich Skalarverarbeitung, Vektorverarbeitung, Hauptspeicher, Sekundärspeicher und E/A-System gewährleistet. Der Hauptspeicher ist jeweils als Realspeicher definiert, auf den alle CPUs gleichberechtigt direkt zugreifen können. Dieses Prinzip - zusammen mit dem flexiblen Speicherzugriff von der Cray CPU - erlaubt es sowohl dem Benutzer wie dem Betreiber, die mit Speicherverwaltung auf Vektorrechnern verbundene Komplexität zu vernachlässigen und das Leistungspotential des Systems ohne großen Aufwand voll auszuschöpfen.

CPU

Die Cray CPUs ermöglichen schnelle Skalarverarbeitung durch eine kurze Zykluszeit, hohe Leistung bereits bei kurzen Vektoren durch eine kurze Vektor Startup Zeit, hohe Leistung bei langen Vektoren durch eine hohe Speicherbandbreite und eine hohe Leistung bei Strides oder Scatter/Gather Operationen durch eine flexible Architektur im Speicherzugriff.
Durch die verstärkte Einführung von Nichtlinearitäten, komplexeren geometrischen Strukturen und Subgrid oder Multigrid Methoden in die numerischen Modelle wird die Bedeutung einer flexiblen CPU für kurze Vektoren, Strides und Scatter/Gather Operationen weiter zunehmen. Alle CPUs in Cray Rechnern werden deshalb auch zukünftig diese Eigenschaften aufweisen.

Multiprocessing

Die Leistungsfähigkeit einer einzelnen CPU - in echter Leistung, nicht theoretischer Peak Rate - wird in den nächsten Jahren nicht in dem Ausmaß erhöht werden können, wie es von den Anwendern gefordert wird. Alle Supercomputer werden deshalb in Zukunft als Multiprozessoren angeboten werden. Cray Rechner sind dabei zum einem zum Multiprogramming, also zur Verbesserung des Durchsatzes einsetzbar, zum anderen können mehrere CPUs eng gekoppelt werden, um in einem echten Multiprocessing Modus an einem Programm zu arbeiten. Die Architektur ist dabei so flexibel, daß Multiprogramming und Multiprocessing parallel im Betrieb behandelt werden können, ohne einander zu stören.
Multiprocessing wird nur dann von den Benutzern in größerem Umfang akzeptiert, wenn es ohne großen Programmieraufwand eingesetzt werden kann und durch den Einsatz kein großer Overhead erzeugt wird. Um Multiprocessing für den Benutzer sehr einfach - oder sogar völlig transparent - zu machen, ist es notwendig, daß die CPUs direkt auf einen gemeinsamen Hauptspeicher zugreifen können. Durch diese Architekur ist es dann möglich, die bei der Parallelverarbeitung anfallende Problematik der Verwaltung und Synchronisierung von lokalen und globalen Datenstrukturen vom Compiler automatisch vornehmen zu lassen.
Um den Overhead gering zu halten, ist zur Synchronisation der CPUs spezielle Kommunikationshardware erforderlich. Gemeinsamer Hauptspeicher und spezielle

Kommunikationshardware sind und bleiben Kennzeichen aller Cray Systeme.

Zugriff zum Hauptspeicher

Ein wesentlicher Teil des Cray Hardware Know-hows liegt im Design eines effizienten Zugriffs zum gemeinsamen Hauptspeicher von allen CPUs, wobei alle CPUs parallel im Multiport-, Stride- und Scatter/Gather-Modus auf den gemeinsamen Hauptspeicher zugreifen können. Bild4 zeigt die Speichereffizienz des größten CRAY Y-MP Systems im Vergleich mit dem größten CRAY X-MP System. Es ist gelungen, beim Übergang von der CRAY X-MP zur CRAY Y-MP Serie, die Speichereffizienz sogar noch weiter zu verbessern, so daß auch bei 8 Prozessoren praktisch keine Speicherdegradation meßbar ist. Simulationen zeigen, daß auch 16 Prozessoren mit der vorhandenen Methode voll unterstützt werden können und daß bei dem erwarteten Fortschreiten der Chip Technologie auch 64 Prozessoren auf einen gemeinsamen Hauptspeicher effizient zugreifen können.

4 . Produktspektrum

CRAY Y-MP Serie

Als Nachfolge der CRAY X-MP Serie hat Cray Research im März 1989 die vollständige CRAY Y-MP Serie eingeführt. Die CRAY Y-MP Serie bietet im Vergleich mit der CRAY X-MP Serie

- höhere Durchsatz- und Einzeljob Leistung
- größere Hauptspeicher
- erhöhte Zuverlässigkeit
- flexiblere Aufrüstbarkeit im Feld
- völlige Software Kompatibilität.

Bild 5 zeigt die CRAY X-MP und CRAY Y-MP Serie im Vergleich. Bild 6 gibt einen Überblick über die Modelle der CRAY Y-MP Serie.

Alle Systeme der CRAY Y-MP Familie arbeiten mit einer Taktzeit von 6 Nanosekunden. Der Hauptspeicher ist im Ausbau von 16 bis 128 MWorten verfügbar, aufgeteilt in 64 bis 256 Speicherbänke. Eine CRAY Y-MP CPU bietet einen Leistungsfaktor von 1.2 bis 1.6 über die CPU eines CRAY X-MP/416 Systems. Die untere Grenze wird dabei für rein skalare und die obere Grenze für hoch vektorisierte Anwendungen erreicht. Durch die verbesserte Speichereffizienz können bei Mehrprozessor Systemen zusätzliche Leistungsgewinne beobachtet werden.
An CRAY Y-MP Systeme ist ein Erweiterungsspeicher mit bis zu 512 MWorten (= 4 Gbyte) Kapazität anschließbar, der über 1 oder 2 Kanäle mit je 1000 Mbyte/Sek. Transferraten mit dem Hauptspeicher verbunden ist. Peripheriegeräte werden von 1 oder 2 leistungsfähigen E/A-Subsystemen (mit je 4 Prozessoren und 12.5 Nanosek. Taktzeit) betrieben. Cray Research hat ein eigenes Magnetplattensystem entwickelt, das eine Kapazität von 5 Gbyte mit einer Transferrate von 10 Mbyte/Sek. kombiniert . Durch Daisy-Chaining ist die Kapazität auf 10 Gbyte erweiterbar. Software Striping zur Erhöhung der Transferraten ist ebenfalls verfügbar. Es sind IBM-kompatible Band- oder Kassettengeräte anschließbar, wobei die höchste am Markt

verfügbare Transferrate von 4,5 Mbyte/Sek. unterstützt wird. Zur Rechnerkopplung und Netzintegration wird eine Palette von Interfaces angeboten, die von direktem Ethernet Anschluß bis zu superschnellen lokalen Netzen (100 Mbyte pro Sekunde) reicht (siehe Bild 7). Bild 8 zeigt eine voll ausgebaute CRAY Y-MP Konfiguration. Im Bild 9 ist das physikalische Erscheinungsbild dieses Systems dargestellt.

CRAY Y-MP Technologie

In den CRAY Y-MP CPUs werden ausschließlich speziell von Cray entwickelte, schnelle Gate Array ECL Chips mit 2500 Gattern verwendet. Diese Chip Technologie ermöglicht es, daß eine gesamte CPU auf einem einzigen Modul - nur 59 cm x 32 cm x 3,5 cm groß - untergebracht werden kann.
Für den Hauptspeicher werden Speicherchips mit einer Zugriffszeit von 15 Nanosekunden eingesetzt.
Zur Kühlung werden die Module im Inneren in einem geschlossenen Kreislauf von einer speziellen Kühlflüssigkeit durchströmt.
Die geringe Anzahl von Komponenten im System und die Austauschbarkeit gesamter CPU- und Speichermodule tragen wesentlich zur hohen Zuverlässigkeit und einfachen Wartbarkeit dieser Systeme bei.

CRAY-2 Serie

Neben der CRAY Y-MP Serie wird weiterhin die CRAY-2 Serie angeboten. CRAY-2 Systeme werden mit 2 oder 4 CPUs und statischem Hauptspeicher bis 128 MWorte angeboten, sowie mit 4 CPUs bei einem dynamischen Hauptspeicher von 512 MWorten. CRAY-2 Systeme mit 512 MWorten (= 4 Gbytes) bieten den größten am Markt erhältlichen Hauptspeicher zur Lösung ungewöhnlich großer Probleme oder zum optimalen Durchsatz in einem gemischten Batch/Interaktiv Betrieb. Die CPU Leistung neuer CRAY-2 Systeme ist etwa um einen Faktor 2 größer als die der ersten ausgelieferten CRAY-2 Systeme.

CRAY X-MP/SE

Als Einstiegsmodell für Neukunden bietet Cray die CRAY X-MP/SE Modelle an. Diese Systeme entsprechen in der eingesetzten Technologie den CRAY X-MP Systemen, sind jedoch in der logischen Architektur voll kompatibel mit der CRAY Y-MP Serie.

5. Software

Betriebssystem

Cray Research hat - als erster Supercomputer Hersteller - bereits 1985 eine Portierung von UNIX für Cray Rechner angeboten. UNICOS - die Weiterentwicklungvon UNIX System V Release 3 für Cray Systeme - enthält heute alle notwendigen internen Verbesserungen und zusätzlichen Features, um UNIX zu einem echten Produktionssystem für Supercomputer zu machen.

Netzintegration

Seit 1985 bietet Cray TCP/IP als das strategische Netzwerk Produkt zur Integration in lokale und verteilte Netze an. Cray Systeme können mit TCP/IP von den verschiedensten Medien aus - von Ethernet bis zu schnellen lokalen Netzen mit 100 Mbyte/Sek. Bandbreite - angesprochen werden.

Netzapplikationen

Standard TCP/IP bietet Konnektivität sowie Remote Login und File Transfer Möglichkeiten. Zur Integration von Supercomputern in ein Rechenzentrum ist es jedoch bei weitem nicht ausreichend. Erst durch Netzapplikationen wird ein Produktionsbetrieb ausreichend unterstützt. Cray Research bietet zum einen die am Markt für UNIX Systeme vorhandenen Applikationen an, zum anderen hat es selbst Applikationen für Aufgaben entwickelt, die speziell für Supercomputer von Bedeutung sind.
Von den Standard UNIX Applikationen zu TCP/IP werden für Cray Systeme angeboten: NFS (Client und Server), X-Windows, Berkeley Sockets, RCP, XDR, ONC, NCS, telnet, rlogin, rcp, rsh, ftp und tftp.
Batch Verarbeitung wird auch in Zukunft für den Einsatz von Supercomputern von großer Bedeutung sein. Standard UNIX bietet nur unzureichende Batch Möglichkeiten und Standard TCP/IP unterstützt Batch Zugriff nicht. Cray Research hat deshalb für UNICOS ein Batch Subsystem entwickelt (NQS = Network Queuing System). NQS ist neben dem Einsatz bei der Batch Verarbeitung auch als ein allgemeines File Queuing System ausgelegt - eine wichtige Feature, die in UNIX fehlt - zum anderen ist es netzwerkfähig, d.h. Cray bietet für andere UNIX Systeme (Sun, DEC, Apollo, Silicon Graphics) ebenfalls ein Queuing System an (RQS = Remote Queuing System), das mit NQS zusammen ein gemeinsames Job und File Queuing System bildet. TCP/IP wird dabei als Transportschicht für die NQS-RQS Kopplung eingesetzt.
Bild 10 und 11 zeigen die Integration von Cray Systemen in eine Workstation Umgebung über TCP/IP und die dabei verwendeten Applikationen.

Compiler

CFT77 ist der gemeinsame, autovektorisierende und autoparallelisierende FORTRAN 77 Compiler für alle Cray Systeme.
Für C und Pascal werden autovektorisierende Compiler angeboten. Lisp und ADA Compiler stehen ebenfalls zur Verfügung.

Tools

Eine große Anzahl von Utilities und Tools zur Unterstützung der Programmentwicklung stehen zur Verfügung. Neben den Standard UNIX Tools stellt Cray eine Vielzahl speziell entwickelter Werkzeuge zur Verfügung, die sowohl im Batch als auch interaktiv genutzt werden können.

6. Parallelverarbeitung

Cray war Pionier bei der Einführung von Parallelverarbeitung für FORTRAN Programme mit der Freigabe von Cray Multitasking im Jahre 1983. Mit der Einführung von Mikrotasking bot Cray 1985 als erster Hersteller Parallelverarbeitung in portabler Form mittels Compiler Direktiven an. Heute ist durch die "Autotasking" Feature in Cray FORTRAN Compiler Parallelverarbeitung völlig automatisch ohne Benutzer Eingriff möglich. Dabei erzeugt der Compiler einen äußerst effizienten Code.

Der Cray Compiler analysiert Standard FORTRAN Programme auf Parallelisierbarkeit und er kann - wenn keine Abhängigkeiten bestehen - das Programm auf mehrere Prozessoren verteilen. Im Falle von geschachtelten Schleifen wird er möglichst die äußerste Schleife parallel abarbeiten, wobei eine eventuell mögliche Vektorisierung der innersten Schleife voll erhalten bleibt. Auch nicht geschachtelte Einzelschleifen können vom Compiler bei gleichzeitiger Vektorisierung parallelisiert werden. Erreichbare Speedups durch Parallelverarbeitung sind begrenzt durch die im Programm vorhandene Parallelität. Bild 12 zeigt, daß für den Standard Linpack Test bei einer Matrix Größe von 100 x 100 (geringe Parallelität) ein Faktor von 2,47 und bei einer Matrix Größe von 1000 x 1000 ein Faktor von 6,96 erzielt werden konnte.

7 . Anwendungssoftware

Nahezu alle wichtigen Software Pakete für technisch-wissenschaftliche Anwendungen stehen für Cray Systeme zur Verfügung. Cray unterhält eine Gruppe von Spezialisten für verschiedene Anwendungsbereiche, die Vertreiber von Software Paketen bei der Umstellung und Optimierung von Anwendungssoftware unterstützt. Cray wirkt dabei als Katalysator. Die treibende Kraft zur Umstellung und Optimierung von Anwendungssoftware für Cray Systeme ist das Eigeninteresse des Anbieters, sein Produkt in einer guten Implementierung auf dem weltweit am weitesten verbreiteten Supercomputer anzubieten.

8 . Zukunft

Heute im Labor verfügbare Chip Technologie zusammen mit neuen von Cray entwickelten Packungs- und Kühlverfahren wird eine Verbesserung aller Komponenten eines Cray Systems ermöglichen, d.h. kürzere Taktzeiten, leistungsfähigere Einzel-CPUs, mehr CPUs im Gesamtsystem, größere Hauptspeicher, größere und schnellere Erweiterungsspeicher, leistungsfähigere E/A Systeme und Magnetplatten mit mehr Kapazität und höheren Tranferraten. Die Gesamtarchitektur der Cray Systeme hat sich als äußerst flexibel und leistungsfähig erwiesen. Da es möglich ist, die Leistung aller Komponenten gleichmäßig zu steigern, kann die heutige Systemarchitektur auch für die nächste Generation von Cray Rechnern beibehalten werden.

Den Leistungssteigerungen, die mit der heute allgemein eingesetzten Silikon Technologie erzielt werden können, sind jedoch durch die physikalischen Eigenschaften von Silikon Grenzen gesetzt. Das Erreichen dieser Grenzen ist bereits heute abzusehen. Cray Research hat sich deshalb das Ziel gesetzt, im CRAY-3 Projekt unter der Leitung von Seymour Cray den ersten Supercomputer in Gallium-Arsenid Technologie zu entwickeln. Durch die schnelleren Schaltzeiten und die geringere Wärmeabgabe bietet Gallium-Arsenid das Potential für noch wesentlich leistungsfähigere Supercomputer.

Neuinstallationen von Cray Systemen pro Jahr

Systeme / Prozessoren

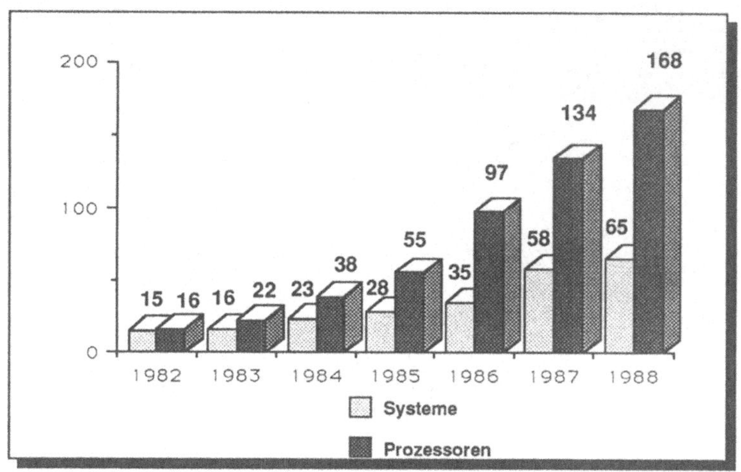

Bild 1

Cray Investitionen in Forschung und Entwicklung

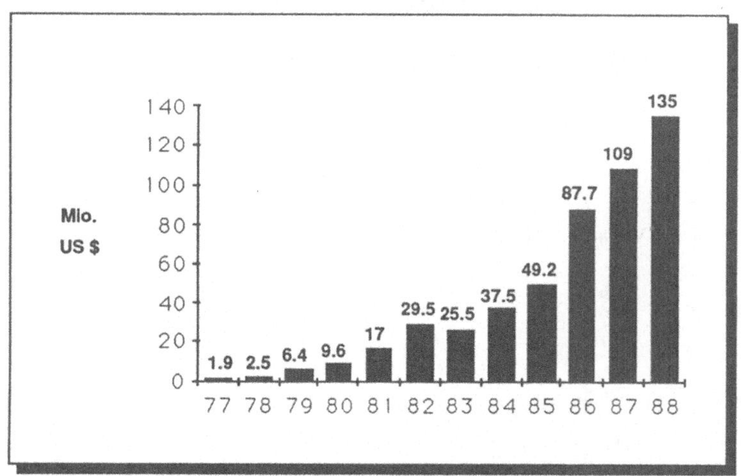

Bild 2

CRAY System Architektur

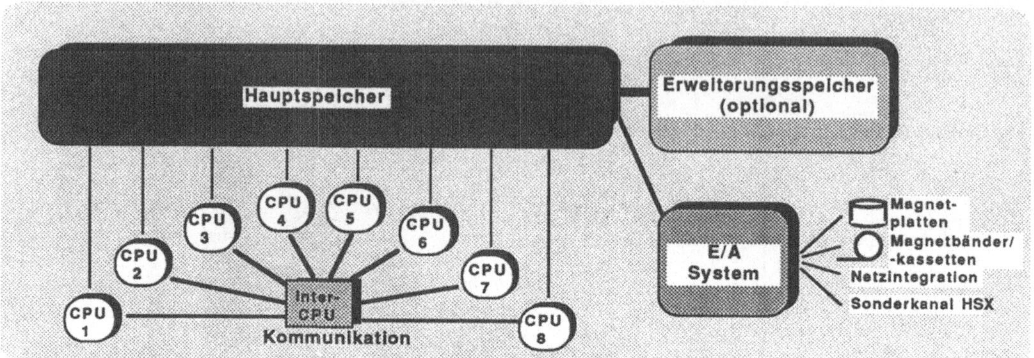

Bild 3

Speicher Effizienz

Vergleich zwischen CRAY Y-MP8 und CRAY X-MP/416

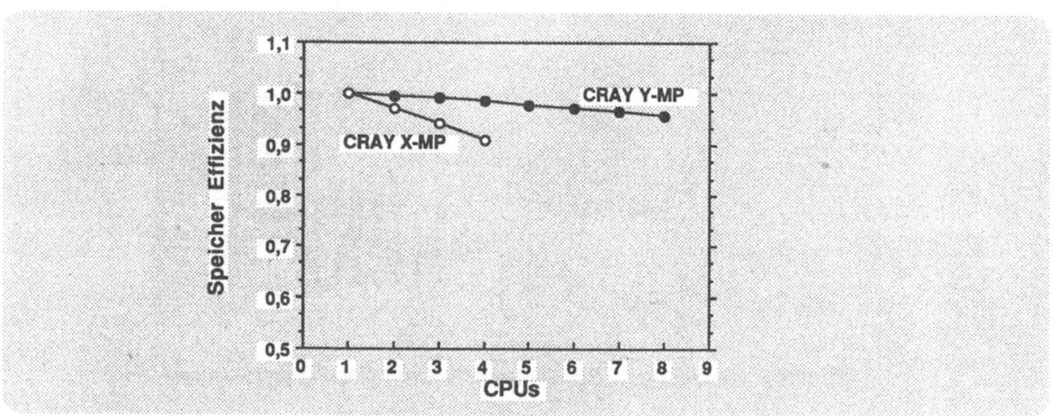

Bild 4

Vergleich CRAY Y-MP mit CRAY X-MP

Architektur

	CRAY X-MP	CRAY Y-MP
Anzahl CPUs	1 - 4	1 - 8
Taktzeit	8.5 Nanosek.	6 Nanosek.
Hauptspeicher	4 - 16 MWorte	16 - 128 MWorte
Speicherbänke	16 - 64	64 - 256
E/A Subsystem	1	1 - 2 (verbessert)
maximale Floating Point Rate	1411 Mflops	4000 Mflops

Bild 5

CRAY Y-MP Konfigurationen

FRAME	CPUs	128 MWorte	64 MWorte	32 MWorte	16 MWorte
8	8	Y-MP8/8128	Y-MP8/864	Y-MP8/832	
	4	Y-MP8/4128	Y-MP8/464	Y-MP8/432	
4	4		Y-MP4/464	Y-MP4/432	Y-MP4/416
	2		Y-MP4/264	Y-MP4/232	Y-MP4/216
	1		Y-MP4/164	Y-MP4/132	Y-MP4/116
2	2			Y-MP2/232	Y-MP2/216
	1			Y-MP2/132	Y-MP2/116

Bild 6

Cray Netzwerk Integration

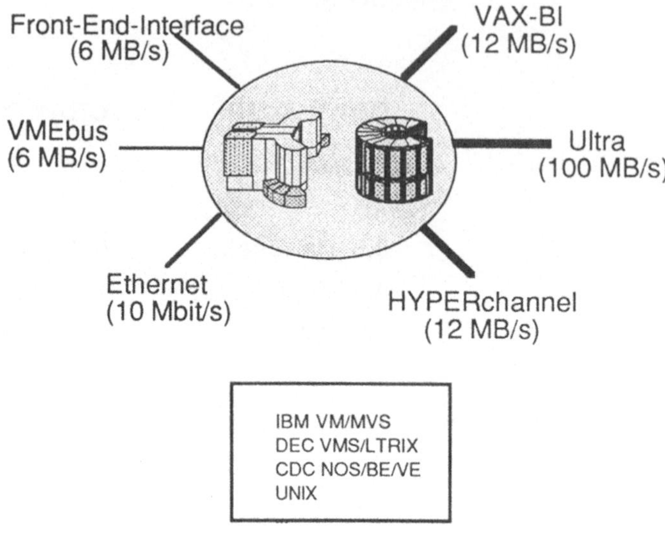

IBM VM/MVS
DEC VMS/LTRIX
CDC NOS/BE/VE
UNIX

Bild 7

CRAY Y-MP8 Konfiguration

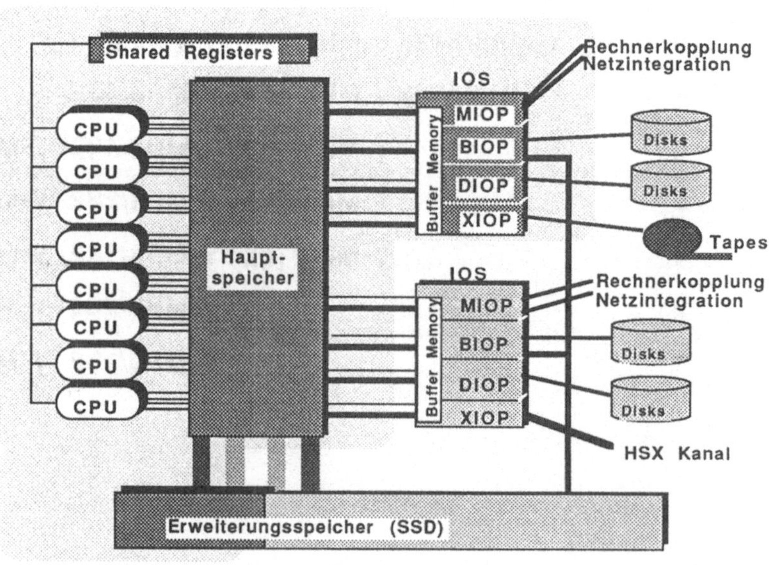

Bild 8

CRAY Y-MP SYSTEM

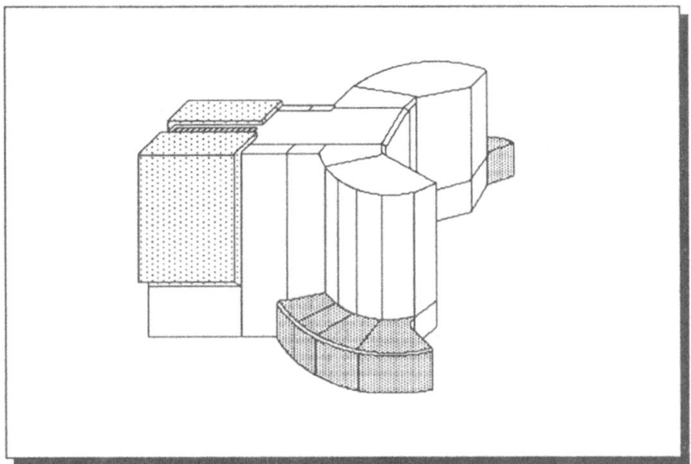

Bild 9

Cray-Workstation Umgebung

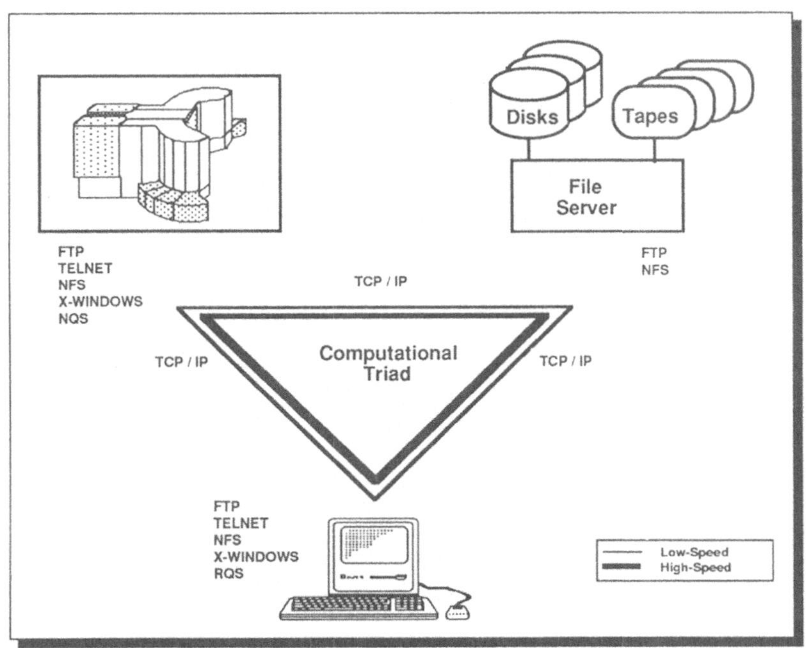

Bild 10

Cray-Workstation Umgebung

z. B verteilte Programm Entwicklung

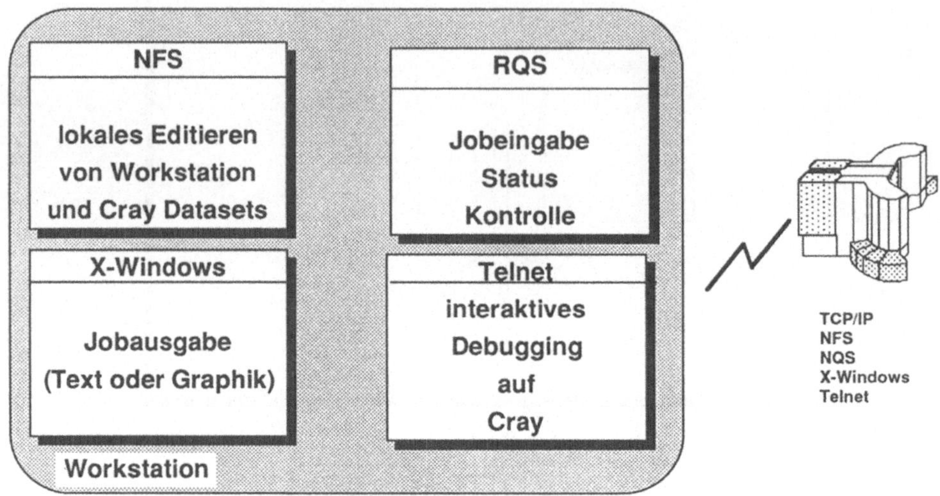

Bild 11

Beispiel für Speedup

Verbesserungsfaktoren für den LINPACK Benchmark mit Autotasking auf einer CRAY Y-MP8

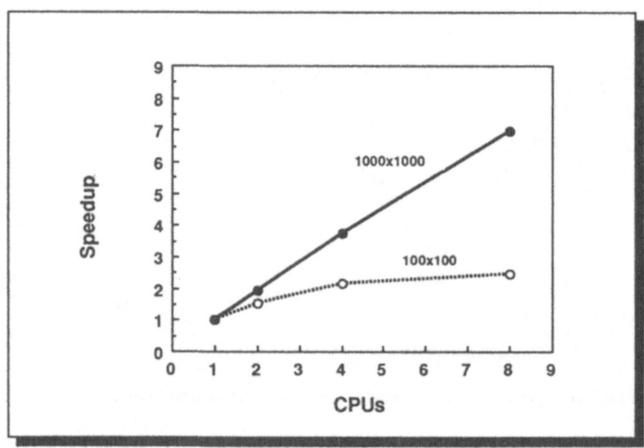

Bild 12

Die Architektur der ETA 10

Wolfgang Bez

Control Data GmbH
Marienstraße 11–13
D–7000 Stuttgart 1

Zusammenfassung

Die ETA 10 Rechnerserie von CONTROL DATA ist eine Familie von Vektorrechnersystemen mit bis zu acht Prozessoren. Der Rechner ist erstmalig in dieser Leistungsklasse ganz aus CMOS Komponenten aufgebaut. Die CPU–Architektur garantiert hohe Vektorisierung durch mikroskopische Parallelverarbeitung. Der Systementwurf gestattet die gleichzeitige Verwendung von schneller SRAM und hochintegrierter DRAM Speichertechnologie in einer zweistufigen Speicherhierarchie mit lokalem und globalem Hauptspeicher sowie virtueller Speicherverwaltung. Der globale Hauptspeicher dient bei synchroner und asynchroner Parallelverarbeitung als Shared Memory mehreren Prozessoren. Die lose Kopplung der Einzelprozessoren führt zu effizienter Parallelisierung makroskopischer Tasks mit geringen Systemverlusten.

Einleitung

Mit der ETA 10 Serie kann CONTROL DATA den Anspruch erheben, die bisher leistungsfähigste Familie von Großrechnern für den technisch–wissenschaftlichen Markt geschaffen zu haben. Trotz dieses technologischen Führungsanspruchs wurde erreicht, daß die Rechner in einem ökonomisch vernünftigen Rahmen von Anschaffungs- und Betriebskosten liegen. Dies war aus drei Gründen möglich:

- Die hohe Leistung wird mit produktionstechnisch günstiger CMOS Technologie erreicht.
- Die Rechner verfügen über lokalen und globalen Hauptspeicher und erschließen damit die virtuelle Speichertechnik auch für vektorisierte Anwendungen.
- Dem Betreiber wird die Möglichkeit geboten, statt eines herstellereigenen Betriebssystems das voll standardisierte UNIX System V zu nutzen. Die ETA 10 wird damit zum vollständig kompatiblen Element im UNIX–Verbund eines modernen Rechenzentrums.

Diese drei Eigenschaften sind Schlüsselmerkmale des ETA 10 Systems. Im vorliegenden Artikel werden sie im Zusammenhang der ETA 10 Systemarchitektur näher untersucht.

Die ETA 10 Familie umfaßt derzeit 44 Modellvarianten mit einem Leistungsspektrum von 1:27, vom luftgekühlten Einstiegsmodell im Abteilungsrechnerformat bis zum Höchstleistungsrechner mit acht Prozessoren.

Alle Modellvarianten sind von der Hardware her identisch. Sie unterscheiden sich durch die Taktzeit, die Anzahl der Prozessoren und den Speicherausbau. Die unterschiedliche Taktzeit wird hauptsächlich durch eine unterschiedliche Umgebungstemperatur erreicht. Die langsameren Modelle P und Q werden bei Raumtemperatur betrieben, während die Modelle E und G auf die Temperatur von flüssigem Stickstoff gekühlt werden. Durch diese kryostatische Kühlung - eine Neuentwicklung des Hauses CONTROL DATA - wird die CPU-Leistung um etwa den Faktor zwei verbessert. Die luftgekühlten Modelle P und Q stellen an die Betriebsumgebung keine höheren Anforderungen als herkömmliche Abteilungsrechner. Den Leistungsdaten aus Bild 1 läßt sich jedoch leicht entnehmen, daß es sich trotzdem um reinrassige Höchstleistungsrechner handelt, die sich von den großen stickstoffgekühlten Modellen zwar in der Anzahl der Prozessoren und im Speicherausbau unterscheiden, ihnen jedoch in der Prozessorleistung nur wenig nachstehen.

Modell	P	Q	E	G
Taktzeiten (Nanosekunden)	24	19	10.5	7
Prozessoren	1-2	1-2	1-4	2-8
Lokaler Speicher (MBytes)	32-64	32-64	32-128	32-128
Globaler Speicher (MBytes)	64-512	64-512	256-1024	512-2048
Peak Performance (MFLOPS)	750	946	3.420	10.280
Kühlung	Luft	Luft	flüssiger Stickstoff	flüssiger Stickstoff

Bild 1: ETA 10 Leistungsspektrum

Technologie

Die ETA 10 ist der erste Höchstleistungsrechner ganz aus CMOS. Diese Neuentwicklung ist ein technologischer Sprung mit weitreichenden Auswirkungen. CMOS läßt sich wesentlich kostengünstiger fertigen und auch betreiben als andere Halbleiter. CONTROL DATA kann deshalb mit der ETA 10 den ersten luftgekühlten Rechner mit allen Leistungsmerkmalen eines Höchstleistungs-Vektorrechnersystems anbieten. Dank der kostengünstigen CMOS Technologie ist aber auch das Preis-/Leistungsverhältnis bei den größeren, stickstoffgekühlten Modellen wesentlich besser als mit anderer Technologie.

Viel überraschender als das überlegene Preis-/Leistungsverhältnis, das man von CMOS erwartet hat, ist jedoch das absolute Leistungsniveau, das sich mit dieser immer noch als langsam geltenden Technologie erreichen läßt. Obwohl der Superlativ "schnellster Rechner" abgenutzt klingt und sich mit gewissem Recht jedem System bezüglich irgendeiner mehr oder minder wichtigen Eigenschaft zubilligen läßt, muß man trotzdem feststellen, daß ein ETA 10 Modell G derzeit in einem breiten Spektrum von Anwendungsprogrammen das leistungsfähigste System am Markt darstellt, sowohl was die Geschwindigkeit des Einzelprozessors angeht, wie auch die Durchsatzleistung des Mehrprozessorsystems. Kryostatisch gekühltes CMOS ist die derzeit leistungsfähigste Hardwaretechnologie am Markt.

Material	Geschwindigkeit (Picosec/Mikrometer)	Entfernung (Mikrometer)	Laufzeit (Picosec)
Chip	$7.5 * 10^{-2}$	2K	150
PC Board	10^{-2}	150K	1500
Coaxialkabel	$5 * 10^{-2}$	900K	4500

Bild 2: Signallaufzeiten zwischen verschiedenen Baugruppen

Wie kann die langsame CMOS Technologie plötzlich ein solches Leistungsniveau erreichen? Der Schlüssel hierzu liegt letztlich in der endlichen Ausbreitungsgeschwindigkeit elektronischer Signale. CMOS hat zwar längere Schaltzeiten als andere Halbleitertechnologien, jedoch sind die Signallaufzeiten zwischen Baugruppen, durch die hohe Integrationsdichte der CMOS Bauelemente kürzer. Die gesamte CPU der ETA 10 konnte auf einer Platine untergebracht werden, womit die langen Signalwege zwischen den verschiedenen Leiterplatten des herkömmlichen CPU-Moduls ganz entfallen. Durch den Wegfall dieser längsten Signalverzögerung wird die Rechnertaktzeit merklich reduziert. Dies ist im Bild 2 dargestellt.

Um die kostengünstige CMOS Technologie auch für Höchstleistungssysteme nutzbar zu machen, mußten drei technologische Barrieren überwunden werden.

Entwurf schneller Logik

Die logischen Grundelemente wie Addierer oder Register, die aus CMOS-Gate-Arrays aufgebaut sind, wurden so entworfen, daß die Schaltzeiten dieser Elemente möglichst kurz sind. Es wurden insgesamt etwa 90 verschiedene Mikrochips entwickelt, auf denen jeweils ein Funktionsblock der CPU untergebracht ist. Jeder Chip hat mit 20.000 Gate-Arrays etwa die Komplexität eines Mikroprozessors. Eine einzelne CPU setzt sich aus 240 dieser Funktionsblöcke zusammen. Neben den CPUs gibt es im ETA 10 System zwei weitere Hochleistungsprozessoren: das Shared Memory Interface und das Communication Buffer Interface. Sie sind in derselben Weise aufgebaut und haben etwa die Komplexität der CPU.

Kühlung mit flüssigem Stickstoff

Es wurde eine Kühltechnik mit flüssigem Stickstoff entwickelt und zur Serienreife gebracht, mit der die Schaltzeiten der Halbleiter-Bauelemente noch einmal um etwa den Faktor zwei reduziert werden können. Stickstoff dient in diesem Prozeß nicht eigentlich als Kühlflüssigkeit zum effizienten Transport der erzeugten Wärme, sondern wurde wegen seines niedrigen Siedepunkts (-196 Grad Celsius) ausgewählt. Bei dieser Temperatur ist der Ohm'sche Widerstand der hochfrequenten Logikschaltkreise herabgesetzt, womit die Schaltzeiten kleiner werden.

Hohe Integration

Die ganze CPU des Vektorrechners befindet sich auf einer einzigen Leiterplatte. Da jeder Mikrochip der CPU über 240 Pins verfügt, müssen auf dieser Leiterplatte 80.000 Verbindungen untergebracht werden. Hierzu mußte eine Platine mit 44 Verdrahtungsebenen entwickelt werden, in die Verbindungswege mit einer Gesamtlänge von 2 km geätzt sind. 80.000 hochpräzise Bohrungen verbinden die Verdrahtungsebenen. Der gesamte Fertigungsprozeß für die Leiterplatte ist vollständig automatisiert. Auch das Auflöten der Mikrochips auf die Leiterplatte wird von Robotern durchgeführt.

Mit diesen Maßnahmen ist es gelungen, ein Rechnersystem zu entwickeln, das heute eine Leistungsspitze von über 10 GFLOPS erreicht. Durch die kostengünstige Technologie und Produktionstechnik bleibt dieses Rechnersystem dennoch in einem sehr ökonomischen Kostenrahmen.

Mikroparallelität

Im Mittelpunkt der ETA 10 Architektur steht Vektorisierung. Der Vektorisierungsgrad eines Programms, der von der Rechnerarchitektur abhängt, ist auf der ETA 10 am höchsten. Die Vektorisierbarkeit eines Programms ist grundsätzlich eingeschränkt durch skalare Programmteile und durch die Startupzeit von Vektorinstruktionen. Die gesamte Ausführungszeit setzt sich damit aus drei Einzelbeiträgen zusammen:

$$T = T_S + T_V + T_A$$

Die Vektor-Ausführungszeit T_A ist die Zeit, in der aus den Vektorpipelines Rechenergebnisse strömen. T_V ist die Vektorstartupzeit, also die Zeit, in der die Vektorpipelines zwar arbeiten, aber noch kein Element des Ergebnisvektors bereit ist. T_S ist eine Vektor-Leerzeit, in der keine Vektorinstruktionen ausgeführt werden, z.B. weil skalare Instruktionen ausgeführt werden müssen oder weil die CPU wegen Speicher- oder Registerkonflikten überhaupt steht. Die Summe $T_S + T_V$ ergibt eine Vektor-Overheadzeit oder effektive Startupzeit für das Programm.

Während für einzelne Programmteile oder Programme ein einzelner Beitrag (z.B. T_S oder T_A) durchaus dominieren mag, sind über das Spektrum von Supercomputer-Anwendungen gesehen alle drei Beiträge zur Ausführungszeit eines Programms wichtig. In der ETA 10 Architektur wird die gesamte Ausführungszeit eines Programms optimiert, nicht nur einzelne Teilbeiträge. Aus diesem Grund wird beispielsweise auf eine spektakuläre Vektor-Leistungspitze bewußt verzichtet. Diese läßt sich zwar durch einfache architekturelle Maßnahmen wie Halbierung der Vektor-Taktrate unter Beibehaltung der (skalaren) Taktzeit oder Verdopplung der Vektorpipelines leicht erreichen, führt aber nur zu einer Reduktion der Vektor-Ausführungszeit

T_A, während die Vektorstartupzeit ansteigt. Hingegen wird in der ETA 10 ein Bündel von Maßnahmen ergriffen, um alle drei Beiträge zur Ausführungszeit balanciert zu reduzieren.

Das Hilfsmittel dazu ist Parallelverarbeitung auf mikroskopischer Ebene. Mikroparallelität ist die gleichzeitige Ausführung von mehreren Skalar- oder Vektoroperationen in getrennten Funktionseinheiten einer CPU. Beispiele für Mikroparallelität sind mehrere Vektor-Addierwerke (parallele Vektorpipelines), welche die Vektor-Ausführungszeit reduzieren; zusätzliche Vektor-Funktionseinheiten für logische Operationen zur Erhöhung des Vektorisierungsgrades eines Programmes; überlappte Vektorinstruktionen zur Reduktion der Vektor-Startupzeit; parallele Ausführung von Skalar- und Vektorinstruktionen zur Reduktion der Vektorleerzeit. Alle diese Maßnahmen und weitere sind in der ETA 10 getroffen. Durch das Zusammenwirken dieser Funktionen auf mikroskopischer Ebene erhält die ETA 10 CPU ihre Leistung. Dies ist in Bild 3 zusammengefaßt.

Eta 10: Mikroskopische Parallelität

Skalaroperationen	143 Mflops
64-Bit Vektoroperationen	571 Mflops
32-Bit Vektoroperationen	1142 Mflops
Boole'sche Vektoroperationen	2286 Mflops

Bild 3: Leistungsdaten des ETA 10 G Einzelprozessors

Mikroparallelität muß unterschieden werden von einer Aufteilung kleiner Programmteile auf verschiedene Betriebssystem-Tasks und verschiedene CPUs. Mikroparallelität ist eine Eigenschaft der Hardware und funktioniert mit minimaler Unterstützung durch den Compiler. Die Aufteilung in Mikro-Tasks ist dagegen hauptsächlich eine Anforderung an die Software, nämlich Compiler und Betriebssysten, mit vergleichsweise geringer Unterstützung durch die Hardware. Mikroparallelität führt deshalb zu einer wesentlich günstigeren Ausnutzung des Systems und ist, wenn in der Hardware vorhanden, einer mikroskopischen Aufteilung auf separate Prozessoren vorzuziehen.

Hoher Vektorisierungsgrad

Die Zeit Ts, in der keine Vektorinstruktionen ausgeführt werden können, wird in der ETA 10 Architektur hauptsächlich durch vier verschiedene Maßnahmen klein gehalten:

Überlappung von Skalar- und Vektorinstruktionen, ein mächtiger Vektorinstruktionssatz, dynamisches Nachladen der Vektorpipelines und eine hohe Skalargeschwindigkeit.

Die ETA 10 CPU ist in Bild 4 schematisch dargestellt. Skalar- und Vektorprozessor verfügen jeweils über eigene Pipelines, die unabhängig voneinander arbeiten. Während eine Vektorinstruktion ausgeführt wird, können die skalaren Funktionseinheiten parallel dazu aktiv sein. Durch den großen Registersatz von 256 Skalarregistern werden Speicherkonflikte zwischen Skalar- und Vektorprozessor weitgehend vermieden. Parallelität von Skalar- und Vektorinstruktionen kann bedeuten, daß ein Programm mit einen Skalaranteil von 50 % auf der ETA 10 voll vektorisierbar ist, da die skalare Zeit voll von Vektorinstruktionen überdeckt wird. Mit diesem in Fortran demonstrierbarem Beispiel wird deutlich, daß der Vektorisierungsgrad eines Programms durch die Trennung von Skalar- und Vektorprozessor wesentlich gesteigert wird.

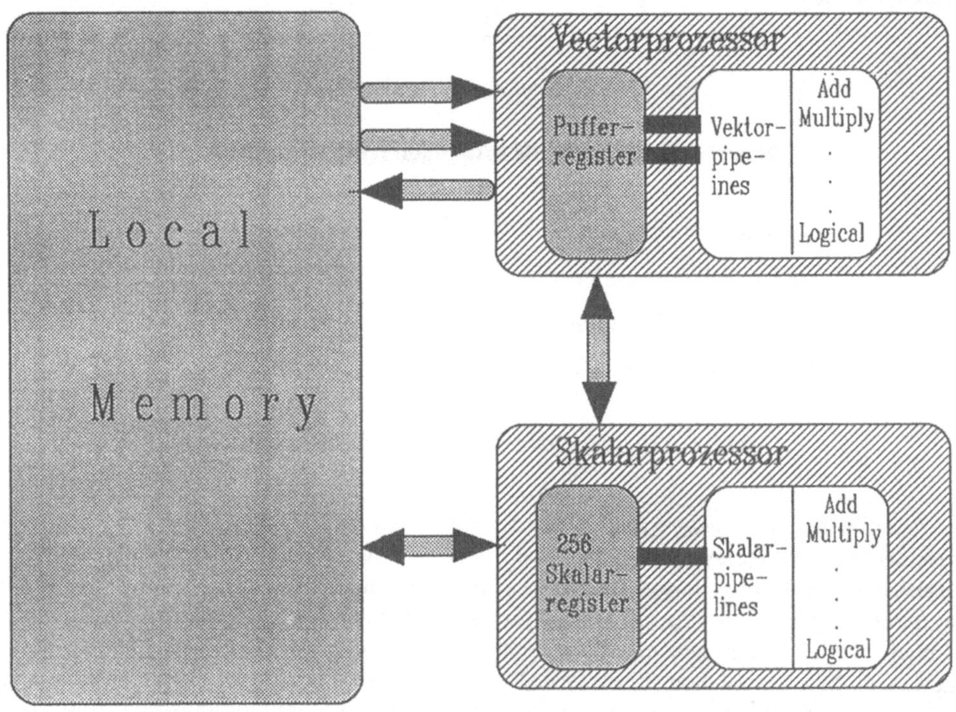

Bild 4: Schema der ETA 10 CPU.

Eine weitere Verringerung der Vektor-Leerzeit wird durch die Architektur des Vektorprozessors erreicht. Dies ist in Bild 5 dargestellt. Der Vektorprozessor verfügt neben den üblichen arithmetischen Funktionseinheiten für Addition- und Multiplikation über Vektorpipelines für logische Verarbeitung von Gleitkomma-Feldern und Boole'schen Feldern oder Bitvektoren. Durch diese zusätzlichen Pipelines können auf der ETA 10 auch Programmteile vektorisiert werden, die üblicherweise im Skalarprozessor abgearbeitet werden müssen. Ein besonders wichtiger Anwendungsfall ist die Vektorisierung von Vorwärtsverzweigungen. Auch sehr komplexe Verzweigungsbedingungen werden durch die Logik-Pipelines in der ETA 10 effizient vektorisiert. Der Datenfluß im Vektorprozessor beruht auf Pufferregistern, die aus dem lokalen Speicher dynamisch nachgeladen werden, während eine Vektorinstruktion ausgeführt wird. Die Vektorinstruktion muß zum Nachladen der Register nicht unterbrochen werden. Dies führt zu einer Reduktion der Vektor-Leerzeit, da auch für längere Vektoren keine Neuberechnung von Adressen und Vektorlängen durchgeführt werden muß und weil Bankkonflikte für die gesamte Dauer der Vektorinstruktion aufgelöst sind.

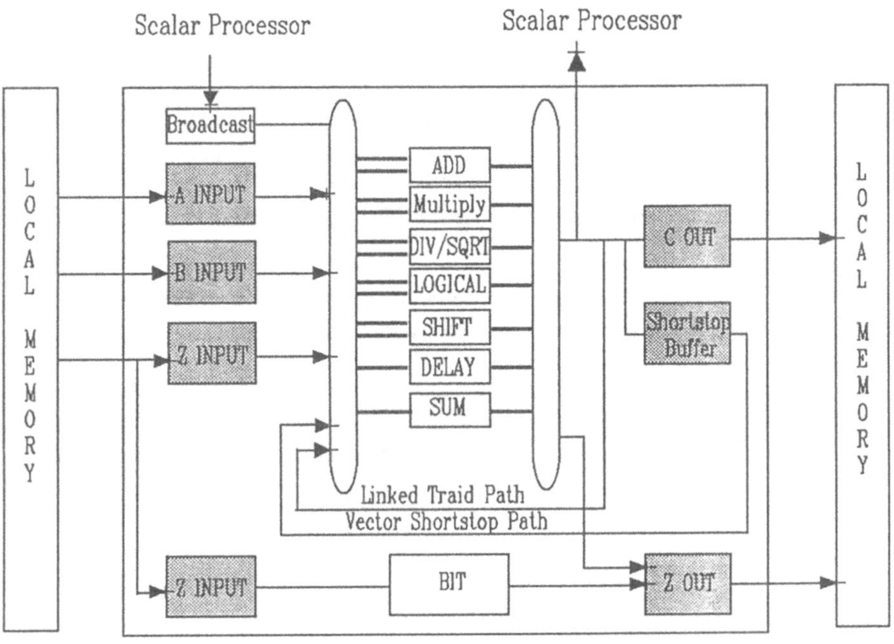

Bild 5: ETA 10 Vektorprozessor

Durch obige Maßnahmen kann auf der ETA 10 ein großer Teil von Skalarinstruktionen vermieden werden und der Vektorisierungsgrad eines Programmes steigt beträchtlich an. Für die verbleibenden Programmteile, die entweder skalar abgearbeitet werden müssen, oder die skalar schneller ablaufen als vektoriell verfügt die ETA 10 über einen schnellen Skalarprozessor. Die skalaren Funktionseinheiten sind wie die Vektorfunktionseinheiten als Pipelines ausgelegt und können somit in jedem Takt eine Rechenoperation ausführen. Für die ETA 10 G ergibt sich damit eine maximale Skalarleistung von 143 Mflops.

Die hohe Geschwindigkeit der skalaren Pipelines muß in Verbindung mit der großen Anzahl von 256 Skalarregistern und einem Instruktionspuffer gesehen werden, der 80 Befehle aufnehmen kann. Dadurch steht die hohe Geschwindigkeit der Skalarpipelines nicht nur als kurzzeitige Leistungsspitze zur Verfügung sondern kann auch über größere Programmteile hinweg aufrechterhalten werden. Beispielsweise erreicht die vielbenutzte Bibliotheksroutine MXMA zur Matrixmultiplikation in ihrem skalaren Zweig, der für kurze Vektorlängen durchlaufen wird, eine Leistung von 54 Mflops. Ein Unterprogramm zur rekursiven Berechnung eines Polynoms mit dem Hornerschema erreicht 79 Mflops.

Durch Minimierung des Skalaranteils, Überlappung von Skalar- und Vektorinstruktionen und einer hohen skalaren Ausführungsgeschwindigkeit, erlaubt die ETA 10 Architektur eine hohe Vektorisierbarkeit von Programmen.

Lokaler und Globaler Hauptspeicher

Die ETA 10 Speicherarchitektur wurde konzipiert, um beide heute gängigen Speichertechnologien in einem Systen verwenden zu können: schnelleres SRAM und höher integriertes DRAM. Die Notwendigkeit hierzu sieht man leicht ein. Um 1 GWord (= 8192 MByte) Hauptspeicher zu bauen - die heutige Anforderung an einen Größtrechner -, benötigt man 319.488 SRAM Chips der Integrationsdichte 256 KBit. Dies ist weder von den Produktionskosten noch der Stromversorgung her eine praktikable Anzahl. Dagegen reichen 79.872 DRAM Chips in 1-Mbit Technologie oder 19.968 4-Mbit Chips aus.

Eine zweistufige Speicherhierarchie mit schnellerem lokalen und langsamerem globalem Hauptspeicher ist jedoch auch von der Programmierung her sinnvoll. Einerseits gibt es die Anforderung, daß Hauptspeicher- und Pipelinegeschwindigkeit balanciert sein müssen, um die Vektorpipelines ohne Unterbrechung mit Daten versorgen zu können. Hierzu ist die schnellste Speichertechnologie notwendig. Andererseits gibt es neben solch "schnellen" Datenstrukturen in einem Programm auch viel "langsamere". Beispielsweise ist in der Matrix-Vektor Multiplikation

```
do i = 1,N
C(1:N) = C(1:N) + A(1:N,i) * B(i)
```

der Vektor C eine schnelle Datenstruktur, da er in jeder der N Vektorinstruktionen benötigt wird. Dagegen ist die Matrix A eine N-mal langsamere Datenstruktur, da ihre Spaltenvektoren A(1:N,i) nur je einmal benutzt werden, ebenso das nur skalar benutzte Feld B.

Die Implementierung dieses Algorithmus in der ETA 10 Speicherhierarchie ist in Bild 6 gezeigt. Das zweidimensionale Feld A befindet sich im globalen Hauptspeicher, während im lokalen Hauptspeicher nur die Ausschnitte von A gehalten werden, die gerade für die Berechnung gebraucht werden. Dagegen sind die kleineren eindimensionalen Felder B und C dauernd im lokalen Speicher.

Die Aufteilung in globalen und lokalen Hauptspeicher führt zu einer beträchtlichen Einsparung. Im obigen Beispiel benötigt man bei einer Vektorlänge N=1.000 acht MByte Hauptspeicher für die Felder A, B und C. Dagegen werden auf der ETA 10 nur wenige 100 KByte des lokalen

ETA 10 Memory Hierarchy

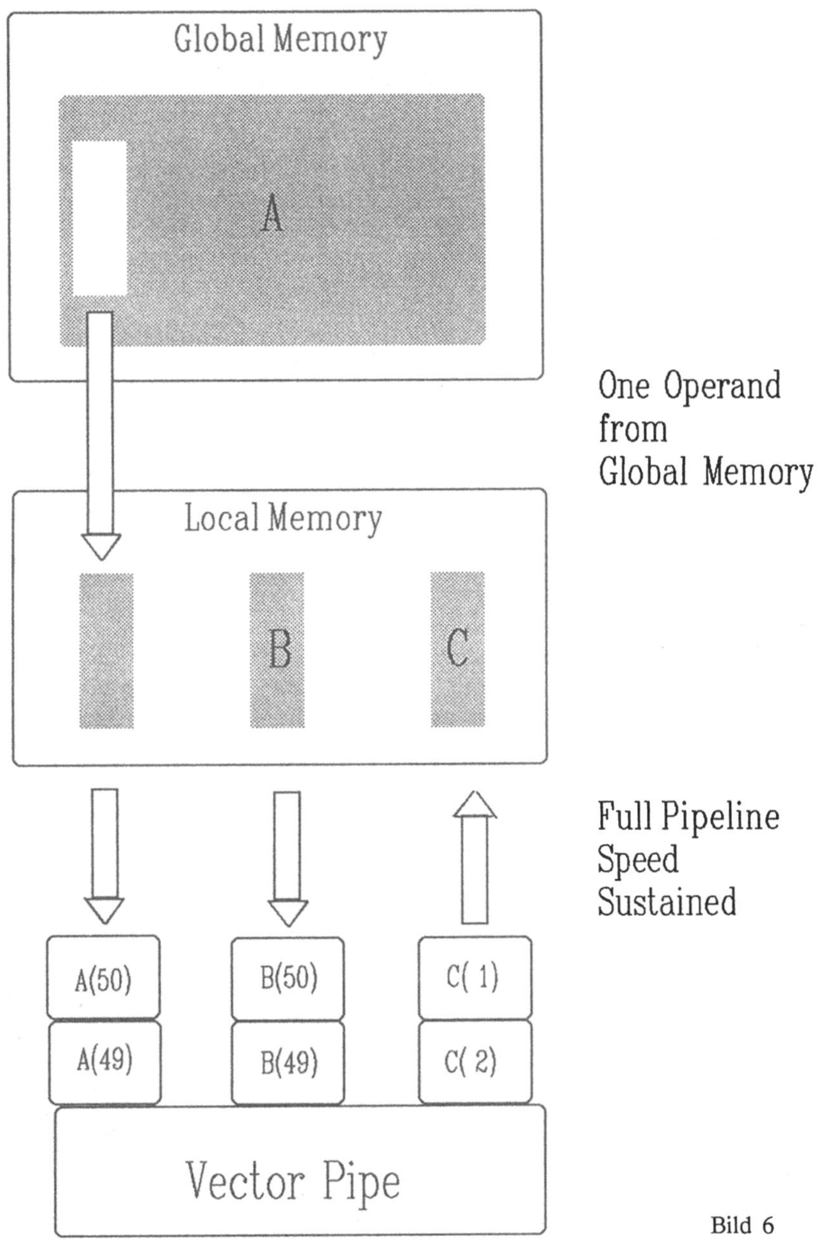

Bild 6

Speichers belegt. Mit der preiswerten DRAM Technologie vergrößert man so den aufwendigen lokalen Speicher effektiv um den Faktor 10.

Im Beispiel der Matrix-Vektor Multiplikation benötigt die langsame Datenstruktur A bereits eine beträchtliche Speichergeschwindigkeit. Der Algorithmus läßt sich nur dann in einer zweistufigen Speicherhierarchie ausführen, wenn sich die Geschwindigkeiten der beiden Speicher nicht allzusehr unterscheiden. Wird der Faktor 10 in den Zugriffszeiten stark überschritten, so wird die Verweilzeit des Problems zu lang. Langsame Magentplatten reichen deshalb als Sekundärspeicher nicht aus.

Darüber hinaus gibt es noch eine Vielzahl wesentlich langsamerer Datenstrukturen, für die der globale Hauptspeicher eingesetzt wird. Beispielsweise ist das Programm, aus dem obige Matrix-Vektor Multiplikation stammt, offensichtlich eine sehr langsame Datenstruktur, da während der gesamten Ausführungszeit des Algorithmus nur wenige Instruktionen im Speicher sein müssen.

Weitere Beispiele solch langsamer Datenstrukturen sind I/O-Puffer, die in einem UNIX System einen merklichen Teil des Hauptspeichers belegen, oder Teile des Compiler-Run-Time Systems. In all diesem Fällen kann aufwendiger SRAM Hauptspeicher ohne die geringste Leistungseinbuße durch kostengünstigen DRAM Speicher ersetzt werden.

Virtuelle Seicherverwaltung

Eine mehrstufige Speicherhierarchie ist, abgesehen von der Möglichkeit verschieden schneller, vielleicht sogar elektronischer Platten, ohne virtuelle Speicherverwaltung nicht möglich. Für einen Vektorrechner gilt auch das Umgekehrte: Ohne abgestufte reale Speicher ist die virtuelle Speichertechnik nur eingeschränkt nutzbar. Dies liegt an der Geschwindigkeit der Vektorinstruktionen. Während ein Datensatz der Größe 1 MWord (= 8 MByte) in der CPU eines schnellen Skalarrechners vielleicht 1 sec verweilt, wird er im Vektorprozessor in 1/100 sec abgearbeitet. Für den Skalarrechner ist deshalb eine Paging-Rate von 10 MByte/sec ausreichend, der Vektorrechner benötigt 1.000 MByte/sec. Im ersten Fall genügt eine Speicherhierarchie mit Hauptspeicher und schnellen Platten, während ein Vektorrechner ohne schnellen Sekundärspeicher nicht auskommt. Ohne globalen Hauptspeicher ist bei naiver Benutzung des virtuellen Adreßraums die Gefahr des Seitenflatterns groß. Mit einer gut abgestuften Speicherhierarchie führt die virtuelle Speichertechnik dagegen zu einer sehr effizienten Auslastung des Systems.

Das Beispiel der Matrix-Vektor Multiplikation soll dies wieder verdeutlichen. Ohne virtuelle Speicherverwaltung belegt die Matrix 8 MByte Hauptspeicher über die gesamte Ausführungszeit des Programms, selbst wenn das Feld A in seiner vollen Größe nur selten gebraucht wird. Auf der ETA 10 belegt die Matrix A dagegen selbst während der Matrix-Vektor Multiplikation nur wenige 100 KByte lokalen Speicher, in der restlichen Zeit kann sie sich im globalen Speicher oder auf der Platte befinden. Der lokale Speicher bleibt auf diese Weise für häufiger gebrauchte Datenstrukturen frei. Dies erhöht den Durchsatz des Systems spürbar.

Makroskopische Parallelverarbeitung

Während beim Einzelprozessor Vektorisierung im Mittelpunkt steht, baut das Multiprozessorkonzept der ETA 10 auf makroskopischer Parallelverarbeitung auf. Dabei ist zwischen asynchroner Verarbeitung, also der Bearbeitung vollkommen unabhängiger Tasks auf mehreren Prozessoren, und der Bearbeitung synchroner Tasks zu unterscheiden. Für einen Höchstleistungsrechner mit wenigen Prozessoren und vielen Benutzern ist die effiziente Bearbeitung asynchroner Tasks für die Durchsatzleistung des Systems wichtig. Synchrone Parallelverarbeitung erlangt jedoch mit steigender Anzahl der Prozessoren ebenfalls eine wachsende Bedeutung.

Die ETA 10 Mehrprozessorarchitektur ist im Bild 7 dargestellt. Das System besteht aus bis zu acht autonomen Rechnern mit eigenem lokalem Hauptspeicher, die in einem globalen Shared Memory gemeinsame Daten halten können und die über einen schnellen Speicher Nachrichten austauschen. Die Speicherhierarchie mit lokalem und globalem Speicher, die schon für den Einzelprozessor große Vorteile bezüglich Speicherverwaltung und -auslastung aufweist, bringt beim Zugriff durch mehrere Prozessoren noch größeren Nutzen. Bei einem einstufigem Hauptspeicher haben die Prozessoren direkten Zugriff auf die gleiche Speicherbank. Dadurch steigt die Anzahl der Speicherkonflikte mit der Anzahl der Prozessoren nichtlinear an. Die betroffene CPU ist blockiert bis der Speicherkonflikt aufgelöst ist. Dies führt zu einer schlechten CPU-Auslastung, die man nur vermeiden kann, wenn man die Anzahl der Speicherbänke mit der Anzahl der Prozessoren nichtlinear erhöht. Die Kopplung von mehreren Prozessoren über einen einstufigen Hauptspeicher ist deshalb nur für eine kleine Anzahl von Prozessoren möglich. Diese Einschränkung gilt sowohl für asynchrone wie auch für synchrone Parallelverarbeitung.

Das Problem ungenügender CPU-Auslastung durch Speicherkonflikte wird in der zweistufigen ETA 10 Speicherhierarchie von vornherein vermieden. Ein Prozessor kann im lokalen Speicher eines anderen Prozessors keinen Bankkonflikt erzeugen. Andererseits können Speicherkonflikte im gemeinsamen Shared Memory nicht zu einer schlechten CPU-Auslastung führen, da der Prozessor nicht blockiert ist. Er kann in dem großen lokalen Hauptspeicher andere Aufgaben bearbeiten, während der Speicherkonflikt im Shared Memory aufgelöst wird. Der Datentransfer zwischen lokalem und globalem Speicher ist asynchron und behindert die CPU nicht. Die ETA 10 hat deshalb unabhängig von der Anzahl der Prozessoren eine gleich gute Auslastung des Einzelprozessors. Dies ist für die Durchsatzleistung eines Systems mit mehreren Prozessoren wichtig.

Multitasking

Bei der synchronen Parallelverarbeitung auf mehreren Prozessoren kommen zum Problem der gemeinsamen Speichernutzung Systemverluste durch Kommunikation hinzu. Bei der Aufteilung eines Programms in synchrone Tasks gibt es Punkte, an denen verschiedene Subtasks erzeugt werden und Punkte, an denen diese wieder zusammengeführt werden. Dies führt zu einem nicht unerheblichen Verwaltungsaufwand für die CPUs und zu Wartezeiten an den Synchronisationspunkten. Die Anzahl der Synchronisationspunkte muß deshalb möglichst klein gehalten werden. Auf der ETA 10 werden aus diesem Grund vorzugsweise makroskopische Tasks auf mehrere Prozessoren verteilt, bei denen der Verwaltungsaufwand gegenüber der produktiven CPU-Zeit klein ist. Mikroskopische Programmteile, wie z.B. einzelne

Communication Buffer
CPU 1
CPU 8
CPU
Local Memory
Shared Memory
Disk

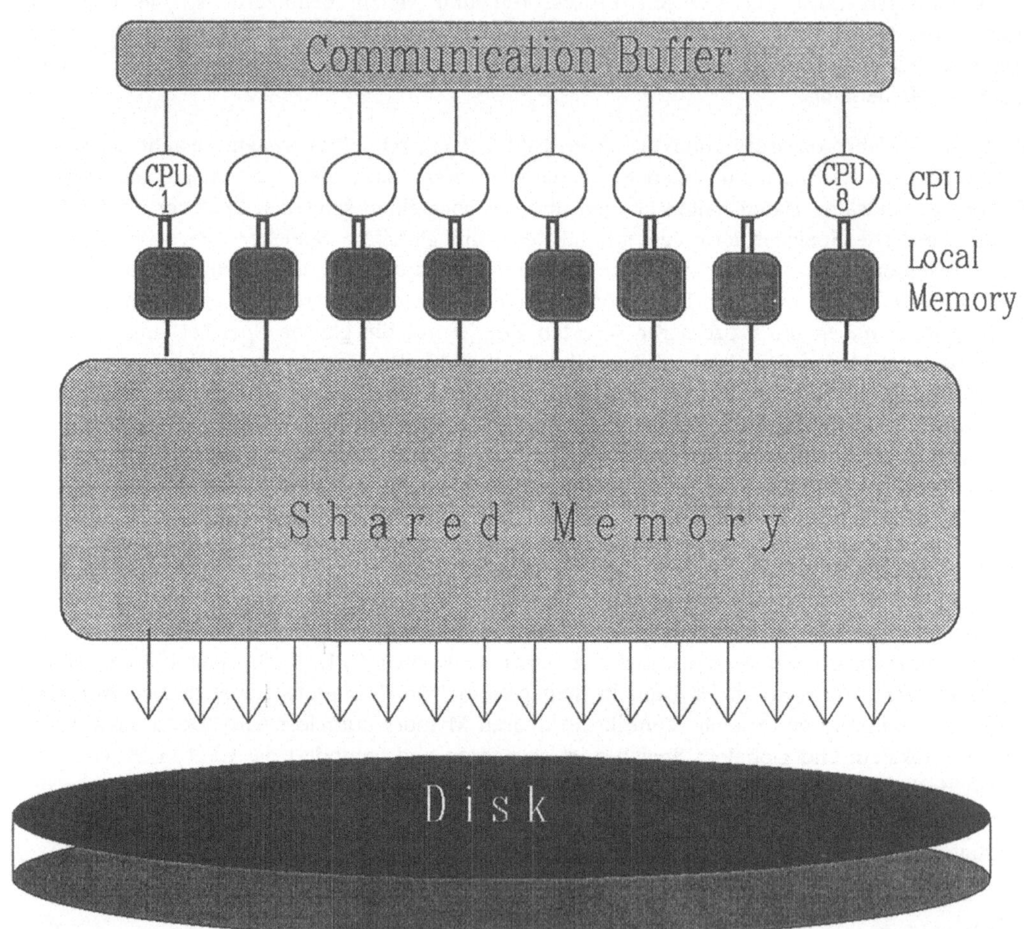

Bild 7

Vektorinstruktionen, werden dagegen innerhalb einer Task ohne Verwaltungsaufwand direkt durch die Hardware parallelisiert.

Die bevorzugte Strategie zur Erzeugung makroskopischer Tasks ist die Parallelisierung weit außen liegender Schleifen, unter der Voraussetzung, daß die einzelnen Schleifendurchläufe voneinander unabhängig sind. Dies wird dem Compiler durch Direktiven mitgeteilt. Der Compiler generiert dann Systemaufrufe an eine Multitasking-Library und das Programm wird auf diese Weise automatisch auf mehrere Prozessoren verteilt.

Die Parallelisierung von Schleifen über makroskopische Programmteile hat gegenüber einer automatischen Erzeugung mikroskopischer Tasks durch den Compiler den Vorteil höherer Effizienz. Autoparallelisierung beschränkt sich heute noch auf eng geschachtelte Schleifen. Diese werden auf der ETA 10 jedoch wesentlich effizienter durch Mikroparallelität in der CPU ausgeführt. Andererseits können Schleifen, die zu einer hohen Lokalität der Tasks führen, nur in wenigen Fällen vom Compiler analysiert werden. Die ETA 10 bietet durch automatische Parallelisierung auf mikroskopischer Ebene und Benutzerdirektiven für Makroparallelität einen Weg zur effizienten Nutzung des Systems in beiden Fällen.

An Overview of The HITACHI S-820 Supercomputer System

Michihiro Hirai, Shun Kawabe, Hideo Wada

Kanagawa Works, Hitachi, Ltd.
1 Horiyamashita, Hadano-shi,
Kanagawa-ken, 259-13 JAPAN
Shizuo Goto
Software Works, Hitachi, Ltd.
549-6 Shinano-machi, Totsuka-ku, Yokohama-shi,
Kanagawa-ken, 244 JAPAN

Abstract

The HITACHI S-820 has made a debut as one of the most powerful supercomputers in the world, with a peak arithmetic performance of 3 GFLOPS. Like its predecessor S-810, the first Japanese-made supercomputer, it consists of a scalar processor and a vector processor. As the scalar processor has the same architecture as a general-purpose mainframe, the whole complex fits well in conventional operating environments. Central to the high computation speed is the vector processor with its multiple-pipeline structure and large vector register memory. The use of the semiconductor Extended Storage dramatically reduces I/O time, contributing to faster job turnaround and balanced system performance. A high degree of parallelism is incorporated inside the vector processor as well as between the vector and the scalar processors. The hardware technology employed in the system, which is the key to high performance and supreme reliability, includes the field-proven state-of-the-art high-speed logic LSIs originally developed for Hitachi's top-of-the-line mainframes, a 256K bit CMOS RAM with an access time of 45 nsec, and a vector register LSI which combines logic and RAMs on a monolithic chip. A variety of software products have also been developed to fully exploit the hardware capabilities. They include a vectorizing compiler FORT77/HAP with enhanced vectorization capability, an easy-to-code differential equation solver DEQSOL E2, and a mathematical subroutine library MATRIX/HAP. In a benchmark with Lawrence Livermore Laboratory's 14 Kernels, the S-820 scores 355 (417 with a biCMOS version of the Main Storage) MFLOPS (algebraic average), among the highest in the industry.

1. Introduction

As science and technology advance in scale and complexity, demand for sheer numerical calculation power is accelerating. Furthermore, as society becomes more sophisticated, the use of the supercomputer is spreading into a variety of fields thus far unthought-of. To meet increasing power demand and diversifying application needs, Hitachi has developed the S-820 supercomputer, with the following design objectives:

(1) world-class performance
(2) large system capacity
(3) ease of use
(4) high reliability
(5) ease of installation

Combining the state-of-the-art hardware technology with innovative logic design and the ad hoc vector architecture, the top-of-the-line model S-820/80 achieves a maximum arithmetic throughput of 3 GFLOPS (Giga/Billion Floating-point Operations Per Second) or a sustained speed of well over 2 GFLOPS. This paper presents an overview of the S-820 supercomputer, primarily focusing on performance considerations.

2. Factors Affecting Performance

The overall performance of a supercomputer system is determined by a number of factors as illustrated in Fig. 2.1. Accordingly, achieving a performance goal requires multiple approaches from different perspectives. Generally speaking, vector hardware performance, which is often measured in MFLOPS (Million Floating-point Operations Per Second), can be improved by advanced hardware -- semiconductor and packaging -- technology and smart logic design.

In real-life environments, however, an increase in vector hardware performance does not necessarily mean an increase of the same rate in actual performance observed for a given job, especially when the vectorization ratio -- the ratio of the vectorizable (vectorized) code to the entire code of the job in terms of dynamic execution time -- is not high enough. The vectorization ratio, often the key factor in determining actual performance, can be improved by a rich vector instruction set and a powerful vectorizing compiler. Another determining factor of actual job performance in terms of Elapsed (E) time is input/output (I/O), especially when a large amount of data is to be processed. An advanced storage organization with an additional level in hierarchy solves this I/O problem effectively.

The overall systems throughput, measured in terms of how many vector jobs can be executed per unit time, reflects all the hardware and software factors, and is also particularly sensitive to how efficiently the system's resources are utilized. In this regard, the degree of parallelism among multiple processors, e.g., between the Scalar Processor and the Vector Processor, is crucial.

The design of the S-820 has taken all these factors into consideration, bringing forth a number of improvements over its predecessor S-810 in architecture, logic structure, hardware technology and software.

3. Architecture and System Organization

3.1 Overview

Apart from high performance, the design goals included ease of use, and affinity with ordinary EDP (electronic data processing) environments has been emphasized. Thus, VOS3, Hitachi's

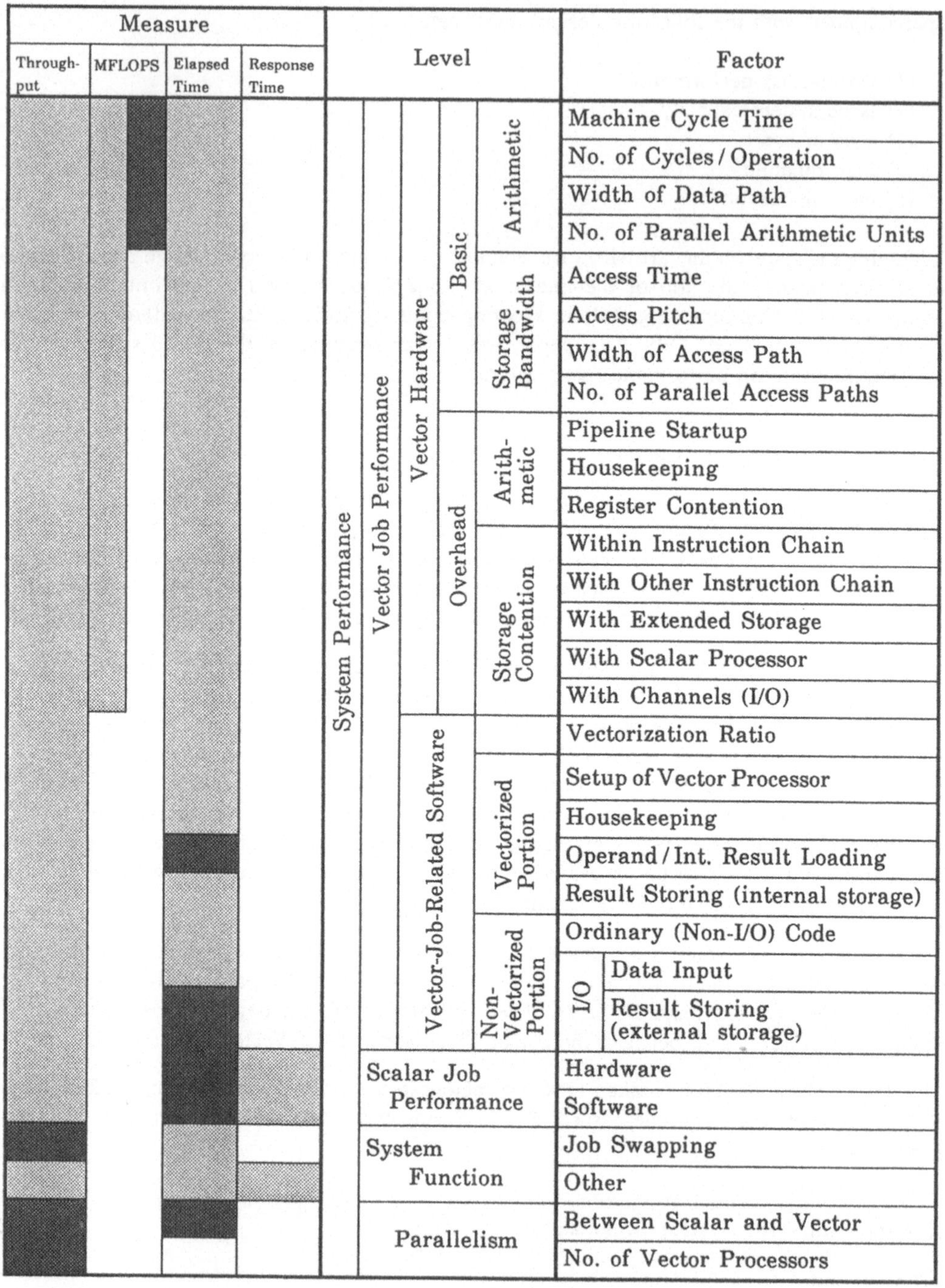

Measure				Level					Factor	
Through-put	MFLOPS	Elapsed Time	Response Time							
				System Performance	Vector Job Performance	Vector Hardware	Basic	Arithmetic	Machine Cycle Time	
									No. of Cycles / Operation	
									Width of Data Path	
									No. of Parallel Arithmetic Units	
								Storage Bandwidth	Access Time	
									Access Pitch	
									Width of Access Path	
									No. of Parallel Access Paths	
							Overhead	Arith-metic	Pipeline Startup	
									Housekeeping	
									Register Contention	
								Storage Contention	Within Instruction Chain	
									With Other Instruction Chain	
									With Extended Storage	
									With Scalar Processor	
									With Channels (I/O)	
						Vector-Job-Related Software			Vectorization Ratio	
								Vectorized Portion	Setup of Vector Processor	
									Housekeeping	
									Operand / Int. Result Loading	
									Result Storing (internal storage)	
								Non-Vectorized Portion	Ordinary (Non-I/O) Code	
									I/O	Data Input
										Result Storing (external storage)
					Scalar Job Performance				Hardware	
									Software	
					System Function				Job Swapping	
									Other	
					Parallelism				Between Scalar and Vector	
									No. of Vector Processors	

Fig. 2.1 Vector Processor Performance Factors

Standalone Configuration

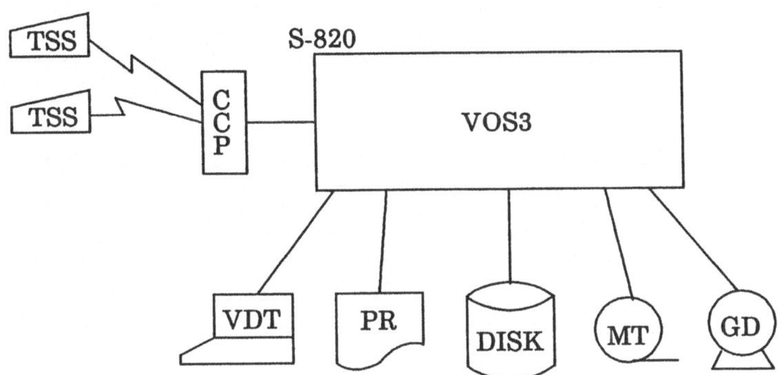

Loosely-coupled Configuration

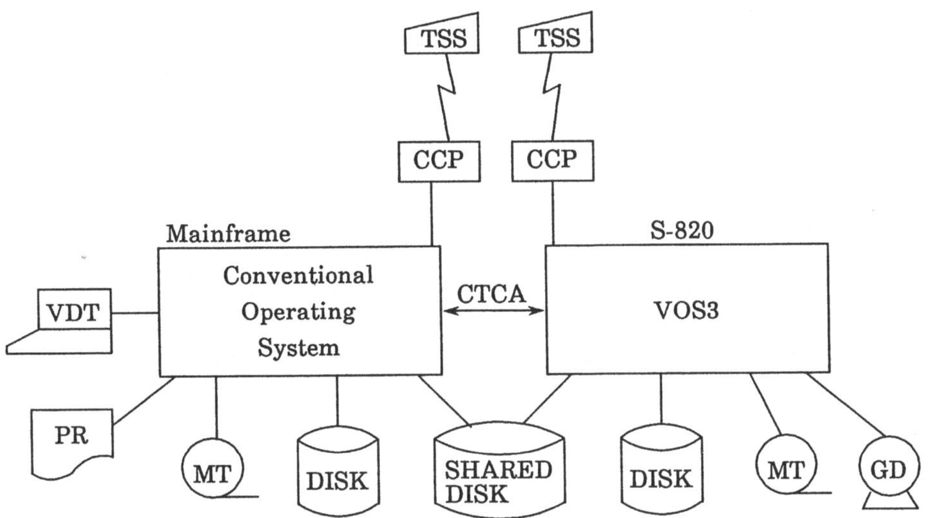

Legend)

CCP : Communication Control Processor
CTCA: Channel-to-Channel Adapter
GD : Graphic Display
MT : Magnetic Tape
PR : Printer
TSS : TSS (Time Sharing System) Terminal
VDT : Video Display Terminal (for system operation)
VOS3 : Virtual Operating System 3

Fig. 3.1 Operating Environments

proprietary operating system for large-scale mainframes, has been chosen as the primary operating system for the S-820 so that the user can take advantage of the rich array of software products accumulated through his conventional operations.

Along this line, as illustrated in Fig. 3.1, the S-820 has been designed to operate both in a loosely-coupled configuration and in a standalone configuration. In the former, the S-820 concentrates on numerical computation as a back-end subsystem while the front-end mainframe executes conventional jobs such as compilation and performs system functions. In the latter, the standalone S-820 executes both front end and back-end jobs by itself. Consequently, the S-820 processor complex comprises a Scalar Processor and a Vector Processor, along with other essential component units. As summarized in Fig. 3.2, the Scalar Processor employs the architecture of Hitachi's M-Series mainframes in consideration of compatibility, connectivity and ease of migration. The Vector Processor, on the other hand, has its own vector architecture suited for high-speed engineering/scientific computation.

The vector architecture includes a set of 90 ad hoc instructions, a large stack of vector registers, a vector processing timer, and a large-capacity Extended Storage

Scalar Processor		Vector Processor	
HITACHI M-Series Architecture		**Extended Vector Architecture**	
M-Series instruction set	216	Vector instruction set	90
General - purpose registers	16	Vector registers	32 sets
Floating - point registers	16	Vector mask registers	16
Control registers	16	Scalar registers	32
Address translation		Vector address registers	48
Storage protection		Vector address translation	
TOD clock		Vector processing timer	
CPU timer			
Clock comparator			
Extended channel subsystem			

Fig. 3.2 Architecture of S-820

which serves as an internal storage for keeping intermediate results and for job swapping. The instruction set has been enriched by adding seven instructions to the predecessor S-810's, including those for list vector (indirect addressing), to speed up such operations as gather/scatter. The basic components of the system are the same as the S-810's, except that their sizes have been enhanced to match the ever increasing system capacity and performance demand.

Table 3.1 S-820 Specifications

<table>
<tr><th colspan="3">Model</th><th>S-820/80</th><th>S-820/60</th><th>S-820/40</th><th>S-820/20</th></tr>
<tr><td rowspan="20">Scalar and Vector Processors</td><td colspan="2">Peak Throughput of Arithmetic Units (GFLOPS)</td><td>3</td><td>1.5</td><td>0.75</td><td>0.375</td></tr>
<tr><td colspan="2">No. of Vector Instructions</td><td colspan="4">90</td></tr>
<tr><td rowspan="7">Registers</td><td>General Registers</td><td colspan="4">16(32bit)</td></tr>
<tr><td>Floating-point Registers</td><td colspan="4">16(64bit)</td></tr>
<tr><td>Control Registers</td><td colspan="4">16(32bit)</td></tr>
<tr><td>Vector Registers</td><td>32 x 512 words</td><td>32 x 256 words</td><td colspan="2">32 x 128 words</td></tr>
<tr><td>Vector Mask Registers</td><td>16 x 512 bits</td><td>16 x 256 bits</td><td colspan="2">16 x 128 bits</td></tr>
<tr><td>Scalar Registers</td><td colspan="4">32 (64bit)</td></tr>
<tr><td>Vector Address Registers</td><td colspan="4">48 (32bit)</td></tr>
<tr><td rowspan="3">Data Formats</td><td>Fixed-point</td><td colspan="4">32bit</td></tr>
<tr><td>Floating-point</td><td colspan="4">32, 64bit</td></tr>
<tr><td>Logical</td><td colspan="4">64bit</td></tr>
<tr><td colspan="2">Vector Processing Timer</td><td colspan="4">Yes</td></tr>
<tr><td colspan="2">Buffer Storage (K bytes)</td><td colspan="3">256</td><td>128</td></tr>
<tr><td rowspan="6">No. of Pipeline Elements</td><td>Add/Logical</td><td>4</td><td>2</td><td>1</td><td>1</td></tr>
<tr><td>Multiply/Add</td><td>4</td><td>2</td><td>1</td><td>1</td></tr>
<tr><td>Divide</td><td>1</td><td>1</td><td>1</td><td>1</td></tr>
<tr><td>Mask Operation</td><td>1</td><td>1</td><td>1</td><td>1</td></tr>
<tr><td>Vector Load</td><td>4</td><td>2</td><td>1</td><td>0</td></tr>
<tr><td>Vector Load/ Store</td><td>4</td><td>2</td><td>1</td><td>1</td></tr>
<tr><td rowspan="2">Main Storage</td><td colspan="2">Capacities (M bytes)</td><td>128-512</td><td>64-256</td><td>32-256</td><td>32-128</td></tr>
<tr><td colspan="2">Error Checking/ Correction</td><td colspan="4">1-bit error corretion, 2-bit error detection</td></tr>
<tr><td rowspan="3">Extended Storage</td><td colspan="2">Capacities (G bytes)</td><td>0.5-12</td><td>0.5-6</td><td>0.5-6</td><td>0.25-3</td></tr>
<tr><td colspan="2">Maximum Transfar Rate (G bytes /sec)</td><td colspan="3">1 or 2</td><td>1</td></tr>
<tr><td colspan="2">Error Checking/ Correction</td><td colspan="4">2-bit error correction</td></tr>
<tr><td rowspan="3">Input/ Output Processors</td><td colspan="2">No. of Channels</td><td colspan="4">16, 32, 48, 64</td></tr>
<tr><td colspan="2">Maximum Data Rate/ Channel (M bytes/sec)</td><td colspan="4">6</td></tr>
<tr><td colspan="2">Total Aggregate Channel Data Rate (M bytes/sec)</td><td colspan="4">288</td></tr>
</table>

To provide budget–tight users with an easy entry to the supercomputer world and a smooth path of future growth, the S–820 is offered in four models: Models 20, 40, 60 and 80 in the ascending order of performance. Table 3.1 presents the specifications of the S–820.

The Vector Processor can basically operate concurrently with the Scalar Processor. During compilation, a DO loop in the source code is converted ("vectorized") to one or more vector instructions for the Vector Processor, and an instruction for starting the Vector Processor (EXVP (Execute Vector Processing) instruction) is inserted into the code for the Scalar Processor. During the execution step, the Scalar Processor, upon encountering an EXVP instruction, activates the Vector Processor, which, in turn, executes the series of vector instructions associated with it, while the Scalar Processor proceeds with the subsequent scalar operation. Subsection 4.2.3 will discuss the parallelism between the Scalar Processor and the Vector Processor in more detail.

3.2 Extended Storage

Whereas the vector instruction set is one of the key architectural contributors to performance in terms of reduced CPU (processor) time, the Extended Storage dramatically reduces elapsed time, another popular measure of performance.

As illustrated in Fig. 3.3, the Extended Storage is hierarchically situated between the Main Storage, where programs and their data (operands) reside when they are to be executed, and the disk units, where they reside when they are not immediately needed. The Main Storage, made of fast semiconductor memory chips, tends to be limited in capacity due to cost impact. As a result, a program with a large amount of data does not fit at one time in the Main Storage, and its execution requires lengthy input/output (I/O) operations between the Main Storage and the disk(s) via a channel. For such large programs, the disk I/O limits the actual elapsed time, even if the vector performance is high.

The Extended Storage, also made of semiconductor memory chips, serves as a highspeed temporary storage for computation results. The capacity as large as 12 Gbytes (giga (=billion) bytes) often eliminates the need for disk I/O for many jobs, which results in significant reductions in elapsed time or job turnaround time. Fig. 3.4 well illustrates the effect of the Extended Storage [1]: a five– to six–fold improvement in elapsed time performance has been achieved. The reduced frequency of running the I/O supervisor (part of the operating system) is also visible in the form of reduced CPU time.

Two synchronous instructions are provided for moving data (intermediate results) from the Main Storage to the Extended Storage and vice versa. "Synchronous" means that the Scalar Processor waits for the completion of this instruction, instead of proceeding further and being interrupted later. For the user's convenience, there is no need to rewrite the I/O statements in the FORTRAN source code: the compiler automatically (by the user's choice) replaces them with appropriate synchronous move instructions.

The Extended Storage also serves as a work storage for job swapping, which contributes to increased system throughput. Invisible to the user, the operating system is provided with an asynchronous move instruction, which is similar in format and operation to an input/output instruction.

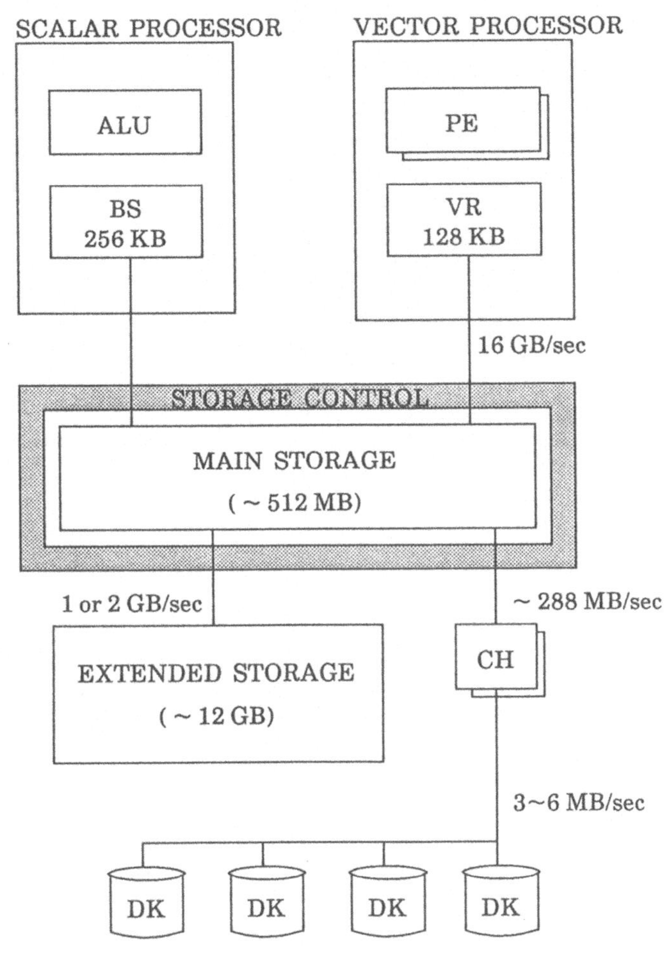

Legend)

ALU	: Arithmetic and Logical Unit
BS	: Buffer Storage
CH	: Channel
DK	: Disk
KB	: K bytes (kilobytes)
MB	: M bytes (megabytes)
PE	: [Arithmetic] Pipeline Element
VR	: Vector Registers

Fig. 3.3 Storage Hierarchy (S-820 / 80)

3.3 Vector Register

During execution, vector operands reside in the Main Storage and are fetched into the Vector Processor as necessary. Likewise, the results of computation are stored into the Main Storage.

(A) Elapsed Time for Plasma Stability Calculation

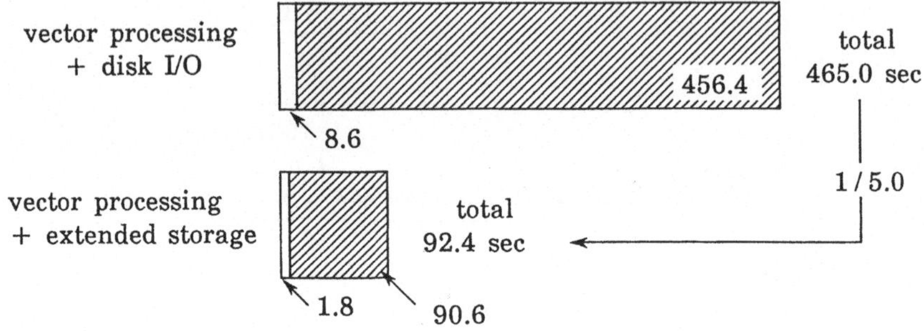

(B) Elapsed Time for Molecular Orbital Calculation

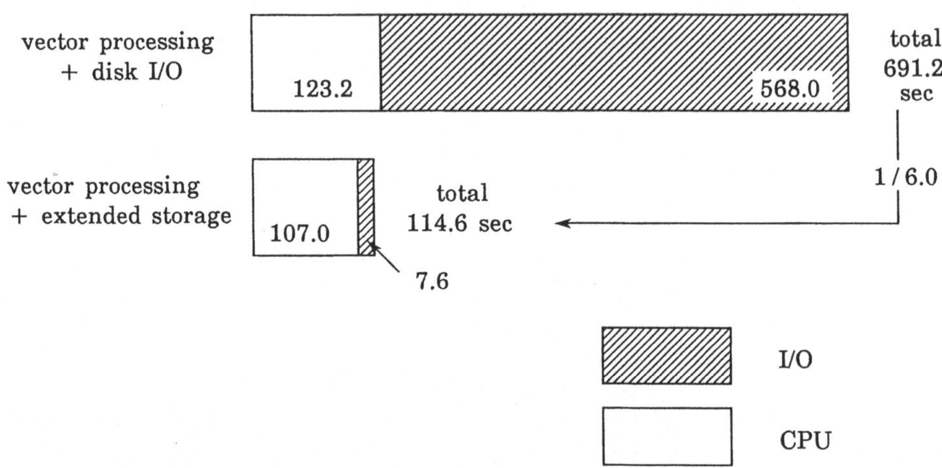

Fig. 3.4 Benefit of Extended Storage

In many instances, operands tend to be used more than once, and the results of computation tend to be referenced later in the same program. If operands and computation results are always to be stored in and fetched from the Main Storage, accesscontention would cause wait in the Vector Processor and impact performance, even with a large storage bandwidth.

Addressing this problem, the S–820 employs a vector register architecture: a large stack -- as much as 128 Kbytes on Model 80 -- of vector registers composed of highspeed bipolar memory LSIs is provided to hold a large amount of vector operands and intermediate results inside the Vector Processor which are likely to be re–used within a short period of time. As shown in Table 3.1, this is equivalent to 32 sets of vectors, each having a maximum of 512 64–bit elements.

3.4 Vector Instruction Set

To increase the vectorization ratio, i.e., to allow as many DO loops to be vectorized as possible, the S–820 has 90 specially defined instructions for vector operations. They include not only arithmetic instructions but also list vector instructions for gather/scatter operations, macroinstructions for compound (double–arithmetic) operations, and compare instructions to generate mask vectors which allow vectorization of conditional (IF) statements. The Vector Processor contains 16 vector mask registers with up to 512 mask bits each (seeTable 3.1).

Table 3.2 lists the vector instructions arranged by kind.

Table 3.2 List of Vector Instructions

Kind	No. of Instructions
load/store (including list vector)	20
move	7
simple arithmetic	13
macro (compound arithmetic)	12
convert	2
compare	13
search	7
logical	7
mask	5
control	4
Total	90

4. Logic Structure

4.1 Overview

As illustrated in Fig. 4.1, the S–820 Model 80 processor complex consists of the following component units:

- one Scalar Processor
- one Vector Processor
- one Storage Controller
- one Main Storage with the capacity ranging from 128 Mbytes to 512 Mbytes
- one Extended Storage with the capacity ranging from 512 Mbytes to 12 Gbytes
- one or two Input/Output Processors (IOPs), each of which contains from 8 to 32 channels
- one Service Processor (SVP)
- one or two Console Devices
- an appropriate number of Power Distribution Units (PDUs) depending upon the configuration

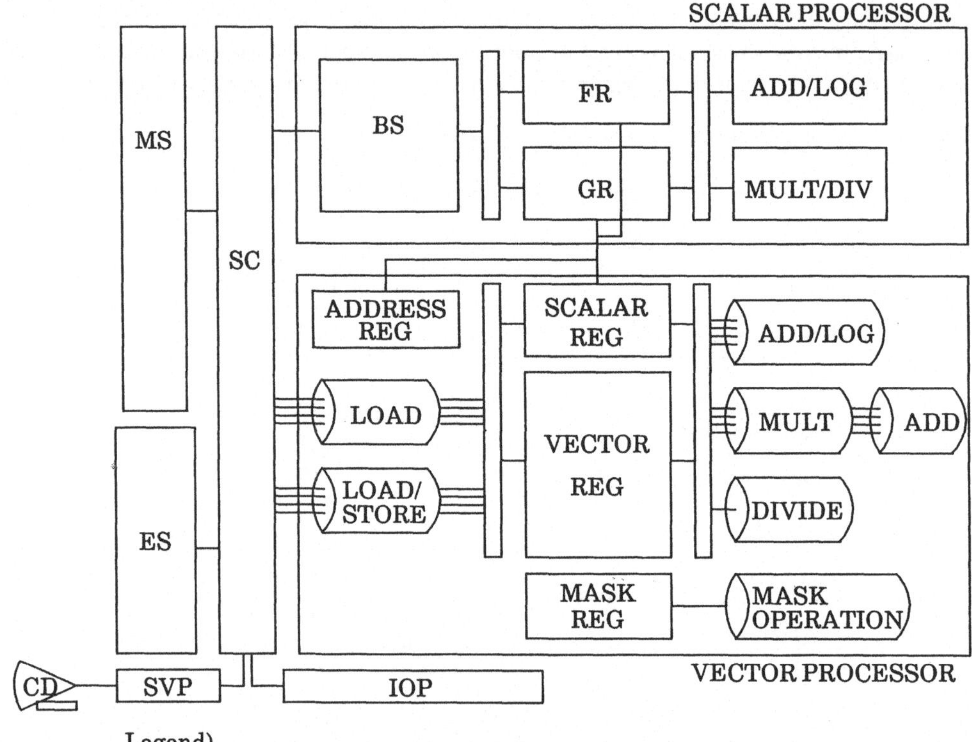

Fig. 4.1 Processor Organization of S–820/80

The Scalar Processor is, in terms of logic structure, substantially similar to the Instruction Processor of the M-680H, Hitachi's top-of-the-line mainframe (uniprocessor). It employs a 31-bit virtual addressing scheme.

The Vector Processor contains several floating-point arithmetic units (pipeline elements) and an array of vector registers, and executes vector instructions at high speed; its structure and operation will be discussed in more detail in Section 4.2. In Fig. 4.1, the four lines coming in or out of each resource (denoted by a cylinder) means that there are four identical units each for Model 80. The number is smaller two for Models 60, 40 and 20 (seeTable3.1).

The Storage Controller performs data transfer between the Main Storage and any of the Extended Storage, the Scalar Processor, the Vector Processor and the IOPs, solving contentions among them. The Main Storage serves as an ordinary processor storage which contains programs, data and system tables. The Extended Storage constitutes an intermediate level in the storage hierarchy and provides excellent potentials for significant elapsed time and system performance improvements, as discussed in Section 3.2.

The channels, housed in Input/Output Processors (IOPs), transfer data between the Main Storage (via the Storage Controller) and input/out devices, over an industry standard protocol. The microprocessor-based Service Processor (SVP), in combination with a Console Device (CD) attached to it, monitors and controls the operation of the processor complex and performs system functions such as initial program load (IPL), and reliability, availability and serviceability (RAS) functions.

4.2 Vector Execution Control

This section discusses the design features of the Vector Processor from the performance point of view.

4.2.1 Parallel Construction [2]

As illustrated in Fig. 4.1, the S-820 Model 80 has four add/logical operation units, four multiply-and-add units and a divide unit for arithmetic operations. A multiply-and-add unit consists of a multiply subunit and an add subunit in a cascade connection. The twelve(12) arithmetic units, namely, the add/logical operation units, the multiply subunits and the add subunits, together with the load or the load/store units and rows of vector registers, form "pipelines" in that operands go through them vector element after vector element in a pipeline manner. Each of these units/subunits is called a pipeline element. The minor models (Models 60, 40 and 20) have fewer pipeline elements.

The pipeline elements can operate simultaneously with each other. Each pipeline element produces a 64-bit result every four (4) nanoseconds (nsec), which is the clock cycle of the Vector Processor. The S-820 Model 80 has altogether 12 pipeline elements, and hence has a maximum arithmetic throughput of:

$12 \times (1/(4 \times 10^{-9} \text{sec})) = 3$ GFLOPS.

The maximum number of arithmetic operations performed per instruction per machine cycle on a pair of operands (vector elements) by the S–820's vector instruction set is two (2). Therefore, the maximum single–instruction execution speed is 2 GFLOPS, as in the case of the Vector Multiply and Add instruction. However, thanks to the parallel structure of the add/logical units and the multiply–and–add units, two dissimilar instructions can be executed simultaneously, one using the former and the other using the latter, in which case the maximum arithmetic throughput of 3 GFLOPS can be achieved. Although a carefully coded synthetic program has scored more than 2.5 GFLOPS as "sustained performance", real–life programs will see somewhat lower performance due to various overhead and the difficulty in taking full advantage of the parallelism all the time. The divide unit cannot operate simultaneously with other arithmetic units/subunits.

Table 4.1 shows arithmetic execution speeds of some vector instructions on the S–820 Model 80.

Table 4.1 Vector Instruction Execution Speed (S–820/80)
(on 64–bit floating–point operands)

unit: MFLOPS

Add	1000
Multiply	1000
Divide	250
Multiply and Add	2000

4.2.2 Elementwise Parallel Processing [2]

One of the load units, one of the load/store units, a pair of rows of vector registers and one of the arithmetic units form a pipeline, also called a section; there are multiple pipelines in Models 80 and 60.

One way to take advantage of the parallel pipelines is to execute multiple vector instructions on them. This is not always easy, however, since complete mutual independency of these instructions must be guaranteed.

The S–820 employs elementwise parallel processing, in which one vector instruction monopolizes all the pipelines of one kind (add/logical or multiply–and–add), allocating different vector elements to different pipelines. Fig. 4.2 illustrates elementwise parallel processing on Model 80 with four pipelines (sections), taking a vector inner (scalar) product operation between two 80–element arrays (operands) as an example.

The vector elements of Array A (first operand) are loaded into four rows of vector registers via four load units; the vector elements of Array B (second operand) are loaded into another set of four rows of vector registers via four load/store units; multiplication and addition are performed on four pairs of vector elements simultaneously in the four multiply–and–add units. In each pipeline, the result of multiplication is accumulated into the accumulator inside the multiply–and–add unit one cycle after another. When all the vector elements (operands) are exhausted, the four partial sums contained in the four accumulators are added together to produce the final result S at the postprocessing stage.

As indicated, the total execution time is composed of the startup time a, the core execution time (20 cycles) and the postprocessing time b. Generally, with a vector size of N, the total execution time Te is expressed as follows:

$$Te = a + (N/4) + b.$$

a and b do not depend upon the vector size, i.e., the number of vector elements per operand (array), and are relatively small.

Without elementwise parallel processing, the total execution time Tn would be:

$$Tn = a + N + b.$$

With a large size of the vector (array), Te = Tn/4, i.e., elementwise parallel execution is nearly four times as fast as serial pipeline execution.

4.2.3 Linking and Signaling [3]

During compilation, a DO loop in source code, if vectorizable, is converted to a series, or a chain, of vector instructions. For each vector instruction, the Scalar Processor prepares the necessary information such as vector length and addresses of the first vector elements of the operands. In a conventional design like that of the predecessor S–810, the Scalar Processor prepares and loads such information for the entire chain of vector instructions into the registers in the Vector Processor before starting the latter, since the latter, once started, would proceed to the end of the chain at its own pace, without regard to the status of the Scalar Processor. Likewise, the Scalar Processor, when it comes to a point where it needs the result of the vector computation, waits for the completion of the execution of the entire chain by the Vector Processor. Thus, as shown in Fig. 4.3 (on the top), the degree of parallelism between the scalar and the vector operations is rather low.

The S–820 introduces parallelism here. It employs two new functions, called linking and signaling, to allow overlapping between scalar processing and vector processing. During compilation, the compiler examines the code, determines which portion of the scalar code can overlap with which portion of the vector code, and inserts an instruction or a flag accordingly.

As illustrated in Fig. 4.3 (on the bottom), the Scalar Processor starts the Vector Processor even in the middle of the setup operation for the entire chain when it (actually the compiler) determines that the latter can go ahead without requiring further information from the former up to a certain point in the chain. One such stretch can be one or more vector instructions. While the Vector Processor is executing the first stretch of vector instructions (the first portion of the chain), the Scalar Processor proceeds with setup operation for the next stretch (the next portion of the chain) and, upon completing it, sends a start signal to the Vector Processor again. This process is called linking, and enhances simultaneous operation of the two processors. The Vector Processor, upon completing the first stretch, starts executing the next.

Similarly, when the Vector Processor determines, by encountering a signaling flag turned on by the compiler beforehand, that the result awaited by the Scalar Processor is now ready in a scalar register, it instructs the latter to resume the scalar operation while it continues the remaining

$$S = \sum_{i=1}^{80} A_i \cdot B_i = A_1 \times B_1 + A_2 \times B_2 + \cdots + A_{80} \times B_{80}$$

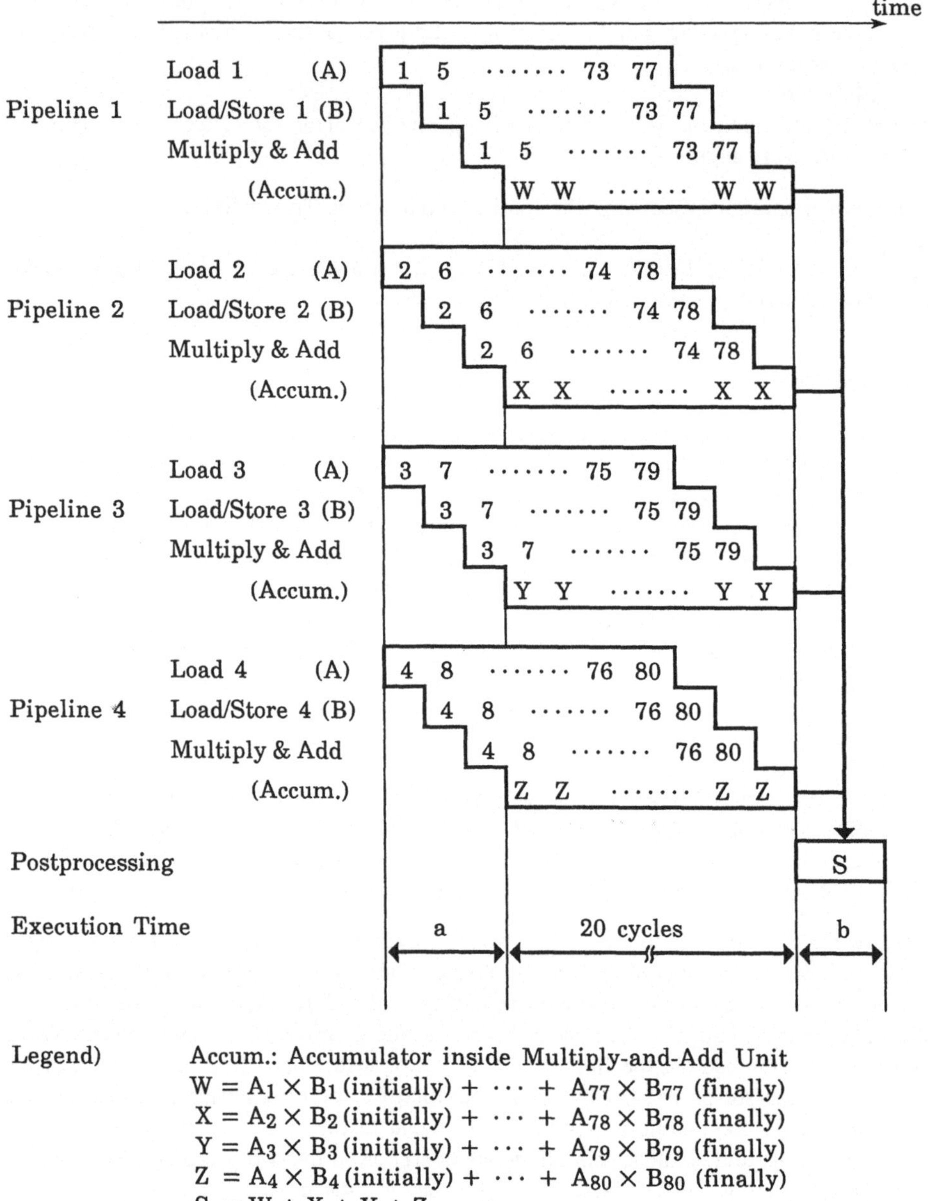

Fig. 4.2 Flow of Elementwise Pipeline Processing

Conventional Design (S-810)

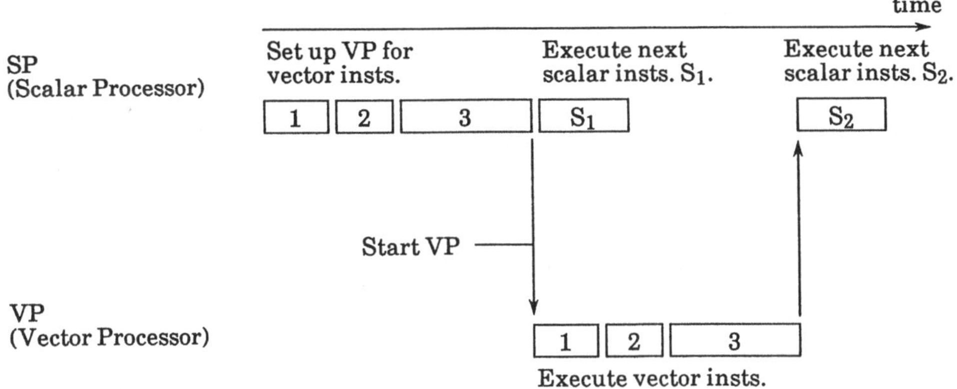

S_1: A series of scalar instructions which does not need the results of the vector computation.
S_2: A series of scalar instructions which needs the results of the vector computation (e.g., (2)).

S-820

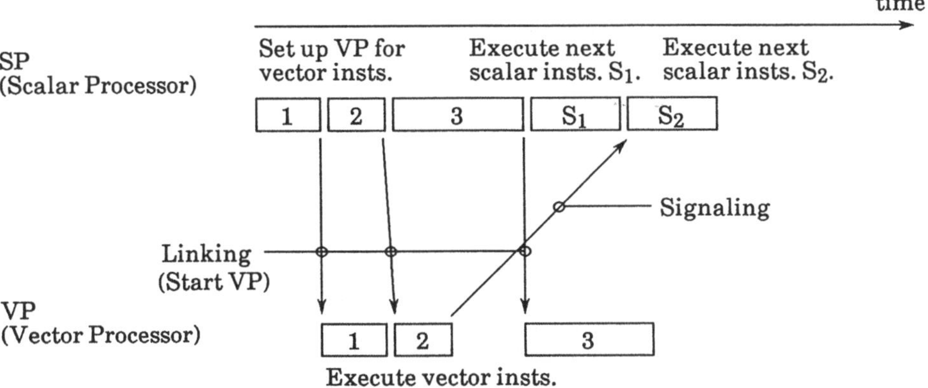

Fig. 4.3 Scalar-Vector Parallelism: Linking and Signaling

vector operation. This process, called signaling, also enhances simultaneous operation of the two processors.

The parallelism thus enhanced by linking and signaling between the Scalar Processor and the Vector Processor reduces elapsed time and increases system throughput.

4.2.4 Instruction Stacking [3]

With the machine cycle time diminishing to as small as 4 nsec, the time required for the Vector Processor's instruction control sometimes becomes critical since it calls for sequential logic by nature and signal propagation delays between various component units are not negligible. Fig.4.4 illustrates the situation for the switching from one instruction to the next.

Inst. #1 $X_i = A_i + B_i$ $(i=1, ..., 8)$

Inst. #2 $Y_i = C_i + D_i$ $(i=1, ..., 8)$

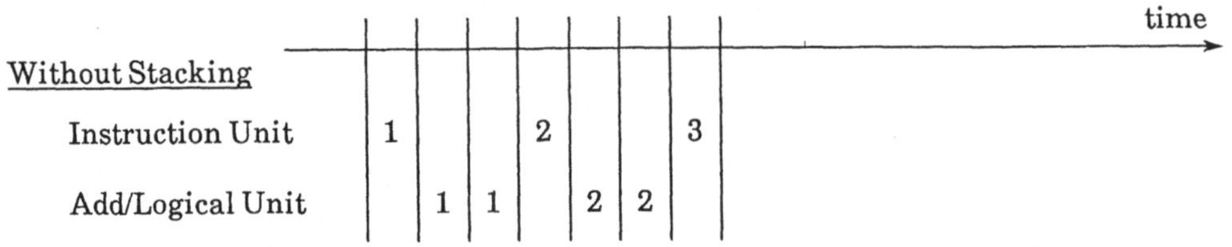

Without Stacking (→ time)

Instruction Unit	1			2			3
Add/Logical Unit		1	1		2	2	

Execution Time = 3 cycles for (2 × 4 =) 8 vector element pairs

With Stacking (→ time)

Instruction Unit	1						
Instruction Stack	1	2		3			
Add/Logical Unit		1	1	2	2	3	3

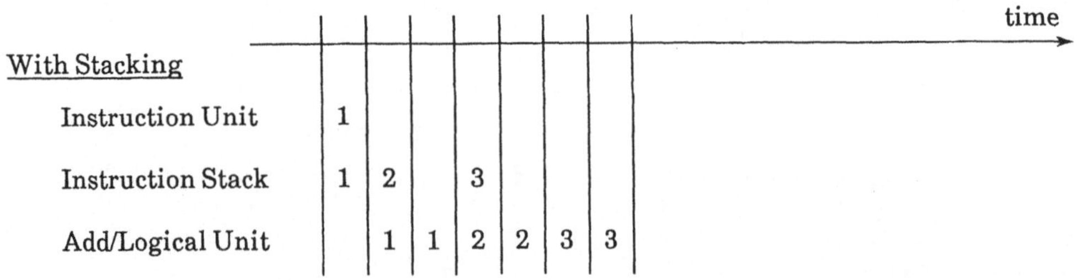

Execution Time = 2 cycles for (2 × 4 =) 8 vector element pairs

The numbers in the time chart denote the instruction numbers.

Fig.4.4 Instruction Stacking

In a conventional design (without instruction stacking), the instruction control at the end of execution of the first instruction proceeds as follows:

(i) The arithmetic unit (here, four add/logical units collectively) notifies the instruction unit, which decodes vector instructions and distributes appropriate orders to various resources inside the Vector Processor, of the completion of execution of the first instruction.
(ii) The instruction unit picks up, out of its instruction buffer, the second instruction which is to use this arithmetic unit.
(iii) The instruction unit sends the decoded second instruction to this arithmetic unit.
(iv) The arithmetic unit starts executing the second instruction.

For the reasons mentioned above, this process takes one machine cycle, and there occurs a break (idle time) of one machine cycle in the arithmetic unit between the first and the second instructions, as illustrated in Fig. 4.4 (top).

The instruction stacking structure employed by the S-820 eliminates such a break (idle time) and shortens the effective instruction execution time. Each one of the major resources is provided with a local instruction stack, i.e., a buffer of decoded instructions. Because of the elementwise parallel instruction scheme, identical pipeline elements, e.g., the four add/logical units, are all allocated to one vector instruction at a time and hence are collectively given one instruction stack. The resources provided with an instruction stack are the add/logical units, the multiply-and-add units, the load units and the load/store units. As the instruction stack is loaded, independently of the progress in the resource, with decoded vector instructions as they become available, the resource (e.g., the add/logical unit) can almost always find the required next vector instruction in the local instruction stack when it finishes executing the current one. Thus, as shown in Fig. 4.4 (bottom), there is no break (idle time) in the resource, and the effective instruction execution pitch is shortened accordingly by one machine cycle.

The saving of one machine cycle thus achieved is significant especially when the vector length, or the size of the vector, is relatively small.

4.3 Storage Control

Generally, the structure of a system's internal storage must be so designed as to provide a sufficient bandwith, i.e., must be able to feed the arithmetic units with data as fast as required by them. Otherwise, the arithmetic units would wait for the arrival of data, and this loss of time would surface as performance overhead.

The bandwidth between the Storage Control (Main Storage) and the vector register stack of the S-820/80 is 16 Gbytes/sec, which may appear to be rather small when one considers the maximum arithmetic throughput of 3 GFLOPS: on the average 2 x 2 (operands) x 8 (bytes) = 32 Gbytes/sec might be "sufficient" (Note that each multiply-and-add pipeline requires only one -- instead of two -- pair of vector operands for two operations in a machine cycle. Thus, 2 x 2 x 8 instead of 3 x 2 x 8. Also, when one is to consider result storing as well, this should be a little bit higher). Most actual programs, however, do not exercise the arithmetic units at maximum duty all the time. They contain some scalar operands as well, which do not require Vector Processor -to- Main Storage accesses. The existence of the vector registers helps significantly reduce storage access frequency since operands and intermediate results tend to be reused within the same program. On the whole, the bandwidth of 16 Gbytes/sec should be sufficient for the S-820/80 in practical sense.

Even with a sufficient bandwidth, some loss of time may be observed from time to time due to contention at resources, especially access contention at the Main Storage, when a particular storage bank is congested with multiple access requests. Such contention also shows up as performance overhead, which means reduced vector performance.

To reduce as much access contention as possible, the S–820 organizes the banks of the Main Storage with a carefully designed addressing scheme in consideration of a cyclic nature of the operand address pattern.

5. Hardware Technology

Whereas the number of machine cycles per instruction (operation) can be generally reduced by increasing the amount of logic circuits and improving the control structure, hardware technology is the key factor determining the bare hardware speed, which is often represented by machine cycle.

A 64 K bit and a 256 K bit biCMOS (bipolar complementary metal oxide semiconductor) memory chips have been initially developed for the Main Storage, with a chip access time of 20 nsec, to satisfy the required bandwidth. A 256 K bit CMOS (complementary metal oxide semiconductor) memory chip with a chip access time of 45 nsec is now employed in the Main Storage of the economical version of the S–820. The Extended Storage uses an industry–standard 1 M bit CMOS chip.
To allow cooling only by air, the S–820 packages an LSI chip on a ceramic substrate with high thermal conductivity; these substrates are then surface–mounted on a multilayer printed circuit board called a package.

Table 5.1 Hardware Technology Used in S–820

<table>
<tr><th>Component</th><th colspan="2">Characteristic</th></tr>
<tr><td>LSI (bipolar)</td><td colspan="2">2,000 / 5,000 gates
0.2 / 0.25 nsec</td></tr>
<tr><td>RAM (bipolar)</td><td colspan="2">4K / 16 K bits
4.5 / 12 nsec</td></tr>
<tr><td>VR LSI</td><td colspan="2">2,500 gates + 6,912 bits
2.5 nsec</td></tr>
<tr><td>MS SRAM (CMOS / bi CMOS)</td><td>256K bits
45 nsec</td><td>64K/256K bits
20 nsec</td></tr>
<tr><td>ES DRAM</td><td colspan="2">1M bit
120 nsec</td></tr>
<tr><td>PK (package)</td><td colspan="2">72 LSIs / PK
22 layers</td></tr>
<tr><td>PL (platter)</td><td colspan="2">21 PKs / PL
22 layers</td></tr>
</table>

In addition to the state-of-the-art logic and memory LSIs used in Hitachi's large-scale mainframe M-680H, the S-820 employs several newly developed semiconductor components. Essential in achieving the machine cycle time of 4 nsec is the VR (Vector Register) LSI, which is built on bipolar technology and contains 6,912 bits of memory and 2,500 gates of logic including the data registers. The chip access time is 2.5 nsec to allow an vector register access pitch (cycle) of 4 nsec required by the logic (arithmetic unit).

Table 5.1 summarizes the hardware technology used in the S-820.

6. Software

6.1 Overview

A powerful set of easy-to-use software packages have been developed to help the user take full advantage of the S-820's hardware capabilities. Table 6.1 lists major program products available on the S-820.

Table 6.1 Major Program Products Available on S-820

Category	Name	Description
System Software	VOS3/HAP/ES	System control program based on general-purpose mainframe operating system (VOS3)
	FORT77/HAP	Vectorizing FORTRAN compiler supporting FORTRAN77 language specification
	FORT/ASSIST FORT/VF FORT77/TD	Tools for programming, debugging and tuning
Appli-cation Software	DEQSOL E2	Differential equation solver based on a high-level language
	SGRAF	Program which visualizes simulation results
	MATRIX/HAP	Library of vectorized matrix calculation subroutines
	ISAS II	Structural analysis package

VOS3/HAP/ES, the primary control program, is a multiple virtual operating system which supports the vector architecture in addition to the Hitachi M-Series (scalar) architecture. It drives vector jobs in parallel with conventional scalar jobs, both in a standalone and in a loosely-coupled configuration, while managing the Main Storage and the Extended Storage efficiently.

FORT77/HAP compiles ("vectorizes") FORTRAN source code into object code with high efficiency, as discussed in Section 6.2 in detail.

DEQSOL E2 directly accepts differential equations in their original mathematical expressions, dramatically reducing programming chores. With this product, the number of lines (statements) in source code can be an order of magnitude smaller, and the program becomes very visible and manageable.

In addition, a variety of off-the-shelf, third-party application packages are being converted to vector versions for the S-820.

6.2 Vectorizing Compiler FORT77/HAP

A compiler with a powerful vectorizing capability is indispensable in exploiting hardware performance potentials of any supercomputer. The vectorizing FORTRAN compiler FORT77/HAP makes full use of the advanced architecture of the S-820 and employs various techniques in achieving the performance objective.

To increase vectorization ratio, which is the key indicator of object code efficiency, FORT77/HAP first takes advantage of the rich vector instruction set:

- Use a compare instruction, which generates a mask vector for elementwise selection of operation/no-operation, in conjunction with a conditional ("IF") statement.
- Use a list vector instruction for indirect addressing in which the subscript of a vector (array) is another vector (array).
- Use a vector macroinstruction for a compound operation consisting of multiple operations, such as sum of products, inner (scalar) product, first order iteration and element sum.

To further improve vectorization ratio, it then attempts to minimize and isolate the unvectorizable portions by rearranging source statements. For a DO loop which it failed to vectorize because it could not resolve data dependencies, it also analyzes the flow of the data outside the DO loop to determine whether the DO loop is inherently unvectorizable. Take the following program, for example:

```
      K1 = K + 1                    (1)
      .
      .
      DO 10 I = 1, N
         A (I + K1) = ....          (2)
               ... = A (I + K)      (3)
   10 CONTINUE
```

Looking only at statements (2) and (3), it is impossible to determine which subscript, I + K1 or I + K, is larger than the other; therefore, this DO loop cannot be vectorized. By expanding the scope of analysis beyond the boundaries of the DO loop and examining statement (1), the compiler can now determine that K1 > K, and can vectorize the DO loop.

FORT77/HAP attempts to vectorize not only unit DO loops but also multifold DO loops. Here, a standalone (single-fold) DO loop and the innermost one in a nest of DO loops (multifold DO loop) are called a unit DO loop. The above-discussed techniques apply to unit DO loops. FORT77/HAP uses the following techniques to vectorize multifold DO loops:

- Exchange the innermost loop with the outer loop.
- Decompose the multifold loop into a unit loop.
- Divide the multifold loop.

The following example illustrates the exchanging of the innermost loop with the outer loop:

Before

```
          DO 20 J=1,N
          DO 10 I=1,N
             A(I,J)=A(I-1,J) + A(I-2,J)
 10       CONTINUE
 20 CONTINUE
```

This loop cannot be vectorized because one statement contains I, I-1 and I-2 as subscripts (indexes), with I being varied.

After

```
          DO 20 I=1,N
          DO 10 J=1,N
             A(I,J)=A(I-1,J) + A(I-2,J)
 10       CONTINUE
20 CONTINUE
```

This new innermost loop can be vectorized.

Another example shown below, which applies the Gaussian elimination method to a system of linear equations [4], demonstrates how dividing a multifold DO loop can make it vectorizable.

Before (cannot be vectorized)

```
DO 200 J=K+1,N
  IF (IPK.NE.K) THEN
    W=A(IPK,J)
    A(IPK,J)=A(K,J)
    A(K,J)=W
  END IF
```

```
        DO 100 I=K+1,N
          A(I,J)= A(I,J)+A(I,K)*A(K,J)
100       CONTINUE
200     CONTINUE
```

After (can be vectorized)

```
      DO 201 J=K+1,N
        IF (IPK.NE.K) THEN
          W=A(IPK,J)
          A(IPK,J)=A(K,J)
          A(K,J)=W
        END IF
201 CONTINUE
      DO 110 J=K+1,N,2
        DO 100 I=K+1,N
          A(I,J)=A(I,J)+A(I,K)*A(K,J)
          A(I,J+1)=A(I,J+1)+A(I,K)*A(K,J+1)
100     CONTINUE
110   CONTINUE
```

Incidentally, this last example uses also the technique of unrolling, which expands one statement into multiple statements in order to minimize software overhead associated with loop control for the "DO 200" loop by reducing the loop count. Basically, the scalar or unvectorized loop, in this case the "DO 110" loop, benefits from unrolling, as the S-820 employs elementwise parallel processing and expanding one statement into multiple statements does not particularly increase parallelism in the Vector Processor.

Furthermore, as discussed in Subsection 4.2.3, FORT77/HAP enhances the degree of parallelism between the Scalar Processor and the Vector Processor by utilizing linking and signaling.

7. Performance

7.1 Summary of Design Considerations for Performance

Fig. 7.1 summarizes which design considerations and features of the S-820 have addressed which of the performance factors discussed earlier in Chapter 2. As indicated, most of the major factors have been given proper considerations, which has resulted in not only extremely high arithmetic throughput in a single vector processor but also well-balanced system performance.

7.2 Some Benchmark Results

A number of benchmark jobs are being used in the industry to help compare the performance of different supercomputers [5]. Among the most popular are Lawrence Livermore laboratory's 14 Kernels and 24 Kernels. The high end model S-820/80 (standard commercial version with the 256 K bit CMOS Main Storage) scores 355 and 340 MFLOPS on the arithmetic average,

Level						Factor	Design Consideration/Feature	Code
System Performance	Vector Job Performance	Vector Hardware	Basic	Arithmetic		Machine Cycle Time	High speed/density LSI & packaging	T
						No. of Cycles / Operation	Amount of logic & efficient control logic	L
						Width of Data Path		
						No. of Parallel Arith.Units	Elementwise parallel processing	
				Storage Bandwidth		Access Time	High-speed LSI & high-density packaging	T
						Access Pitch		
						Width of Access Path	Amount of logic & efficient control logic	L
						No. of Parallel Access Paths		
			Overhead	Arith-metic		Pipeline Startup	Efficient control logic	
						Housekeeping		
						Register Contention		
				Storage Contention		Within Instruction Chain	Efficient control logic	
						With Other Instruction Chain		
						With Extended Storage		
						With Scalar Processor		
						With Channels (I/O)		
		Vector-Job-Related Software				Vectorization Ratio	Intelligent compiler & inst. set	C, A
			Vectorized Portion			Setup of Vector Processor	Intelligent compiler	C
						Housekeeping		
						Operand / Int. Result Loading	Vector registers	A
						Result Storing (int. storage)		
			Nonvect. Portion			Ordinary (Non-I/O) Code	Powerful scalar processor	S
					I/O	Data Input	Fast channel	
						Result Storing (external storage)	Extended Storage	A
	Scalar Job Performance					Hardware	Powerful scalar processor	S
						Software	Efficient systems software	O
	System Function					Job Swapping	Extended Storage	A
						Other	Powerful scalar processor	S, O
	Parallelism					Between Scalar and Vector	Linking & signaling	A(L)
						No. of Vector Processors		

Legend) A: Architecture C: Compiler L: Logic Design O: Operating System
S: Scalar Processor T: Technology

Fig. 7.1 Summary of Design Considerations and Features for Performance

respectively, among the highest in the industry (The 256 K bit biCMOS version scores 418 and 363 MFLOPS, respectively).

8. Conclusion

The HITACHI S-820 has been developed as one of the most powerful supercomputers in the world, delivering a peak arithmetic throughput of 3 GLFOPS on a single vector processor. The world class performance has been achieved by first analyzing the factors determining performance and then effecting a number of improvements in architecture, logic design, compiler and hardware technology. The key performance features include the advanced vector instruction set, the Extended Storage, elementwise parallel execution, linking, signaling, and the intelligent vectorizing compiler FORT77/HAP.

Special Note

The information presented here in pertains to the Japanese domestic version of the S-820. It should be noted that the specifications of the S-820, if and when offered outside Japan, may change without notice.

References

[1] H. Wada, et. al.: "Performance Enhancement by Extended Storage on Hitachi Supercomputer S-820 System", Proceedings of the Fourth International Conference on Supercomputing, Santa Clara, 1989

[2] T. Odaka, et. al.: "Development of Hitachi Supercomputer S-820 System", Proceedings of the Third International Conference on Supercomputing, Boston, 1988, pp, 71-77

[3] H. Wada, et. al.: "High-speed Vector Instruction Execution Schemes of Hitachi Supercomputer S-820 System", Proceedings of the International Conference on Parallel Processing, 1988, pp. 291-298

[4] C. Oguni: FORTRAN77, Maruzen, 1985 (Japanese)

[5] C. Eoyang, et. al.: "The Birth of the Second Generation: The Hitachi S-820/80", Proceedings of Supercomputing '88, 1988, pp. 296-303

SIEMENS Dual Scalar Supercomputer

Peter Wüsten

Siemens AG, DV 17
Otto-Hahn-Ring 6
D-8000 München 83
Federal Republic of Germany

1. Introduction

The usage of Supercomputers by universities, research institutes and increasingly by industrial research and development centers demand new functions and higher performance of future supercomputers. Besides the infinite requirement of raw MIPS respectively MFLOPS, large direct access memory in the area of Gigabytes is necessary to reduce the elapsed time of new applications.

To satisfy these needs, SIEMENS introduces in Europe the S-Series, a new family of Supercomputers, manufactured and developed by FUJITSU Ltd.

2. Architecture

The basic archticture of the VP-Series is known since 1983 (Fig. 1).

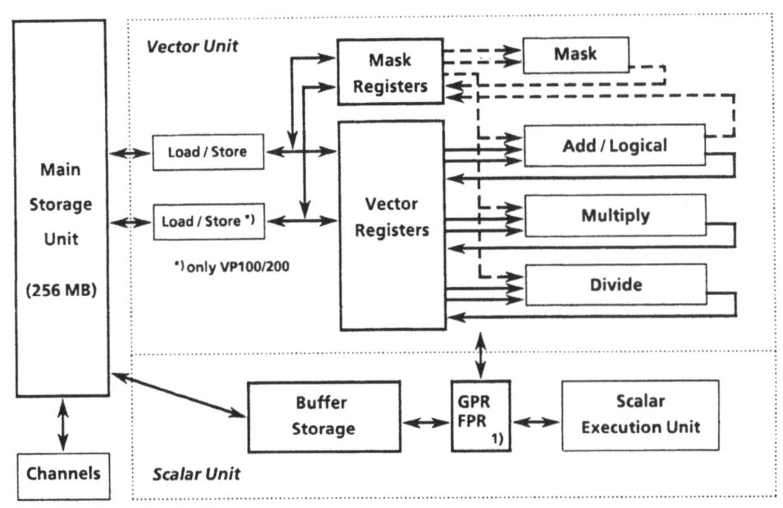

VP Series: System Architecture (Fig. 1)

The vector processor comprises the vector and scalar units, the main memory and the I/O processor. The data transfer rate between main memory and vector register is from 1 Gbyte/s up to 4 Gbyte/s depending on the model. Data transfer is effected via the load/store units. Operations on the mask registers are carrried out in the mask unit. Five of the six units (the 2 load/store units, the mask unit and 2 of the 3 arithmetic units) can operate in parallel.

This architecture has been enhanced by the successor product family VP-EX, mainly by introducing a new so called multifunctional pipe. (Fig. 2)

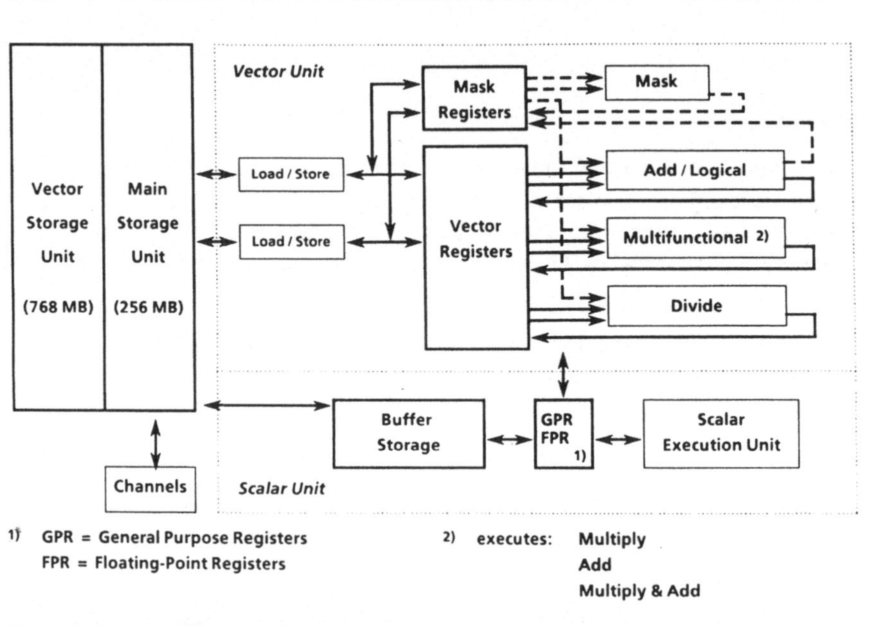

VP200-EX Architecture (Fig. 2)

Within one machine cycle this pipe executes one ADD- and MULTIPLY-instruction. The machine cycle of the VP-EX family is model dependent. By consequence, the fastest model VP400-EX executes 8 instructions in the multifunctional pipe every 7 nsec. The second enhancement was the introduction of 1 Gigabyte main memory, where the upper 768 MB could be accessed only by the vector unit. In the S-Series (Fig. 3) this architecture is kept and enhanced by the following features:

- two multifunctional pipes
- two mask-pipes
- 2 GB Main Storage
- 8 GB Global Storage
- 2 Scalar Processors for one Vector Unit.

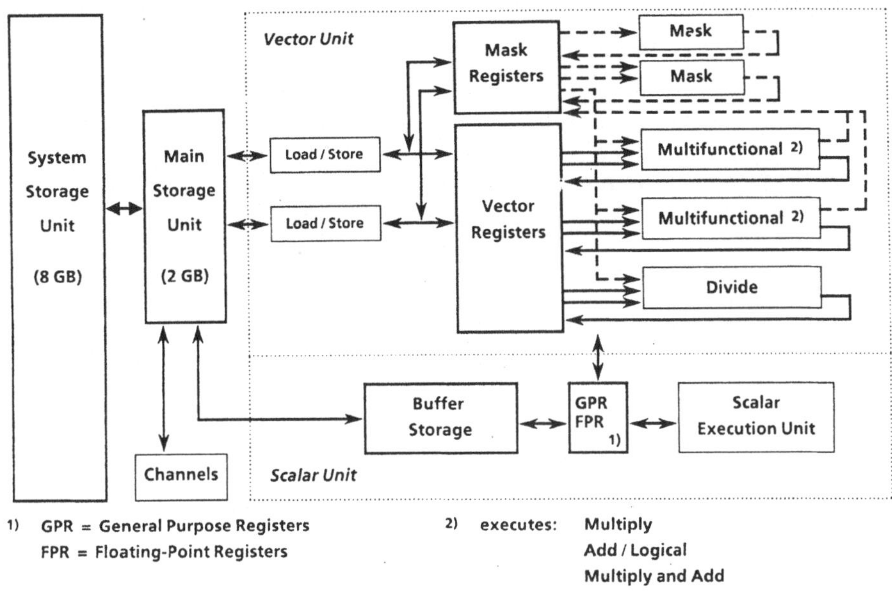

S Series: System Architecture (Fig. 3)

The two multifunctional pipes can work in parallel with the ability of chaining the vector instructions, thus improving the sustained performance. The following table shows some of the instructions, which can be executed within one multifunctional pipe creating one result during one machine cycle:

Operation	EXAMPLE
Add	V=V+V
Multiply	V=V*V
Triadic (scalar)	V=V+S*V
Triadic (vector)	V=V+V*V

Having two of these multifunctional pipes, any combination of Add and Multiply can be executed parallel (2x Add, 2x Mult., 2x Triad., 1x Triad. +1x Add, 1x Triad. + 1x Mult.).

The second mask-pipe allows the compiler easily to calculate the sum of "1"s in the mask registers to optimize compiler strategies.

The main storage can now be expanded up to 2 Gigabytes memory, accessable by scalar and vector unit. In addition to this memory a global storage unit up to 8 Gigabytes capacity is available for large user files and can be used as swapping area by the operating system.

The outstanding feature of the new S-series is the DUAL SCALAR Architecture. Measurements of the utilization of the vector unit have shown, that even high vectorizable jobs are using the vector unit only less than 50 % of its capacity. To use this capacity the S-series systems allow two scalar units to share one vector unit.

Vector Processor System

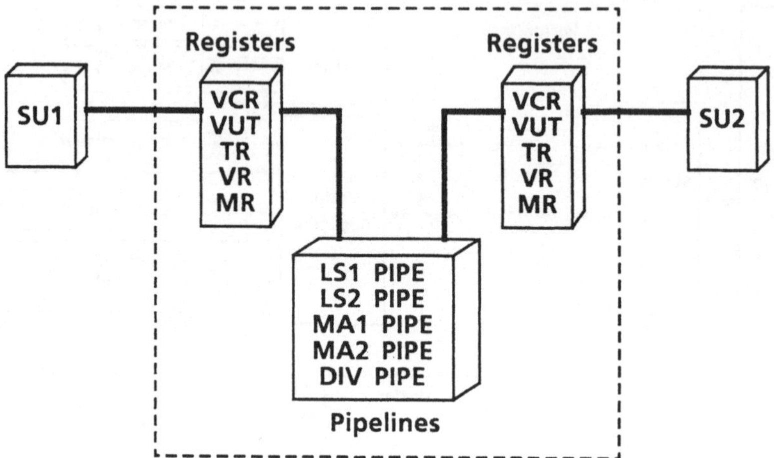

- Two sets of vector- and mask registers in VU
- Controlling of shared VU by hardware

S Series: Shared VU (Fig. 4)

Fig.4 shows the usage of the doubled set of vector registers avoiding to save these registers during task switching. By this combination the throughput of the system can be improved up to a factor of 2.

3.Technology and Performance

Based on the latest technology the S-series is using:

15000 gates / chip ECL-LSI with 80 picosec delay time,

64 KBit	RAM	1,6	nsec	access time
1 MBit	SRAM	35	nsec	"
4 MBit	DRAM	100	nsec	"

Thus achieving 4 nsec cycle time for the vector unit and 8 nsec cycle time for the scalar unit. Depending on the model the following peak performance can be achieved:

VP50-EX:	285	MFLOPS	S100	500	MFLOPS
VP100-EX:	428	MFLOPS	S200	1000	MFLOPS
VP200-EX:	857	MFLOPS	S400	2000	MFLOPS
VP400-EX:	1714	MFLOPS	S600	4000	MFLOPS

Compared with the VP-EX-Series the scalar speed is increased 3 times, respectively 6 times in case of the DUAL SCALAR-Architecture.

Combined with the large amount of main memory and global storage, the throughput of the new series will increase dramatically.

4. Operating System and Networking

Based on the upward compatibility of the hardware architecture, the S-Series is controlled by the interactive operating system VSP/I. This operating system manages the hardware resources, jobs, tasks, data and controls interrupts and I/O operations. VSP/I provides all necessary functions to manage the execution of batch jobs and supports interactive sessions without requiring a front end processor (Fig 5).

One main function of VSP/I is the management of the real storage and the virtual address spaces. The real storage is divided into two disjunct sections (VP user area and scalar area) by the so called VP line, which can be varied by the operator. Jobs containing vector instructions (VP jobs) have to run in the VP user area. Scalar jobs, e.g. for compilation or data set manipulation, may run either in the scalar area or in the VP user area. The region size of VP jobs is limited by the real size of the VP user area. Jobs running in the scalar area can use a pageable virtual address space of 2 Gigabytes.

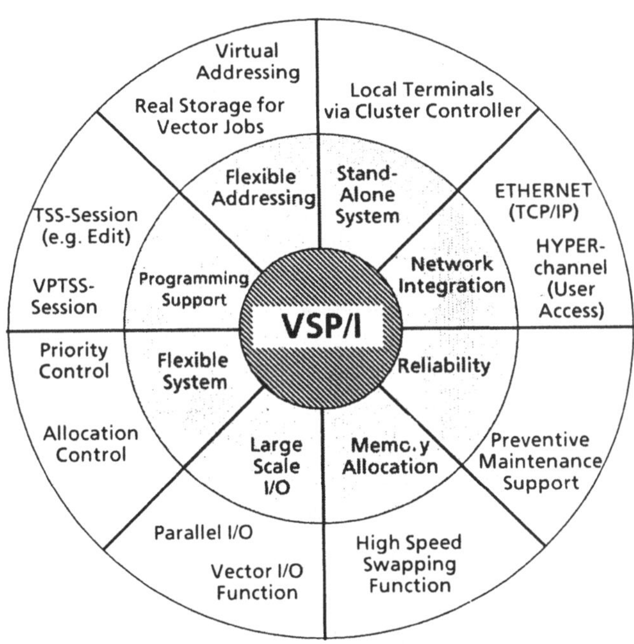

VSP/I Components

(Fig. 5)

To ensure the efficient use of the S–Series, VSP/I supports the connection of local terminals via clusters and offers the possibility of two interactive modes, one for scalar operations (e.g. editing, compiling) and one for executing VP programs (VPTSS session). The user can dynamically switch between both modes according to his needs.

VSP/I offers many tuning functions to optimize the operation of the S–Series for a specific work load. With the CPU allocation control function it is possible to specify the relative amount of CPU resources to be used by individual job groups.

Various additional system products are available for VSP/I, for example to control the access to different resources, to measure and to analyze the performance of the system, and to enhance functions for system managers.

The imbedding of VSP/I into existing planned LAN's and WAN's is already achieved widely by existing installations following our open policy.

Connections to SNA, TRANSDATA, DEC–NET, TCP/IP, HYPERchannel, and other de facto Standards are implemented (Fig. 6).

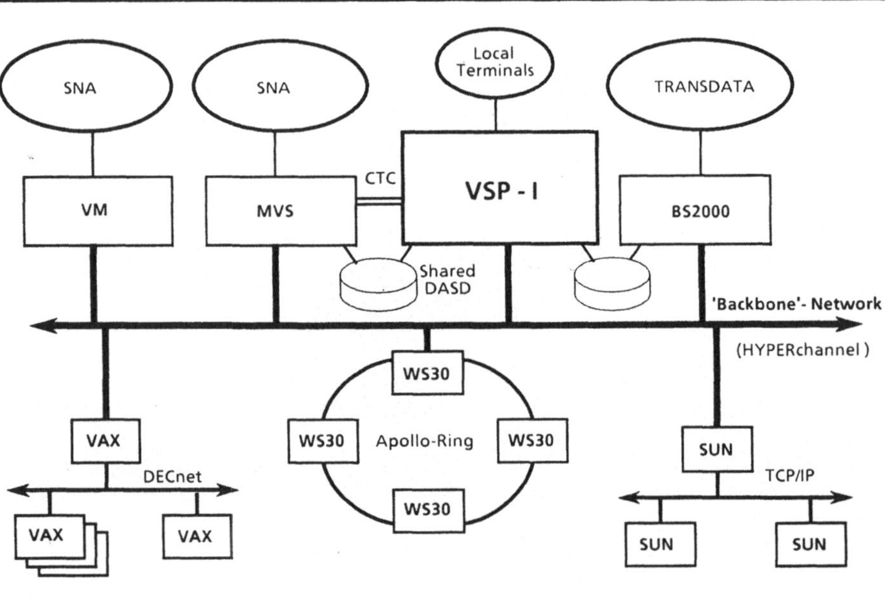

VSP/I: Network Support (Fig. 6)

5. Compiler and Programing Tools

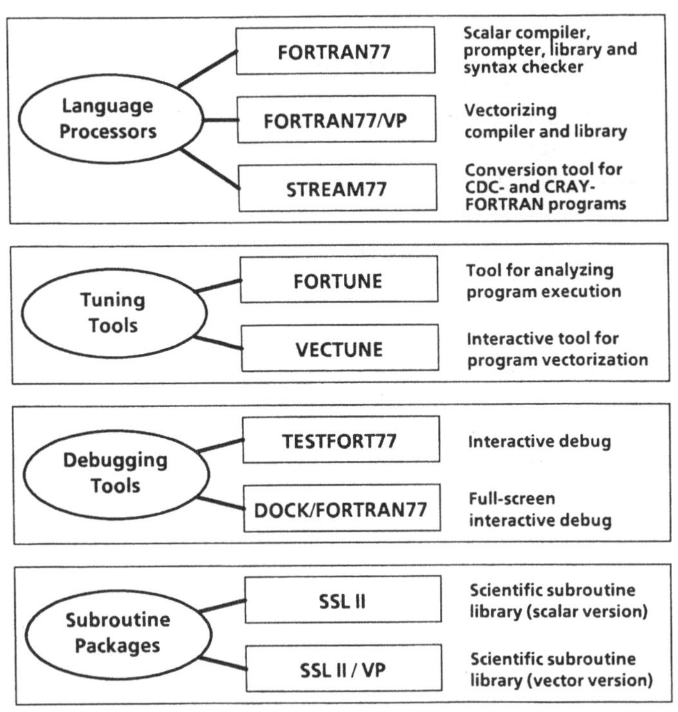

VP-EX Series: FORTRAN Program System (Fig. 7)

The FORTRAN program system with its advanced facilities for optimization, automatic vectorization, tuning and high-speed input/output make program preparation and execution of the S-Series very efficient.

FORTRAN77 Compilers

The language processors FORTRAN77 and FORTRAN77/VP include the scalar and vectorizing compiler and libraries for compiling and executing FORTRAN77 programs. The vectorizing compiler is able to generate efficient object code for programs written in standard FORTRAN automatically using suitable vector instructions. This is the case for simple arithmetic operations (e.g. inner product), complex operations, containing IF statements, and complicated data manipulations involving indirect access to main memory. There is no need to introduce special calls or vector notation. Especially the vector instructions for combinations of multiplication and

addition are intensively used to take advantage of the multifunctional pipelines.
The vector input/output function VIO/F has been extended in such a way that temporary data sets now can be placed in the system storage unit (SSU) with a size of up to 8 Gigabytes. All READ and WRITE statements for a VIO/F file cause a high speed data transfer between SSU and MSU. This reduces the elapsed time of large scale application programs significantly.

Analysis and Conversion of FORTRAN Programs

STREAM77 is a tool for the analysis and conversion of FORTRAN programs. The structural analysis of FORTRAN programs provides various information, such as cross-reference tables and tree structure diagrams. The converter function helps in converting programs written in CRAY or CDC FORTRAN language back into standard FORTRAN77 syntax.

Tuning Tools

The tuning tools FORTUNE and VECTUNE support the program development by providing information that helps to increase the efficiency of FORTRAN77 program execution. FORTUNE is a tool that analyzes the behaviour of FORTRAN programs during execution, indicating which program portions were actually executed and calculating the execution costs for each statement respectively the CPU time spent by each subroutine. VECTUNE (Interactive Vectorizer) is a tool for improving the execution efficiency of FORTRAN programs to obtain maximum performance of the VP System. It is used in a timesharing subsystem environment and displays various tuning messages on the screen.

6. Application Software

Worldwide more than 80 VP installations in science and industry using more than 260 application packages of all kinds. Topics which are covered are

FEM Applications as

ABAQUS
ADINA
FIDAP
MSC/NASTRAN
NISA II
PERMAS
. . .

and **FLUID DYNAMICS**

FIDAP
FIDISOL
FMCS
EUFLEX
NSFLEX
. . .

and recently **Quantum Chemistry**
using
GAUSSIAN '86
HONDO 5
GAMESS
MNDOVP
DISCOVER
CHARMm
. . .

7. Installed Base

Starting in 1985, SIEMENS has installed 7 Vector processor systems in Europe (Table 1).

	Model	Customer	Application	Date
1	VP200, 64MB	IABG, Ottobrunn	structural analysis (NASTRAN) flow simulation (EUFLEX)	04/85
2	VP200, 64MB	SIEMENS ZTI, München	VLSI design (SPICE)	06/85
3	VP100, 32MB	University of Kaiserslautern	general scientific applications	06/86
4	VP200, 128MB	CIRCE, Orsay	general scientific applications	09/86
5	VP50, 64MB	Nuclear Research Center, Karlsruhe	nuclear research, climate simulation	06/87
6	VP100-EX, 256 MB	SIEMENS D, München	system development	05/88
7	VP400-EX, 512 MB	University of Karlsruhe	general scientific applications	11/88

8. Future Outlook

Offering the fastest vector processors as monoprocessors in the world, SIEMENS will be able to satisfy the future demand in scientific and industrial computation by enhancing the S-Series architecture together with the cooperation partner FUJITSU.

Das skalierte Gesetz von Amdahl
Zur Leistungsermittlung von Vektorrechnern*)

Hans-Martin Wacker

DFVLR Deutsche Forschungs- und Versuchsanstalt für Luft- und Raumfahrt
Zentrale Datenverarbeitung
Münchner Straße 20
8031 Oberpfaffenhofen

Zusammenfassung

Die Bestimmung der Leistung von Universalrechnern ist heute bis zu einer ausreichenden Genauigkeit gut möglich. Einerseits besteht eine weitgehende Übereinstimmung bei der Beurteilung von marktgängigen Rechenanlagen durch Anwender und Hersteller, andererseits können noch immer bestehende Unsicherheiten durch qualifizierte Benchmark-Untersuchungen zumindest soweit beseitigt werden, daß eine für eine Beschaffung notwendige Entscheidungsbasis gefunden werden kann. Dabei geht man im allgemeinen davon aus, daß sich das Lastprofil bei einem neu zu beschaffenden Rechner von dem des Vorläuferrechners nicht wesentlich unterscheidet.

Die Situation bei Vektorrechnern und insbesondere bei Supercomputern ist davon völlig verschieden. Selbst Spezialisten beurteilen die Leistung dieser Systeme so unterschiedlich, daß es für den Anwender in den meisten Fällen unmöglich ist, sich ein genügend genaues Bild zu machen. Darüber hinaus verschließen sich Vektorrechner bislang einer objektiven Leistungsbewertung durch Benchmark-Untersuchungen, da man mit einer gravierenden Veränderung der Charakteristik des zu bearbeitenden Lastprofiles rechnen muß, wenn man auf einen Rechner einer anderen Leistungsklasse übergeht [4]. Bis heute gibt es nur sehr unzulängliche Versuche, die Leistung und das Lastprofil eines neu zu installierenden Vektorrechners zu bestimmen [5].

In dem ersten Teil dieser Arbeit wird gezeigt, wie abhängig von den entsprechenden Arbeitsgebieten die Leistung eines neu zu beschaffenden Supercomputers ermittelt werden kann. Es zeigt sich, daß die Einflüsse des Vektorisierungsgrades durch modifizierte Amdahl-Gesetze bestimmt werden. Die "skalierten" Amdahl-Gesetze werden abgeleitet.

Im zweiten Teil dieser Arbeit werden diese Ergebnisse auf den Einsatz von mehreren unterschiedlichen Vektorrechnern angewandt. Es ergeben sich einige interessante wirtschaftliche Alternativen zu dem Einsatz von Supercomputern durch die Kombination von Universalrechnern mit Vektorzusatz und sogenannten Minisupercomputern.

---

*) Ein Teil dieser Arbeit ist gekürzt erschienen in PIK – Praxis der Informationsverarbeitung und Kommunikation, Heft 1, März 1989, S. 44–48, Carl Hanser-Verlag München

1. Einleitung

Im Jahr 1986 führte ein großes deutsches Industrieunternehmen sehr sorgfältige Leistungsuntersuchungen bei Vektorrechnern durch. Die Ergebnisse dieser Benchmarks wurden im Jahr 1987 veröffentlicht. Besonders interessant war dabei der Vergleich zwischen der Cray X MP2 und der IBM 3090-200 VF. Es zeigte sich, daß - bei der gleichen Anzahl von Prozessoren - die Cray etwa die eineinhalbfache Leistung der IBM hatte. Trotz dieses Ergebnisses, das - bezogen auf den Preis - für die IBM 3090 recht günstig war, beschaffte das betreffende Unternehmen eine Cray X MP2 und nicht eine 3090-400 VF, die zum gleichen Preis der Cray X MP2 leistungsfähiger gewesen wäre. Folgende Gründe für die Beschaffung einer doppelt so teuren und eineinhalbmal so leistungsfähigen Rechenanlage wurden genannt:

- Ein Zweiprozessorsystem ist günstiger als ein Vierprozessorsystem.

- Nach der Installation eines leistungsfähigeren Rechners wird sich der Vektorisierungsgrad der Last so erhöhen, daß die Cray X MP auch im Hinblick auf die Wirtschaftlichkeit der IBM 3090 VF überlegen ist.

Beide Argumente sind nicht ohne weiteres einzusehen und erfordern eine gründliche Diskussion. Dabei zeigt es sich, daß eine solch einfach erscheinende Entscheidung heute oftmals nur nach unsachlichen Kriterien getroffen werden kann, da weder objektive Methoden zur Entscheidungsfindung noch die notwendigen Informationen verfügbar sind. Dabei wird es mit einem zunehmenden Angebot von unterschiedlichen Rechnertypen, das vom in Zukunft sehr leistungsfähigen Arbeitsplatzrechner über den Minisupercomputer und den Universalrechner bis zum Supercomputer reicht, immer wichtiger, eine richtige Entscheidung treffen zu können.

Einen wichtigen Beitrag zu dieser Fragestellung leistete J. L. Gustafson [5]. Er nimmt an, daß Supercomputer normalerweise nicht zu der Bearbeitung einer größeren Anzahl von Programmen beschafft werden, sondern zur Lösung größerer Probleme. Weiter nimmt er an, daß der Rechenaufwand der vektorisierbaren bzw. parallelisierbaren Programmteile mit der Problemgröße anwächst, nicht aber die skalaren Teile der Programme.

Eine genauere Analyse der letzteren Annahme zeigt allerdings, daß es offensichtlich fast keine Probleme gibt, die die von Gustafson formulierte Eigenschaft haben. So ist beispielsweise bei der Matrixmultiplikation der nicht vektorisierbare Teil keineswegs von der Problemgröße unabhängig, sondern er wächst mit ihrem Quadrat an. Ähnlich verhalten sich die Lösungsprogramme für Rand- und Anfangswertprobleme, die, wie z. B. die Lösung der Navier-Stokes-Gleichung, eine sehr wichtige Rolle bei der Nutzung von Supereomputern spielen.

2. Wirtschaftlichkeit als Entscheidungskriterium

Die Entwicklung der Informationstechnik bringt in sehr kurzen Abständen neue Halbleiterprodukte, die immer mehr Schaltkreise auf einem "Chip" anbieten und darüber hinaus auch mit immer schnelleren Schaltzeiten die Konstruktion schnellerer Rechner erlauben. Dabei ist es so, daß die neuesten und damit schnellsten Bauelemente - verglichen mit denen der Generation vorher - nur mit einer geringeren Ausbeute gefertigt werden können und deshalb sehr viel teurer sind. Aus diesem Grund sind Rechenanlagen, die auf die neuesten Bauelemente zurückgreifen, zwar schnell, aber auch teuer.

Es ist in vielen Fällen billiger, zwei Zentraleinheiten mit je einer bestimmten Leistung zu bauen, als eine mit der doppelten Leistung des Einzelprozessors. Das gilt insbesondere auch für Mehrprozessorsysteme, die bei einer bestimmten Technologie mehr Leistung anbieten können, oder aber diese Leistung billiger als ein Einprozessorsystem offerieren.

Das ist der Grund für die starken Entwicklungsbemühungen verschiedener Hersteller, wie z. B. Cray und IBM, bei der Einführung von Programmtechniken für die Nutzung von Multiporzessorsystemen. So vielversprechend diese Technik für eine Reihe wichtiger Anwendungen sein mag, so zurückhaltend sollte man bei der Beurteilung derartiger Programmiermethoden bei einem breiten wissenschaftlichen Nutzerkreis sein. Schon heute ist die Qualität der in der Forschung eingesetzten Software keineswegs auf einem befriedigenden Stand. Bei Benchmark-Untersuchungen und bei Programmumstellungen stößt man immer wieder auf fehlerhafte Programme, die in wichtigen Forschungsbereichen eingesetzt werden. Mit einer neuen, komplizierteren Technik zur Software-Erstellung ohne ausreichende Werkzeuge dürfte das Problem der Softwarequalität noch unbeherrschbarer werden.

Für einen Vergleich zwischen Ein- und Mehrprozessorsystemen sollten die Möglichkeiten des "Macrotasking" und des "Microtasking" deshalb zurückhaltend eingeschätzt werden. Dagegen ist die Nutzung derartiger Rechenanlagen durch eine größere Benutzergemeinde die Regel. Teure Supercomputer werden deshalb oft durch Hunderte von Programmen täglich genutzt, damit werden auch mehrere Prozessoren gut ausgelastet. Insbesondere im Tagesbetrieb, wenn viele Programme zur gleichen Zeit bearbeitet werden, sind mehrere Prozessoren ebenso gut wie ein einzelner. Während der Nachtstunden allerdings, wenn die langen Nutzerprogramme verarbeitet werden, gibt es durchaus Unterschiede zwischen Rechnern mit unterschiedlich vielen Prozessoren, sofern dem Nutzer bestimmte Antwortzeiten garantiert werden sollen. Hierbei treten dann Leerzeiten auf, die proportional der Prozessorenanzahl sind.

Angenommen, die maximale Programmlaufzeit - bezogen auf das Einprozessorsystem - sei eine Stunde und die maximal mögliche Programmdurchlaufzeit ("Turn-Around-Time") sei ein Tag, d.h. die Rechenanlage soll morgens leer sein. Dann ergibt sich eine mittlere Leerzeit, wenn die gleichen Programme auf Multiprozessorsystemen der gleichen Gesamtleistung verarbeitet werden sollen, von

$$T_1 = \frac{n}{2} T_{max}$$

$$T_1 = n * 30 \text{ min}$$

Dabei ist n die Anzahl der Prozessoren.

Aus dieser Beziehung ersieht man, daß die Verluste durch Leerzeiten bei kleiner Prozessoranzahl nur wenige Prozent der Gesamtproduktionszeit ausmachen. Erst wenn deren Anzahl größer wird, z. B. 16 und mehr, muß darauf Rücksicht genommen werden entweder durch Reduktion der maximalen Programmlänge oder durch Lockerung der Antwortzeitbedingungen. Der Unterschied zwischen Ein- und Zweirechnersystemen bzw. zwischen Zwei- und Vierrechnersystemen ist, wie man sieht, sehr gering (in dem dargelegten Fall kleiner als 5 %).

Für das größte Problem, das auf einem Rechner bearbeitet werden kann, ist die Antwortzeit ("Turn-Around-Time") für den Nutzer aber entscheidend und nicht die maximale Prozessorleistung. Die Antwortzeit bestimmt sich bei einem "Batch-Job" überwiegend aus der Wartezeit in der Eingangswarteschlange des Rechners und nur in zweiter Linie aus der eigentlichen Ausführungszeit. Damit ist die Gesamtdurchsatzleistung des Systems der entscheidene Faktor, d. h., daß bei vorgegebenen Kosten dasjenige System am besten geeignet ist, das die beste Gesamtdurchsatzleistung bietet. Andererseits ist aber auch bei vorgegebenen Antwortzeitbedingungen das System am besten, das zum niedrigsten Preis die erforderliche Gesamtleistung erbringt, und zwar unabhängig von der Anzahl der Prozessoren.

Die Wirtschaftlichkeit eines Rechners ist deshalb auch für die Bearbeitung großer Probleme in der Forschung ein sehr wichtiges Auswahlkriterium.

3. Ermittlung der Leistung eines Vektorrechners

Lange Zeit wurden Vektorrechner nur nach ihrer Nominalleistung bewertet. Die Cray 2 wurde beispielsweise als ein 2 GFLOPS-Rechner bewertet, die Cray X MP4 hingegen als ein 920 MFLOPS-Rechner, obwohl für die weitaus überwiegende Anzahl von Programmen die Cray X MP deutlich leistungsfähiger ist als die Cray 2. Erst durch die LINPACK-Benchmarkergebnisse, die J. J. Dongarra veröffentlichte, wurde einer größeren Öffentlichkeit bekannt, daß die Leistungen von Vektorrechnern selbst bei fast vollständig vektorisierbaren Programmen durchaus enttäuschend sein können.

Die neueren Veröffentlichungen von Dongarra zeigen bei einigen Vektorrechnern deutlich verbesserte Leistungsergebnisse. Das deutet daraufhin, daß diese Hersteller starke Verbesserungen an ihren Compilern durchgeführt haben. Es ist allerdings zu fragen, ob diese Verbesserungen einer großen Bandbreite von Nutzerprogrammen zugute kommen oder ob es sich nur um auf die LINPACK-Programme gezielten Optimierungen handelt. Hier liegt eine Gefahr in weltweit verbreiteten Benchmarkergebnissen, die nur auf einem Programm basieren.

Bei der Anwendung von Supercomputern zeigt es sich, daß bei Nutzerprogrammen, ähnlich den LINPACK-Programmen, die Nominalleistung eines Vektorrechners bei weitem nicht ausgeschöpft werden kann. Die Gründe hierfür wurden schon wiederholt dargelegt [1] [2]. Es ist deshalb beispielsweise für eine richtige Beschaffungsentscheidung von entscheidender Wichtigkeit, die tatsächliche Leistungsfähigkeit eines derartigen Rechners für das zu erwartende Arbeitsprofil genügend genau zu bestimmen.

Ein Vektorrechner wird vor allem zur Bearbeitung größerer Probleme genutzt, deshalb muß man bei dem Übergang auf einen leistungsfähigeren Vektorrechner damit rechnen, daß sich der durchschnittliche Vektorisierungsgrad der zu bearbeitenden Programme erhöht. Aus diesem Grund können Benchmark-Ergebnisse nicht von einem Rechner auf einen anderen übertragen werden, ohne die zu erwartende Veränderung des Lastprofiles zu berücksichtigen.

Ermittlung der Leistung eines Vektorrechners

Aufbau eines typischen E/S-Programmes

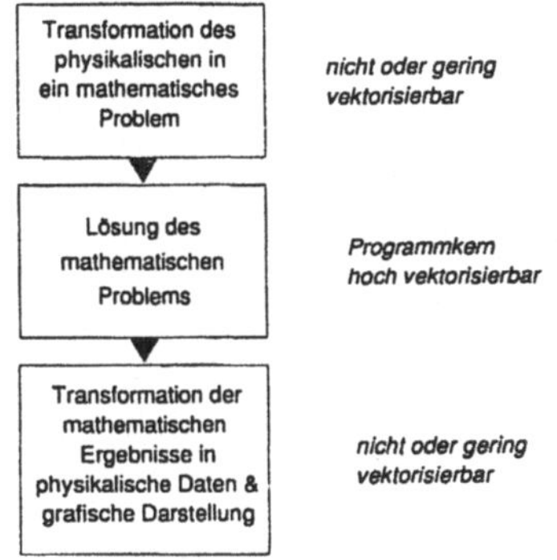

Bild 1

Das Bild 1 zeigt den Aufbau eines typischen Programmes für technisch-wissenschaftliche Anwendungen. Die Ermittlung der Leistung eines Vektorrechners erfordert die Messung der Skalarleistung und der Vektorleistung für repräsentative Programme. Die Vektorleistung wird durch Messung der Leistung für Programmkerne bestimmt, während die Skalarleistung durch die übrigen Programmteile oder einfacher näherungsweise durch Abschalten der Vektorisierung gemessen werden kann. Ist nun auch der mittlere Vektorisierungsgrad der Last bekannt, läßt sich mit Hilfe des **Amdahl'schen Gesetzes** die Leistung des Vektorrechners ermitteln [1]:

$$L = L_s \frac{\beta}{\alpha + \beta(1 - \alpha)}$$

L	Gesamtleistung
L_s	Skalarleistung
L_v	Vektorleistung
α	Vektorisierungsgrad
$\beta = \frac{L_v}{L_s}$	Vektor-Skalar-Verhältnis

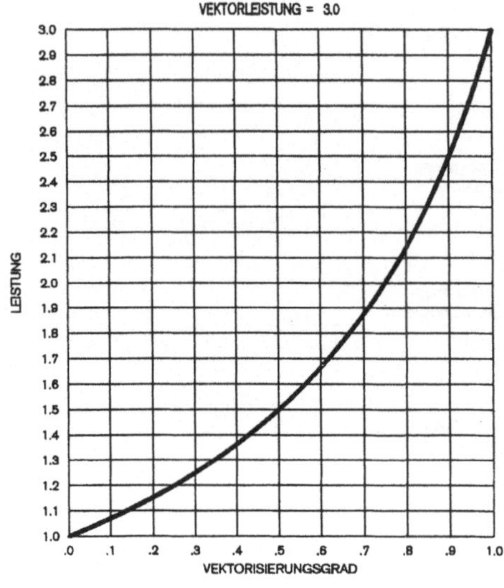

Bild 2

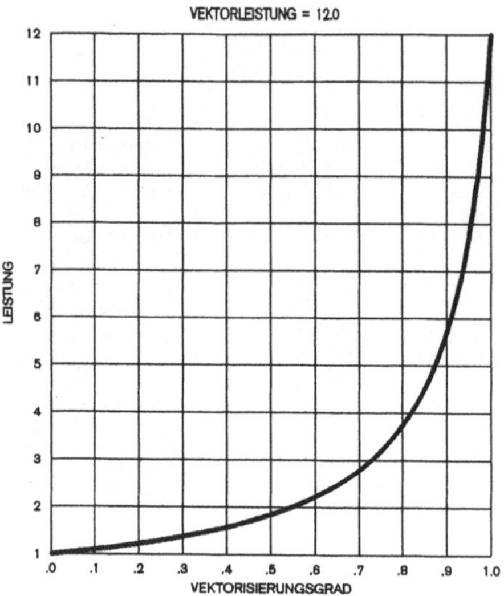

Bild 3

Die Bilder 2 und 3 zeigen eine grafische Darstellung des Amdahl'schen Gesetzes. Dabei ist die Skalarleistung mit 1 angenommen und die Vektorleistung mit 3 bzw. 12. Bild 2 ist repräsentativ für eine IBM 3090 VF und Bild 3 für eine Cray X MP, wenn heute übliche Benchmarkergebnisse [7] [8] zugrunde gelegt werden. Beide Darstellungen zeigen eine nur geringe Leistungsausbeute bei Vektorrechnern, solange der Vektorisierungsgrad nicht wesentlich größer ist als 50 %. Vektorrechner mit einer hohen Vektorleistung im Vergleich zu ihrer Skalarleistung erfordern einen sehr hohen Vektorisierungsgrad für eine gute Ausnutzung.

4. Das skalierte Gesetz von Amdahl

Die Erfahrung mit Vektorrechnern zeigt, daß es durchaus möglich ist, für eine große Palette von Programmen gute Leistungswerte für die Skalar- und Vektorleistungen von Supercomputern anzugeben. Die Skalarleistung ist dabei unkritischer und läßt sich als generelle Konstante bestimmen, die Vektorleistung dagegen hängt in einem gewissen Maß von der Qualifikation der Nutzer und ihrer Ausbildung für Vektorrechner-Softwareerstellung ab; sie muß deshalb als installationsabhängige Konstante ermittelt werden. Sehr viel schwieriger ist es, den Vektorisierungsgrad eines neu zu beschaffenden Vektorrechners vorauszubestimmen. In vielen Fällen behilft man sich dadurch, daß man die potentiellen Nutzer nach dem voraussichtlichen Vektorisierungsgrad ihrer Programme auf dem neuen Rechner befragt. Allerdings ist dieses Verfahren auch problematisch, da Nutzer oftmals den Vektorisierungsgrad ihrer Anwendungen völlig falsch einschätzen. Leider bieten auch die meisten Vektorrechner keine ausreichenden Informationen, die dem Nutzer eine Orientierung sein könnten.

Einen neuen Ansatz zur Bestimmung des Vektorisierungsgrades der Last eines neuen Vektorrechners aufgrund des Vektorisierungsgrades der Last auf einem vorhandenen (Vektor-)Rechner machte J. L. Gustafson [5]. Er nimmt an, daß ein leistungsfähiger Vektorrechner nicht zu der Verarbeitung einer größeren Anzahl von Programmen beschafft wird, sondern zur Lösung größerer Probleme. Er folgert daraus ein Ansteigen des Vektorisierungsgrades der Programme einer Installation, bei dem Übergang von einem leistungsschwächeren System auf ein leistungsfähigeres. Weiter nimmt er an, daß die Rechenzeit nur in dem vektorisierbaren (parallelisierbaren) Teil der Programme mit der Problemgröße anwächst, nicht aber in den skalaren Programmteilen.

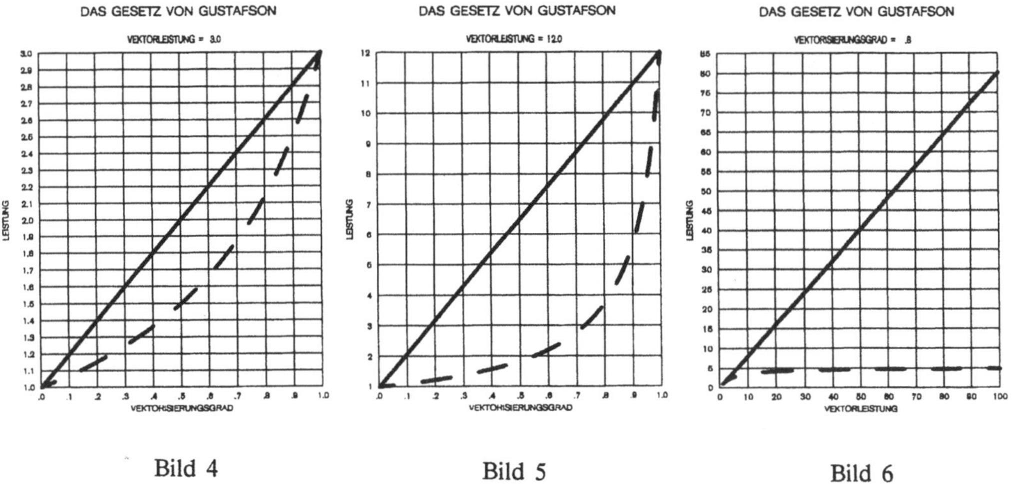

Bild 4 Bild 5 Bild 6

Durch diesen Ansatz ergeben sich neue Amdahl'sche Gesetze, die in den Bildern 4 bis 6 graphisch dargestellt sind. Gustafson nennt diese Gesetze skalierte Gesetze von Amdahl. Bild 4 zeigt die Leistung einer IBM 3090 VF und Bild 5 die einer Cray X MP unter den gleichen Benchmark-Annahmen wie im letzten Kapitel. Bild 6 zeigt die Leistung eines Vektorrechners bei einer 80 %-vektorisierbaren Last in Abhängigkeit von der Vektorleistung. Die gestrichelte Linie zeigt jeweils zum Vergleich das Amdahl'sche Gesetz. Der Unterschied zwischen den eigentlichen und den skalierten Gesetzen ist, wie man aus den drei Bildern sieht, beträchtlich. Insbesondere das Bild 6 zeigt für große Vektorleistungen gravierende Unterschiede von mehr als einer Größenordnung. Zieht man nun die skalierten Gesetze zum Vergleich von Vektorrechnern wie im Kapitel 1 heran, so ergibt sich Bild 7. Dieses Bild zeigt den Vergleich einer IBM 3090-400 VF mit einer Cray X MP2 (bzw. einer IBM 3090-200 VF mit einer Cray X MP1). Die Cray X MP ist für einen Vektorisierungsgrad ab etwa 33 % der IBM 3090 überlegen. Im Gegensatz dazu ist bei dem Amdahl'schen Gesetz der Schnittpunkt der beiden Kurven bei über 80 % [1]. Nach den Annahmen von Gustafson wäre die Entscheidung zugunsten einer Cray X MP, wie in Kapitel 1 dargelegt, voll und ganz zu rechtfertigen. Aus diesem Grund wird von vielen Seiten diese Modifikation des Amdahl'schen Gesetzes geradezu als Sensation gesehen [4].

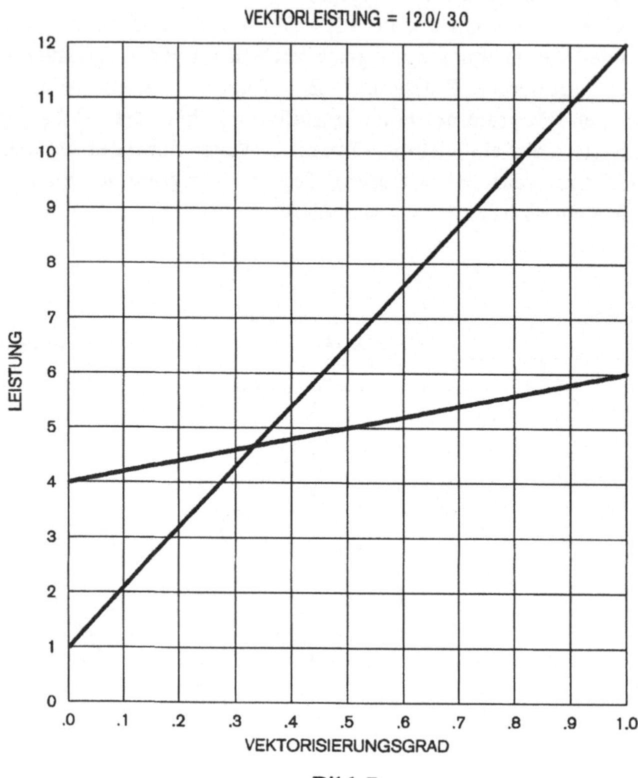

Bild 7

Leider zeigt es sich aber bei einer genaueren Studie der zu bearbeitenden Probleme, daß die Annahme der Unabhängigkeit des Rechenaufwandes für den des Skalarteiles von der Problemgröße, die Gustafson macht, für wichtige Probleme nicht gilt [9]. So zeigt sich schon an dem einfachsten Beispiel der Matrixmultiplikation ein Anwachsen des skalaren Rechenaufwandes mit dem Quadrat der Matrixgröße, während die vektorisierbaren Instruktionen mit der dritten Potenz der Matrixdimension anwachsen. Der Hauptgrund hierfür ist die Vektorisierungsstrategie der heutigen Vektorrechner, die stets nur eine von mehreren geschachtelten DO-Schleifen vektorisieren. Dies führt zu einer grundsätzlichen Änderung der skalierten Gesetze von Amdahl.

Eine wichtige Rolle bei der Anwendung von Supercomputern spielt die Lösung von mehrdimensionalen Anfangs-Randwertproblemen , wie z. B. die Lösung der Navier-Stokes-Gleichung, die das Wettergeschehen beschreibt, die den Luftwiderstandsbeiwert von Fahrzeugen und Flugzeugen bestimmt und neben anderen Gleichungen auch Verbrennungsabläufe in Wärmemaschinen maßgebend beeinflußt. Wichtige weitere Gleichungen, die z. B. für die Verformung von Materialien bei Krafteinwirkung bestimmend sind, haben eine ganz ähnliche Charakteristik.

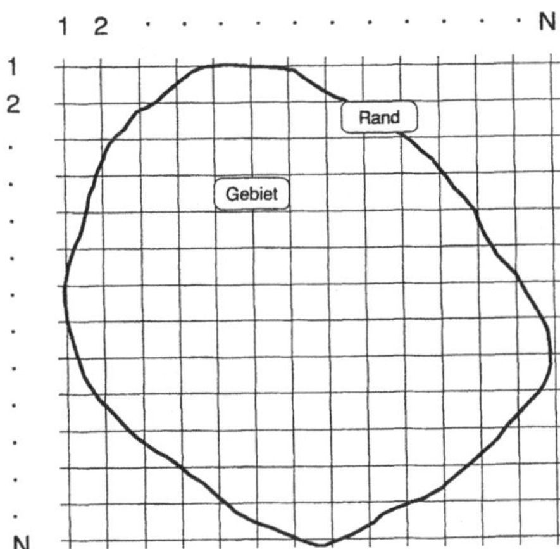

Bei einem zweidimensionalen Problem:
Stützstellenanzahl proportional N^2
Rechenaufwand proportional N^3

Bild 8

Bild 8 zeigt den Aufbau eines Gitters, das zur Lösung eines derartigen Anfangs-Randwertproblemes herangezogen werden kann, der Einfachheit halber in zwei Dimensionen [6]. Der Aufbau eines Programmes zur Lösung eines dreidimensionalen Anfangs-Randwertproblemes besteht aus einer Reihe arithmetischer Ausdrücke, die in geschachtelten DO-Schleifen angeordnet sind:

Arithmetischer Ausdruck I

DO 10 IT = 1,N *Zeit*

Arithmetischer Ausdruck II

DO 10 IX = 1,N *X-Achse*

Arithmetischer Ausdruck III

DO 10 IY = 1,N *Y-Achse*

Arithmetischer Ausdruck IV

DO 10 IZ = 1,N *Z-Achse*

Arithmetischer Ausdruck V

10 CONTINUE

Es sei M die Gesamtanzahl der Gleitkommainstruktionen in dem skizzierten Programmteil, dann ist M proportional zu der vierten Potenz von N:

Anzahl der Gleitkommainstruktionen $M \sim N^4$
vektorisiebar:

$$M_V = a_4 N^4 + O(N^3) = \alpha M$$

nicht vektorisierbar:

$$M_S = a_3 N^3 + O(N^2) = (1 - \alpha) M$$

dabei ist α der Vektorisierungsgrad des Programmes, daraus folgt:

$$a_4 = \alpha \frac{M}{N^4} + O(N^{-1})$$

$$a_3 = \frac{(1 - \alpha) M}{N^3} + O(N^{-1})$$

Bezieht man sich nun ohne Beschränkung der Allgemeinheit auf einen Ausgangsrechner mit der Skalar- und Vektorleistung 1 (Skalarrechner) und legt man eine Ausgangsgittergröße zugrunde, so ergibt sich für den Zielrechner mit einer neuen Gittergröße:

Ausgangsrechner

z.B. Skalarrechner mit der Leistung $L_{S_0} = 1$:

$$M = M_0 , \quad N = N_0$$

Zielrechner

Vektorrechner mit der Leistung L_s und $L_v = \beta L_s$

$$P = \frac{N}{N_0}$$

$$M_0 = \frac{T_0}{L_{s_0}} = T_0$$

$$a_4 = \frac{\alpha T_0}{N_0^4}$$

$$a_3 = \frac{(1-\alpha)\, T_0}{N_0^3}$$

Dabei sind die Konstanten a asymptotische Größen, die für große Gitter bestimmt werden können.

Setzt man die Programmausführungszeit auf dem Zielrechner gleich der Ausführungszeit des Ausgangsproblems auf dem Ausgangsrechner, so läßt sich eine Problemgröße berechnen, aus der dann im nächsten Schritt die Leistung des Zielrechners ermittelt werden kann:

$$T(L_{s,}\beta) = \frac{T_0}{L_s} \{ \frac{\alpha}{\beta} P^4 + (1-\alpha) P^3 \}$$

mit $T(L_{s,}\beta) := T_0$ folgt

$$1 = \frac{1}{L_s} \{ \frac{\alpha}{\beta} P^4 + (1-\alpha) P^3 \}$$

Aus dieser Beziehung kann P bestimmt werden, und damit wird

$$L = \{ \alpha P^4 + (1-\alpha) P^3 \}$$

Die beiden letzten Gleichungen sind das skalierte Gesetz von Amdahl für die Lösung von dreidimensionalen Anfangs-Randwertproblemen.

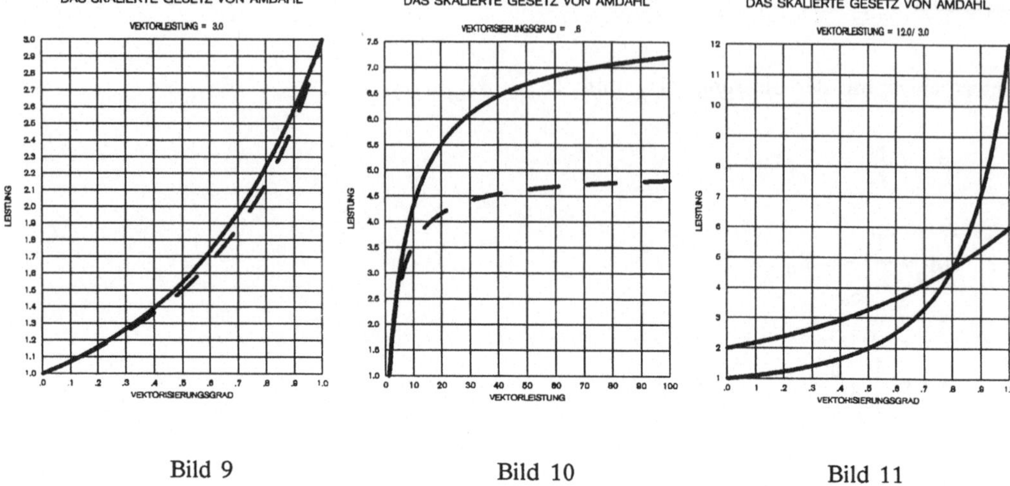

Bild 9 Bild 10 Bild 11

Die Bilder 9 bis 11 zeigen in einer graphischen Darstellung dieses Gesetz. Es zeigt sich, daß der Unterschied zwischen dem skalierten Gesetz von Amdahl (durchgezogen) und dem Originalgesetz nicht sehr groß ist. Das Amdahl'sche Gesetz nähert in diesem Fall die Wirklichkeit besser an als die Beziehung von Gustafson. Auch für einen Vergleich zweier Vektorrechner, wie z. B. IBM 3090 und Cray, ergibt sich wie Bild 11 zeigt, kein wesentlicher Unterschied zu dem Gesetz von Amdahl; der Schnittpunkt der Leistung liegt hier bei 80 %.

Allgemein kann das skalierte Gesetz von Amdahl durch folgende beiden Gleichungen beschrieben werden:

$$1 = \frac{1}{L_s} \left\{ \frac{\alpha}{\beta} P^J + (1-\alpha) P^K \right\}$$

$$L = \{ \alpha P^J + (1-\alpha) P^K \}$$

Dabei ist für $J = K \neq 0$ dieses Gesetz äquivalent zu dem Amdahl'schen Gesetz. Dieser Fall tritt vor allem bei stark nichtlinearen Problemen auf, aber auch an anderer Stelle [9] . Für $J > 0$ und $K = 0$ entspricht es der von Gustafson formulierten Beziehung. Für $J = 3$ und $K = 2$ beschreibt es z. B. Lösungen von zweidimensionalen Anfangs-Randwertaufgaben, die Matrixmultiplikation, die Lösung eines linearen vollbesetzten Gleichungssystems. Für $J = 4$ und $K = 3$ ist es der dargelegte Fall einer dreidimensionalen Anfangs-Randwertaufgabe.

5. Die Leistung von Vektorrechnerkombinationen

Die heute auf dem Markt angebotenen Vektorrechner lassen sich in drei Gruppen einteilen:

Klassifizierung von Vektorrechnern:

– Daten jeweils pro Prozessor –

1. Supercomputer

Cray, VP 200

Skalarleistung	10 MFLOPS
Vektorleistung	120 MFLOPS
Preis ca.	4 MIO. $

2. Universalrechner mit Vektoreinrichtung

IBM 3090 VF

Skalarleistung	10 MFLOPS
Vektorleistung	30 MFLOPS
Preis ca.	2 MIO. $

3. Minisupercomputer:

Convex C2

Skalarleistung	2.5 MFLOPS
Vektorleistung	30 MFLOPS
Preis ca.	1 MIO. $

Dabei ist die hohe Skalarleistung der Universalrechner mit Vektorzusatz und die hohe Vektorleistung der Minisupercomputer jeweils bezogen auf deren Preis bemerkenswert. Es stellt sich die Frage, ob die Kombination eines Universalrechners mit Vektorzusatz für den niedrig vektorisierbaren Teil der Last und ein Minisupercomputer für den hoch vektorisierbaren Teil eine wirtschaftlichere und damit eventuell auch eine bessere Lösung ist als ein Supercomputer.

Will man diese Frage beantworten, so ist es erforderlich, das Profil der zu bearbeitenden Last genauer zu kennen. Es ist hierfür nicht ausreichend, den durchschnittlichen Vektorisierungsgrad der Programme zu wissen, vielmehr muß auch die Verteilung der Last als Funktion des Vektorisierungsgrades bekannt sein.

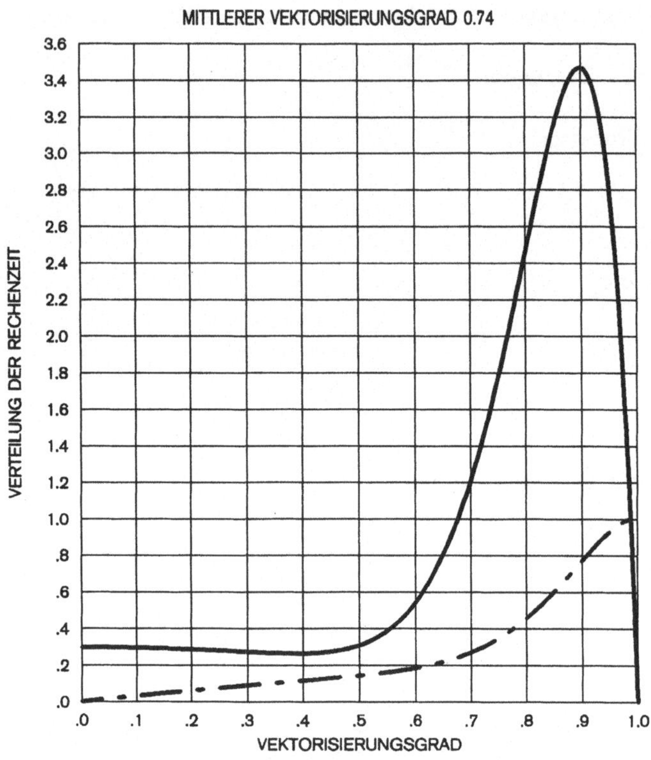

Bild 12

Die Verteilungsfunktion sollte am besten durch Messen des Lastprofiles ermittelt werden. Die heutigen Vektorrechner erlauben es leider häufig nicht, die erforderlichen Daten zu gewinnen, deshalb muß man in diesem Fall versuchen, durch eine sorgfältige Benutzerumfrage brauchbare Daten zu gewinnen, wie z. B. bei der DFVLR, wo die Verteilungsfunktion entsprechend Bild 12 als Grundlage der Beschaffung eines Vektorrechners diente. Die durchgezogene Linie ist die Verteilungsfunktion V, die gestrichelte Linie das Integral über V. Die zur Verarbeitung eines Arbeitspaketes notwendige Rechenzeit bestimmt sich dann aus

$$T = \int_0^1 \frac{N\, V(\alpha)}{L(\alpha)}\, d\alpha$$

Dabei ist N die Anzahl der Gleitkommainstruktionen in diesem Arbeitspaket und L die Leistung nach dem Amdahl'schen Gesetz oder nach dem skalierten Amdahl'schen Gesetz. Setzt man nun zwei Rechner ein, den mit der höheren Vektorleistung für den höher vektorisierbaren Teil der

Leistung von Rechenzentrumskonfigurationen

VAX 8550	CONVEX C2	IBM 3090 VF	CRAY X/Y	Leistung
	Anzahl der Prozessoren			
1	-	-	-	0.25
-	1	-	-	0.80
-	-	1	-	2.0
-	-	-	1	3.1
-	1	1	-	3.1 bei 83%
-	2	1	-	4.1 bei 77%
-	4	1	-	5.9 bei 67%
1	-	-	1	3.8 bei 22%
2	-	-	1	4.4 bei 40%
-	-	2	2	12 bei 67%
-	-	4	2	16 bei 77%
-	-	6	2	21 bei 81%
-	-	2	4	18 bei 45%
-	-	6	4	28 bei 73%

Tabelle 1

Die Leistung ist auf die Skalarleistung der Cray X MP bzw. der IBM 3090 bezogen

Leistung von Rechenzentrumskonfigurationen

VAX 8550	CONVEX C2	IBM 3090 VF	CRAY X/Y	Leistung
	Anzahl der Prozessoren			
1	-	-	-	0.25
-	1	-	-	0.50
-	-	1	-	1.7
-	-	-	1	2.5
-	1	1	-	2.7 bei 83%
-	2	1	-	3.6 bei 76%
-	4	1	-	5.3 bei 66%
1	-	-	1	3.2 bei 21%
2	-	-	1	3.8 bei 33%
-	-	2	2	12 bei 67%
-	-	4	2	17 bei 77%
-	-	6	2	22 bei 81%
-	-	2	4	20 bei 46%
-	-	6	4	32 bei 74%

Tabelle 2

Die Leistung ist auf die Skalarleistung der Cray X MP bzw. der IBM 3090 bezogen

Last und den mit der niedrigeren Vektorleistung für den niedrig vektorisierbaren Teil, so ergibt sich für jeden dieser Rechner eine Verarbeitungszeit für seinen Lastteil:

$$T_1(x) = \int_0^x \frac{N\,V(\alpha)}{L_1(\alpha)}\,d\alpha$$

$$T_2(x) = \int_x^1 \frac{N\,V(\alpha)}{L_2(\alpha)}\,d\alpha$$

Dann ergibt sich mit $T = \mathit{Maximum}(T_1, T_2)$:

$$T \;\; \mathit{Minimum} \;\; \text{für} \;\; T_1(x) = T_2(x)$$

Die Tabelle 1 zeigt die Leistungsdaten mehrerer Zentraleinheiten unter Annahme der in Bild 12 gezeigten Lastverteilung und des Gesetzes von Amdahl. Die Leistungswerte sind bezogen auf die Skalarleistung der Cray X MP bzw. der IBM 3090. In der letzten Spalte ist neben der Leistung einer Rechnerkombination der Grenzvektorisierungsgrad angegeben. Der Lastteil, der höher als der Grenzvektorisierungsgrad vektorisiert ist, wird dabei auf dem Rechner mit der größeren Vektorleistung verarbeitet. In der Tabelle 2 sind dieselben Rechnerkombinationen aufgeführt. Bei dem gleichen Lastprofil bezogen auf eine IBM 3090-200 VF und eine Cray X MP2, wie sie derzeit bei der DFVLR eingesetzt werden, wurde die Leistung berechnet durch das skalierte Gesetz von Amdahl. Dabei ist angenommen, daß sich die Rechnerlast hauptsächlich aus der Berechnung von dreidimensionalen Problemen zusammensetzt.

Ein interessantes Ergebnis aus den Tabellen 1 und 2 ist, daß die Rechnerkombination IBM 3090 VF /Convex C2 die gleiche Leistung hat wie eine Cray X MP, die deutlich teurer ist. Für die DFVLR, die heute eine IBM 3090-200 VF und eine Cray X MP2 betreibt, ist die Frage von hoher Wichtigkeit, wie sich eine steigende Nachfrage nach Vektorleistung am wirtschaftlichsten befriedigen läßt. So kann sowohl die IBM 3090-200 VF als auch die Cray X MP erweitert werden. Abhängig von den Kosten der Erweiterungen läßt sich dann aufgrund der Tabellen 1 und 2 die wirtschaftlichste Lösung finden. Wie die Tabellen zeigen, ist der Unterschied zwischen der Erweiterung der Cray durch zwei Prozessoren und der 3090 durch zwei Prozessoren nicht sehr groß. Eine Erweiterung der 3090 um vier Prozessoren führt zu einer höheren Leistung als eine Verdoppelung der Prozessoranzahl der Cray X MP2.

6. Folgerungen für Parallelrechner

Die beiden Tabellen des letzten Abschnittes zeigen, daß Supercomputer in bezug auf deren Wirtschaftlichkeit durchaus problematisch sind. Falls es möglich ist, den hochvektorisierbaren Teil der Last herauszufiltern, so ist eine Convex-C2 zusammen mit einer IBM 3090 VF ebenso leistungsfähig wie eine Cray Y, die etwa das doppelte kostet. Noch klarer verlieren die großen und größeren Systeme, wenn sie mit dem Wirtschaftlichkeitspotential der RISC-basierten Mikro-Rechnersysteme, wie z.B. der neuen DEC-Station 3100 verglichen werden. Diese DEC-Station hat als Skalarrechner eine Leistung, die mindestens der Skalarleistung einer Convex-C2 entspricht. Für niedrigvektorisierte Programme leistet die DEC-Station 3100 etwa soviel wie eine Convex-C2 (mit einem Prozessor) und kostet dabei nur ein Zwanzigstel. Bei einem Vektorisierungsgrad von 80 % ist die Convex lediglich um einen Faktor drei bei 90 % um einen Faktor fünf überlegen. Noch in diesem Jahr wird die Ankündigung und die Auslieferung von Mikrorechnersystemen erwartet, deren Leistung vier- bis fünfmal höher ist als die der DEC-Station 3100. Damit werden die kleineren Vektorrechner noch 1989 bedeutungslos geworden sein.

Diese Wirtschaftlichkeitsüberlegungen zeigen, daß weder die eigentlichen Supercomputer noch die Mini-Supercomputer sich in Zukunft in einer Vielbenutzerumgebung behaupten werden können. Lediglich für Sonderanwendungen, wie z.B. bei der Wettervorhersage oder bei der "Windkanalsimulation" wird es noch Einsatzmöglichkeiten derartiger Systeme geben. Aber auch bei diesen Anwendungen ist es erforderlich, eine Programmlast mit einem sehr hohen mittleren Vektorisierungsgrad zu haben, um derartig teuere Rechner sinnvoll nutzen zu können. Hohe Vektorisierungsgrade werden aber in der Regel nur dann erreicht, wenn das zu Grunde liegende physikalische bzw. mathematische Problem linear ist. Aber gerade die wichtigsten der heute sehr verbreiteten physikalischen Problemstellungen führen zu mathematisch nichtlinearen Aufgaben: "Crash-Simulation" in der Kraftfahrzeugindustrie, Strömungsrechnungen durch Lösung der Navier-Stokes-Gleichung in der Flugzeug- und Kraftfahrzeugindustrie sowie die Simulation von Verbrennungsvorgängen in der Entwicklung von Kraftfahrzeugmotoren und Flugzeugtriebwerken.

Die hier aufgezeigten Grenzen der Supercomputer sowie die immer stärker werdende Konkurrenz durch Mikrorechnersysteme haben die Aktivitäten zur Entwicklung hochparalleler Rechnersysteme in aller Welt sehr stark stimuliert. Es wird erwartet, daß mit Parallelrechnern neue Leistungsklassen erreicht werden und somit auch bisher unlösbare Probleme behandelt und gelöst werden können. Dabei setzt man vor allem auf die Tatsache, daß die Klasse der parallelisierbaren Probleme viel größer ist als die der vektorisierbaren, da alle vektorisierbaren Probleme auch parallelisierbar sind, nicht aber umgekehrt. Insbesondere für nichtlineare Probleme verspricht der Einsatz von Parallelrechnersystemen neue Perspektiven.

Aus diesem Grund sind deshalb gerade auch bei Parallelrechnern die durch das Gesetz von Amdahl gezogenen Grenzen von erheblichem Interesse. Gustafson hat ausdrücklich die Gültigkeit des von ihm postulierten Gesetzes besonders auch für parallele Rechnersysteme hervorgehoben. Leider zeigt es sich aber, daß die Gesetzmäßigkeiten bei Parallelrechnern nicht von denen der Vektorrechner abweichen.

Die höchste Analogie zwischen Vektor- und Parallelrechnern tritt auf, wenn selbstvektorisierende und selbstparallelisierende Compiler verglichen werden. Während der selbstvektorisierende Compiler in der Regel die innerste von geschachtelten Schleifen vektorisiert, parallelisieren selbstparallelisierende Compiler die äußerste Schleife. In beiden Fällen wird nur eine mehrerer in sich geschachtelter Schleifen vektorisiert bzw. parallelisiert. Daraus folgt dann dieselbe Gesetzmäßigkeit, die zu den skalierten Gesetzen von Amdahl führt.

Selbst wenn ein Programm durch den Programmhersteller parallelisiert wird, ist es unmöglich, den seriellen bzw. nichtparallelisierbaren Programmteil von der Problemgröße unabhängig zu halten. Die Anzahl der Prozesse in einem Programm für einen Parallelrechner muß nämlich mindestens ebenso groß sein wie die Prozessoranzahl, wenn dieser vollständig ausgenutzt werden soll. Die Prozesse müssen jedoch alle erzeugt, gestaltet und beendet werden. Die Aufgabe des Erzeugen, Starten und Beenden der Prozesse selbst läßt sich aber nicht oder nur sehr unvollständig parallelisieren.

Wendet der Programmierer eine einfache und gebräuchliche Technik hierfür an, so ist der Aufwand zur Bearbeitung des nichtparallelisierbaren Programmteiles proportional zur Anzahl der Prozesse und damit auch zur Anzahl der Prozessoren. In diesem Fall gilt das Gesetz von Amdahl in seiner ursprünglichen Form. Wendet man hingegen eine weit aufwendigere Synchronisiertechnik an, bei der ein Prozeß je zwei neue Prozesse startet, die wieder jeweils zwei initiieren usw., so ist der Aufwand hierfür erheblich geringer, er wächst nur noch mit dem Logarithmus der Prozeßanzahl. Doch selbst in diesem günstigsten Fall gilt nicht die von Gustafson postulierte Beziehung der Proportionalität zwischen Leistung und Prozessoranzahl, sondern es ergeben sich skalierte Gesetze von Amdahl, die denen von Bild 9 und Bild 10 ähnlich sind.

Literatur

[1] Wacker, H.-M.: Der Markt für Vektorrechner nach Ankündigung der IBM 3090 VF. PIK - Praxis der Informationsverarbeitung und Kommunikation, Heft 3, Juli 1986, S. 16-20, Carl Hanser-Verlag München

[2] Wacker, H.-M.: Kriterien für den wirtschaftlichen Einsatz von Vektorrechnern. PIK - Praxis der Informationsverarbeitung und Kommunikation, Heft 1, Januar 1988, S. 40-43, Carl Hanser-Verlag München

[3] Meuer, H.-W. (Hrsg): Supercomputer '88 - Anwendungen, Architekturen, Trends - Seminar an der Universität Mannheim, PIK Special 1, Carl Hanser-Verlag München 1988, S.170

[4] Meuer, H.-W.: Supercomputerarchitektur in den 90er Jahren. PIK - Praxis der Informationsverarbeitung und Kommunikation, Heft 4, Dezember 1988, Carl Hanser-Verlag München

[5] Gustafson, John L.: Reevaluating Amdahl's Law. Communications of the ACM, Vol. 31 No. 5, Mai 1988, pp.532-533

[6] Forsythe, G.E.; Wasow, W.R.: Finite Difference Methods for Partial Differential Equations, Wiley & Sons, 1960

[7] Dongarra, J.J.: Supercomputer Performance Considerations - The LINPACK Benchmark: An Explanation. Proceedings of the Seminar Supercomputer '87, Mannheim, 12.–13. Juni 1987

[8] Dongarra, J.J.: Reconstruction Supercomputer Algorithms. Proceedings of the Tutorial Supercomputer '87, Mannheim, 15.–16. Juni 1987

[9] Balram, N.: Belo, C.; Moura, J.M.F.: Parallel Processing on Supercomputers: A Set of Computational Experiments, Proceedings Supercomputing '88, IEEE Computer Society, Order Number 882, pp. 247–257, November 1988

[10] Wacker, H.–M.: Das skalierte Gesetz von Amdahl. PIK - Praxis der Informations-verarbeitung und Kommunikation, Heft 1, Januar 1989, S. 44–48, Carl Hanser–Verlag München

Dem parallelen Rechnen gehört die Zukunft

Karl Solchenbach, Bernhard Thomas, Ulrich Trottenberg

SUPRENUM
Gesellschaft für numerische Superrechner mbH
Hohe Straße 73
5300 Bonn 1

1. Zusammenfassung und Einleitung

Parallelrechner (im engeren Sinne) kennzeichnen die 3. Generation von Superrechnern nach

- Vektorrechnern (1. Generation)
- Multi-Vektorrechnern mit mehreren CPUs und dem Konzept eines gemeinsamen Speichers (2. Generation).

Technologische Grenzen der Vektorrechner: Hier ist die Leistung durch die Anzahl sinnvoll einsetzbarer Pipeline-Stufen und durch technologische Schranken (Aufbautechnik, Integrationsdichte/Wärme, Signallaufzeiten/Lichtgeschwindigkeit) begrenzt.

Architektonische Grenzen der Multi-CPU-Vektorrechner: Den Engpaß stellt hier vor allem das Konzept des gemeinsamen, von allen CPUs gleich schnell zugreifbaren Speichers dar, an dem besonders aus Softwaregesichtspunkten zunächst festgehalten wurde. Durch dieses Konzept wird die Anzahl parallel arbeitender CPUs wesentlich begrenzt.

Die beiden genannten Begrenzungen entfallen bei Parallelrechnern (in engeren Sinne). Hierbei sind die Einheiten des Arbeitsspeichers auf die Prozessoren verteilt, und damit kann die Leistung im Prinzip unbegrenzt gesteigert werden. Man kann Hunderte, Tausende und mehr Prozessoren einsetzen, und man kann auf die teure VHSIC-Technologie (very high speed integrated circuit) zugunsten sehr viel preisgünstigerer VLSI-Technologie (Mikrocomputer-Technologie) verzichten.

Dabei liegt es nahe, den einzelnen Prozessor, z.B. durch Verwendung sehr schneller und preiswerter Vektor-Arithmetikeinheiten, so stark wie möglich - und wie unter Kostengesichtspunkten vertretbar - zu machen.

Die technologischen Möglichkeiten und die bei der 1. und 2. Superrechnergeneration gesammelten Erfahrungen können dabei voll ausgenutzt werden.

1.2. Das Kommunikationsproblem, das viele Jahre - für die Hardware- und vor allem für die Softwareseite - als das zentrale Problem des parallelen Rechnens angesehen wurde, ist heute gelöst:

- Es ist nachgewiesen, daß Parallelrechner - mit flexiblen Verbindungsstrukturen zwischen den einzelnen Prozessoren - sehr kostengünstig aufgebaut werden können.
- Durch konsequente und effiziente Realisierung des Botschaftenkonzepts (message passing) wird die Kommunikation auch von der Systemsoftwareseite her vollständig beherrscht.
- Parallelrechner sind mit Standardprogrammiersprachen (FORTRAN, C etc.) überraschend einfach programmierbar. Dabei sorgen elementare Kommunikationskonstrukte oder high-level Kommunikationsroutinen für Synchronisation und Kommunikation. Verglichen mit der Programmierung herkömmlicher Rechner braucht praktisch kein Mehraufwand getrieben zu werden. Im Gegenteil: Da die Parallelverarbeitung zu den meisten Anwendungen und algorithmischen Strukturen unmittelbarer paßt als die sequentielle Verarbeitung, ist die parallele Programmierung sogar in vielen Fällen eleganter als die konventionelle.
- Das Anwendungsspektrum für Parallelrechner umfaßt alle Aufgaben, für die Vektorrechner geeignet sind, und geht weit darüber hinaus: Viele Algorithmen sind schlecht vektorisierbar, aber gut parallelisierbar. Vektorverarbeitung ist eben eine besonders einfache Spezialform der Parallelverarbeitung.

1.3. In SUPRENUM ist ein Konzept hoher Parallelität und mittlerer Granularität verwirklicht worden (viele Prozessoren, jeder einzelne Prozessor so leistungsstark, wie mit VLSI-Technologie leicht erreichbar), mit einer sehr flexiblen Kommunikationsstruktur auf der Basis eines Hochleistungsverbindungssystems.

In diese Richtung, auf dieses Architekturkonzept hin bewegen sich alle ernstzunehmenden Superrechnerentwicklungen: Die Hersteller herkömmlicher Superrechner erhöhen die Anzahl der parallel arbeitenden Prozessoren wesentlich; die Hersteller hochparalleler Systeme verstärken die Leistung der Einzelprozessoren. Diese Tendenz zur mittleren Granularität mit flexiblen Verbindungsstrukturen wird (von W. Giloi) treffend als "Konvergenz der Superrechnerarchitekturen" bezeichnet.

2. Unbegrenzter Rechenbedarf in den Anwendungen

Superrechner sind zum unentbehrlichen Hilfsmittel für die wissenschaftliche Arbeit geworden, sie haben eine ähnlich zentrale methodische Bedeutung erlangt, wie die wissenschaftliche Theorie und das wissenschaftliche Experiment. In vielen wissenschaftlichen Disziplinen (Aerodynamik, Meteorologie, Teilchenphysik, Chemie/Pharmazie, Plasmaphysik usw.) sind technologische Durchbrüche absehbar, wenn Rechner zur Verfügung stehen, die 10, 100, 1000 mal leistungsfähiger sind als die heutigen Superrechner. Dabei ist kein Ende abzusehen: Jedes mit dem Rechner gelöste Problem zeigt ein komplexeres neues auf, jede Überprüfung der Theorie durch Rechner und Experiment zieht eine Verfeinerung der Theorie nach sich.

Wir nennen einige Beispiele:

In der **Aerodynamik**, einem der ersten und wichtigsten Anwendungsfelder für Superrechner, werden heute Windkanalexperimente durch numerische Simulation ergänzt und in vielen Bereichen auch schon ersetzt.

Da jedoch die heutigen Superrechner in ihrer Leistung begrenzt sind, muß man heute noch wählen: Man kann die volle 3D-Geometrie des umströmten Objekts (z.B. eines Überschallflugzeugs) modellieren, muß sich dann aber mit einem vereinfachten mathematisch-physikalischen Modell (z.B. Vernachlässigung der Reibung: Eulergleichungen) zufrieden geben, oder umgekehrt: Bei Verwendung des vollen mathematisch-physikalischen Modells (Navier-Stokes-Gleichungen) muß man sich mit einer vereinfachten Geometrie (2D- oder grob vereinfacht 3D) begnügen.

Von einem "numerischen Windkanal" könnte man erst sprechen, wenn beides möglich wäre: volle Geometrie und volle Mathematik im gleichen Modell zu berechnen. Bei Verwendung der heute gängigen numerischen Methoden werden dazu Rechner benötigt, die mindestens um den Faktor 10 schneller wären als die schnellsten heute zur Verfügung stehenden Superrechner.

In der **Meteorologie** (mittelfristige Wettervorhersage) ist heute eine 5-Tagesvorhersage mit guter Trefferquote möglich. Die dazu erforderlichen Rechnungen werden auf einem über die Hemisphäre ausgebreiteten Gitter der Maschenweite 100 km ausgeführt, wobei man rund 20 Höhenschichten zugrundelegt. Um eine 10-Tagesvorhersage mit akzeptabler Trefferquote zu ermöglichen, würde ein Gitter der Maschenweite < 20 km mit mindestens 30 Höhenschichten benötigt. Die zugehörigen Rechnungen würden rund 100 mal mehr Rechenzeit erfordern als die 5-Tages-Wettervorhersage.

Turbulenzforschung ist grundlegend für das Verständnis elementarer Phänomene in Strömungsmechanik, Meteorologie, Klimaforschung, Schadstoffausbreitung, Verbrennung u.a. Die zugehörigen Berechnungen werden heute in 3D-Gittern mit 100 Gitterpunkten in jeder Richtung durchgeführt (in einem zeitabhängigen Modell). Aufgrund theoretischer Erkenntnisse weiß man, daß eine Rechnung in einem 3D-Gitter mit je 1000 Gitterpunkten zu Aussagen führen würde, die einen Durchbruch für die Turbulenzmodellierung bedeuten könnten. Da man in den Gittermodellen heute mit zeitexpliziten Diskretisierungen arbeitet, erfordert die Berechnung in dem 1.000^3-Gitter etwa die 10.000-fache Rechenzeit gegenüber dem 100^3-Gitter.

In der **Elementarteilchenphysik** ist mit der Gitter-Eich-Theorie (Quantenchronodynamik) eine grundlegende Theorie vorhanden, die prinzipiell auch durch Experimente (in Teilchenbeschleunigern) überprüft werden kann. Trotzdem können Theorie und Experiment bis heute nicht zur Deckung gebracht werden, da die der Theorie zugrundeliegenden mathematischen Modelle wegen ihrer Komplexität nur viel zu grob numerisch ausgewertet werden können. Für die reine Eichtheorie werden heute Monte-Carlo-Rechnungen auf 4D-Gittern mit je 24 Gitterpunkten in jeder Richtung durchgeführt. Bezieht man die Hadronenmassen in die Berechnungen mit ein, so erlauben die heutigen Rechner nur unrealistische Gitter der

Größenordnung 10^4 . Für die Berechnung der Hadronenmassen auf realistischen Gittern der Größenordnung 100^4 würden wiederum 10.000 mal schnellere Rechner benötigt.

Diese Liste von Beispielen läßt sich beliebig fortsetzen, und zwar was den Superrechnerbedarf sowohl für die Grundlagenforschung als auch für die industrielle Praxis angeht.

Die genannten Aufgaben geben eine Ahnung von den Leistungen, die von den Rechnern morgen und über- morgen erwartet werden.

3. Vektorverarbeitung

Bei der ersten Generation von Superrechnern, zu denen die Cray-1, CDC Cyber 205, Fujitsu VP gehören, setzte die Idee der Parallelität auf sehr niedriger Ebene, im Prozessor an: das Fließband-Prinzip.

Typisch für viele wissenschaftliche Probleme ist, daß innerhalb des gesamten Rechenablaufs häufig die gleiche Rechenoperation (Addition, Multiplikation u.ä.) hintereinander für eine ganze Reihe von Daten durchgeführt werden muß, etwa wenn in einer Schleife die Addition zweier Vektoren programmiert wurde. Dadurch, daß die verschiedenen Teilschritte zur Ausführung einer solchen Operation fließbandartig hintereinandergeschaltet werden (*Pipeline*), können diese nach einer Anlaufphase parallel arbeiten und so aus den eingehenden Daten (Operandenstrom) in jedem Zyklus ein Rechenergebnis erzeugen. Für die verschiedenen arithmetischen und logischen Operationen sind solche Funktionspipelines entweder einzeln hardware mäßig (Cray) oder als multifunktionale, schaltbare Pipelines (Cyber 205) realisiert und in einer zentralen Prozessoreinheit zusammengefaßt (*Pipeline-Prozessor*). Da dieser Fließband-Arbeitsmodus gerade bei solchen Berechnungen sehr effizient ist, die auf - möglichst lange - Vektoroperationen im mathematischen Problem zurückgehen, spricht man hier auch von *Vektorverarbeitung*. Die Superrechner der 1. Generation und damit auch die Klasse der "traditionellen" Supercomputer werden daher auch *Vektorrechner* genannt.

Oft lassen sich Berechnungen auch so aneinanderreihen, daß die Ergebnisse einer Pipeline-Einheit direkt an eine andere Pipeline weiterleiten lassen. Durch diese Verkettung (*Chaining*) läßt sich Parallelverarbeitung bereits auf der Ebene vollständiger Rechenoperationen ausnutzen, mit der entsprechenden Durchsatzsteigerung.

Die Nutzung der Vektorverarbeitung (*Vektorisierung*) bei der Programmierung bereitet i.a. keine größeren Schwierigkeiten, insbesondere wenn die anwendungstypischen Datenobjekte Vektoren und Matrizen sind. Darüberhinaus kann man heutzutage das Vektorisieren auch weitgehend den modernen vektorisierenden Compilern überlassen. Diese erzeugen automatisch aus normalen FORTRAN-Programmen ablauffähigen Vektorcode, wenn auch eine wirklich gute Vektorisierung nur selten erreicht wird.

Im Spektrum neuer Rechnerarchitekturen werden Vektorrechner zu den SIMD-Rechnern gezählt. SIMD (single instruction / multiple data) bezeichnet dabei den Arbeitsmodus eines Rechners, bei dem zentral gesteuert *ein* Befehl gleichzeitig oder fließbandartig auf vielen Daten ausgeführt wird. (Bezüglich einer systematischeren Klassifizierung von Rechnerarchitekturen siehe auch [1].)

Zu den Merkmalen traditioneller Superrechner gehört neben dem Vektorparallelismus im übrigen auch der Einsatz von Höchstgeschwindigkeitstechnologie, d.h. von Prozessor- und Speicherkomponenten mit extrem niedrigen Schaltzeiten (heute im Nanosekunden-Bereich). Diese VHSIC-Technologie ist mit hohem Entwicklungsaufwand, Kühlungsbedarf und relativ geringer Integrationsdichte verbunden. Hier sind inzwischen die physikalischen Grenzen in Sicht, so daß allein mit Hochgeschwindigkeitstechnologie auf ökonomische Weise keine großen Leistungssprünge mehr zu erwarten sind.

4. Multi-Vektorrechner

Die zweite Generation Supercomputer geht daher den Weg der Vervielfachung zur Leistungssteigerung. Die Cray X/MP, Cray-2, ETA-10 können mit mehreren CPUs und zugehörigen Pipeline-Prozessoren ausgestattet werden, die sich die Arbeit an langen Datenströmen teilen können. Auf diese Weise können zum Beispiel Abschnitte einer Schleife (DO-Loop in FORTRAN) auf die verschiedenen Prozessoren verteilt werden (*Microtasking*) oder, wenn es das Rechenverfahren erlaubt, sogar verschiedene Unterprogramme (*Macrotasking*).

Typische Größenordnungen für diese Multivektorprozessor-Rechner sind 2 bis 8 Prozessoren. Pläne für bis zu 64 Prozessoren bestehen, doch steigt der Entwicklungsaufwand mit der Anzahl enorm an. Ein Grund dafür ist das Problem der zentralen Speicherverwaltung. Der Hauptspeicher muß für alle Prozessoren gemeinsam, gleichzeitig und schnell zugreifbar sein (*shared memory*). Das führt zu Zugriffskonflikten, deren Auflösung nur durch zusätzlichen Hardwareaufwand und Zeitverlust beim Programmablauf gewährleistet werden kann. Diese für alle shared-memory Systeme typische Speicherzugriffsproblematik wächst mit zunehmender Zahl und Leistungsfähigkeit der Prozessoren rasch an und wird schon bei kleinen Größenordnungen (30–60 Prozessoren) kaum mehr überschaubar und leistungsbegrenzend.

Die Alternative ist, jeden einzelnen Prozessor in einem Multiprozessorsystem mit einem eigenen Hauptspeicher auszustatten, auf den nur dieser uneingeschränkte Zugriffsrechte hat (*lokaler Speicher, local memory*).

5. Parallelrechner (im engeren Sinne)

Die dritte Superrechner-Generation baut auf dem Konzept solcher Multiprozessor-Rechner mit vielen, unabhängig voneinander arbeitenden Prozessoren und einem so über das Gesamtsystem verteilten Speicher (*distributed memory*, synonym wird auch von *local memory* gesprochen) auf. Sie überwindet damit gleichermaßen die VHSIC-Grenzen und das Shared-memory-Problem. Nur so können heute Rechner konstruiert werden, deren Leistung prinzipiell unbegrenzt ist und im Bereich des technologisch und wirtschaftlich Machbaren liegen, die also eine reale Perspektive für die Anforderungen in den beschriebenen Anwendungsbereichen (vgl. Abschnitt 2.) bieten.

Die Parallelität der Hardware korrespondiert unmittelbar zur Parallelisierung der Aufgaben, die auf Superrechnern zu lösen sind. In der Tat besteht heute kein Zweifel mehr, daß allen Aufgaben des Scientific computing und der numerischen Simulation eine natürliche Parallelität innewohnt, die sich algorithmisch effizient nutzen läßt. Der Grad dieser inhärenten Parallelität steigt dabei mit der Größe der Aufgabe; dies gilt unabhängig von der für die betreffende Aufgabe charakteristischen Datenstruktur, die z.B. durch Gitter, Matrizen und Vektoren, oder Partikel gekennzeichnet sein kann.

Viele Aufgaben sind im übrigen sehr gut parallelisierbar aber nicht gut oder gar nicht vektorisierbar. Als Beispiele seien genannt: Blockstrukturierte Gitter in der numerischen Strömungsmechanik (die verschiedenen Blöcke können auf einem Multiprozessorrechner gleichzeitig, auf einem Vektorrechner nur sequentiell bearbeitet werden [2]); die Assemblierungsphase bei Finite-Element-Anwendungen; Simulationsprogramme wie RELAP (Simulation des Kühlsystems von Kernreaktoren), die aus parallel bearbeitbaren, aber strukturell unterschiedlichen Einheiten bestehen.

Parallele Hardware kann insbesondere dann in einem weiten Problemfeld genutzt werden, wenn sie die Aufteilung in gleichzeitig zu bearbeitende Rechenprozesse, sehr flexibel und effizient unterstützt. Dazu gehört die Möglichkeit, ganze Programmteile (*Tasks*) einer Gesamtaufgabe auf dem Multiprozessor gleichzeitig zu bearbeiten statt nur jeweils einzelner Operationen. Solche nach dem MIMD-Prinzip (Multiple instruction / multiple data) arbeitenden Multiprozessoren sind in den letzten 3 bis 5 Jahren gerade auch in Mikroprozessor-Technologie (VLSI statt VHSIC) von verschiedenen Gruppen entwickelt worden. Dabei wird eine hohe Leistungsfähigkeit der einzelnen Prozessoren heute am kostengünstigsten durch Vektorverarbeitung in den einzelnen Prozessoren erzielt, d.h. durch die Kombination von MIMD-Parallelität und SIMD-Parallelität.

In der Regel lag das Interesse bei diesen Entwicklungen mehr auf der Realisierung paralleler Architekturen, ggf. für spezielle Anwendungen als in parallelen Supercomputern. Kaum eine Entwicklung hat anfangs daran gedacht, die Vorteile von MIMD *und* SIMD-Parallelität zu vereinen und ein hochparalleles System auf Vektorprozessoren aufzubauen (Ausnahme: SUPRENUM). In der Tat gehört eine Menge mehr dazu, ein paralleles Höchstleistungssystem zu entwickeln, als nur ein paar Prozessoren "zusammenzustecken".

6. Kommunikation zwischen Prozessoren

Damit viele Prozessoren effizient an einer gemeinsamen Aufgabe arbeiten können, muß für den dazu erforderlichen Datenaustausch ein leistungsfähiges Kommunikationssystem (hohe Bandbreite) zwischen den Prozessoren zur Verfügung stehen

Ideal wäre eine eigene superschnelle Verbindung von jedem Prozessor zu jedem anderen (z.B. Crossbar) bzw. zu jedem (lokalen) Speicher. Die Komplexität dieses Verbindungsnetzes steigt aber quadratisch mit der Zahl der Prozessoren an und ist mit den heute einsetzbaren Technologien bei größerem p praktisch nicht zu realisieren. Man muß daher auf Verbindungsstrukturen zurückgreifen, die in der Komplexität möglichst niedrig bleiben aber trotzdem gestatten, in wenigen "Sprüngen" (über andere Prozessoren oder Vermittlungspunkte) von einem Prozessor zum anderen Daten zu übertragen. Zu den elementaren Verbindungsstrukturen gehören Ring-, Gitter-, Baum- und mehrdimensionale Würfelstrukturen (*Hypercube*).

Besonders große Flexibilität und ein Übertragungsverhalten, das der Verbindung "jeder-mit-jedem" nahekommt, kann man dadurch erreichen, daß man jeweils eine möglichst große

Anzahl Prozessoren (*Cluster*) lokal über einen parallelen Hochgeschwindigkeitsbus verbindet und die Cluster untereinander wiederum etwa durch eine Hypercube- oder Crossbar-Struktur untereinander verbindet. Solche hierarchischen Strukturen nutzen auf jeder Ebene aus, was technisch optimal machbar ist, und machen den Anwendungsprogrammierer unabhängig von der Prozessor-Topologie.

Die Leistungsfähigkeit des flexiblen Verbindungssystem auf der Hardwareseite kann nur ausgenutzt werden, wenn zur Abwicklung der Kommunikation auf der Softwareseite korrespondierende Systemkomponenten zur Verfügung stehen. Eine Lösung für Parallelrechner mit lokalen Speichern zeichnet sich heute in Form eines "Prozeßkonzepts mit message-passing Kommunikation" ab. Unter einem Prozeß wird hier eine Programmeinheit verstanden, die parallel zu anderen Prozessen ablaufen kann. Eine Anwendung besteht in diesem Sinne aus mehreren oder auch sehr vielen Prozessen, die häufig von einem initialen Prozeß aus gestartet werden. Diese Prozesse besitzen einen lokalen Adreßraum, und die Kommunikation mit anderen Prozessen wird durch das Versenden und Empfangen von Botschaften (das sogenannte message-passing) .abgewickelt.

Hierbei kommt der effizienten Implementierung des message-passing Mechanismus im Betriebssystem eine große Bedeutung zu. Neben der Bandbreite der Kommunikationskanäle ist besonders die "start-up" Zeit, die das Betriebssystem zur Initiierung jeder einzelnen Kommunikation benötigt, als wesentlicher Parameter anzusehen.

Wichtig für die flexible Nutzung von Parallelrechnern ist die Frage der Prozeß-Knoten-Zuordnung. So kann z.B. in einigen frühen Betriebssystemen der ersten allgemein verfügbaren Multiprozessorrechner auf jedem Knoten nur ein Prozeß ablaufen, der dem Knoten statisch zugeordnet wird. Dies bedeutet, daß sowohl die Anzahl der Prozesse wie auch ihre Topologie durch die Hardware vollständig festgelegt ist.

Ein solch starres Konzept, zusammen mit einer statischen Verbindungsstruktur ist in der Regel nur für bestimmte Anwendungsstrukturen ohne Engpaß. Das verteilte Programm sollte dabei nach Möglichkeit Datenaustausch nur jeweils auf "benachbarte", d.h. direkt verbundene Prozessoren beschränken. So ist ein (dreidimensionales) Prozessorgitter gut geeignet, um eine Gitteraufteilung im Beispiel der Flugzeugumströmung aufzunehmen, weniger gut dagegen für eine Vielteilchen-Simulation, wo Fernwirkungen im Modell häufigen Datenaustausch zwischen beliebigen Prozessoren nötig machen (globaler Datenaustausch).

Wesentlich flexibler sind dynamische Prozeßkonzepte, die eine Prozeßerzeugung zur Laufzeit erlauben und mehr als einen Prozeß pro Knoten zulassen. Der Benutzer hat hier die Möglichkeit, die Prozeßtopologie seiner Anwendung anzupassen. Dies ist insbesondere bei Algorithmen mit komplexen und adaptiven Datenstrukturen wünschenswert. Die Abbildung des benutzerdefinierten Prozeßsystems auf die Hardware wird dann von Systemsoftwarekomponenten (Betriebs- und Laufzeitsystem) übernommen. Ebenso ist, sowohl aus Sicht der Programmierung als auch aus Gründen der Kommunikationsleistung, ein automatisches Durchreichen von Botschaften ohne Unterbrechung nicht betroffener Prozessoren für ein flexibles Multiprozessorsystem unabdingbar.

7. Multiprozessor-Effizienz

Ziel des Einsatzes von Parallelrechnern ist es (im Idealfall), eine Beschleunigung (*speed up*) des Rechenprozesses zu erzielen, die der Anzahl *p* der Prozessoren entspricht. Dabei denken wir bei *p* zur Zeit konkret an Größenordnungen von einigen Hundert oder Tausend.

Ein anderes Maß ist die *Multiprozessor-Effizienz* (speed up dividiert durch die Anzahl der beteiligten Prozessoren). Eine Multiprozessor-Effizienz von z.B. 0.8 in Zusammenhang mit einer bestimmten Aufgabe besagt, daß die Prozessoren zu 80% zur Beschleunigung der Bearbeitung beitragen, d.h. 200 Prozessoren würden das Problem rund 160 mal schneller bearbeiten als ein Prozessor (wenn es auf einem Prozessor überhaupt bearbeitet werden kann).

Daß die ideale Effizienz von 1.0 und damit der ideale speed up von p in der Regel nicht erreicht wird, kann u.a. folgende Gründe haben:

- Unausgewogene Lastverteilung. Den beteiligten Prozessoren werden unterschiedliche Rechenlasten übertragen, sodaß unnötige Leerlaufzeiten entstehen. Für statische Datenstrukturen kann dieses Problem des Load balancing als vollständig gelöst angesehen werden, für dynamische Strukturen zeigt die laufende Forschung bereits vielversprechende Ergebnisse. Ein spezieller Fall unausgewogener Lastverteilung entsteht auch durch u.U. unvermeidbare sequentielle Teile, die auf nur einem Prozessor ablaufen. Dies wird häufig als prinzipielle Leistungsschranke für massiv parallele Rechner angesehen (*Amdahl's Law*). Da jedoch mit wachsender Prozessorzahl die Größe der berechenbaren Probleme zunimmt und der sequentielle Anteil relativ geringer wird, ist das Amdahlsche Gesetz für Rechner mit verteiltem Speicher praktisch irrelevant.

- Kommunikationsaufwand. Das Verhältnis von Kommunikationsaufwand und Rechenaufwand hat ebenfalls entscheidenden Einfluß auf die Effizienz einer Multiprozessor-Anwendung. Fein granulare Parallelisierung, etwa die punktweise Aufteilung der Berechnungen bei Gitteranwendungen, führt i.a. zu einem schlechten Verhältnis zwischen Rechenoperationen und Kommunikationsaufwand: Für jeden Verarbeitungsprozeß sind relativ wenige Rechenoperationen zwischen den notwendigen Inter-Prozeß-Datentransfers auszuführen. Eine Aufteilung in (möglichst große) Teilgitter pro Verarbeitungsprozeß kann dieses Verhältnis um Größenordnungen verbessern.

Besonders vorteilhaft wird es für die Effizienz, wenn der Kommunikationsaufwand im Vergleich zum Rechenaufwand gleich um eine Dimension niedriger liegt, wie etwa beim Rand-Austausch zwischen Teilgittern. So kann man für gitterorientierte Anwendungen nachweisen, daß bei Parallelisierung durch Gitteraufteilung für jede feste Anzahl von Prozessoren bei genügend großen Problemen die Effizienz 1 beliebig gut angenähert werden kann [3]. Die theoretische Multiprozessor-Höchstleistung kann also für große Probleme stets erreicht werden.

8. Die Zukunft

Wie in der Einleitung schon angedeutet, konvergieren die Entwicklungslinien für Superrechner auf der Hardwareseite erkennbar gegen MIMD-Parallelrechner mit einer mittleren Anzahl sehr leistungsfähiger Einzelprozessoren. Diese Konvergenz [4] findet von oben und von unten statt: Bei den "konventionellen" Superrechnern wird die Anzahl der Prozessoren deutlich erhöht (8, 16, 32, 64, ...); bei den massiv- und hochparallelen Systemen wird die Leistungsfähigkeit der

Einzelprozessoren wesentlich gesteigert. Außerdem findet eine Verschiebung von SIMD zu MIMD statt. Alle treffen sich in der Mitte.

Auf der Softwareseite ist ebenfalls eine Tendenz zur Vereinheitlichung erkennbar, auch wenn sie vielleicht nicht ganz so schnell realisiert werden kann wie die Konvergenz bei der Hardware. Dabei ist Portierung herkömmlicher Software auf hochparallele Systeme, die durch verteilte Speicher gekennzeichnet sind, zur Zeit noch Gegenstand intensiver Forschungs- und Entwicklungsarbeit. Während für Vektorrechner automatische Vektorisierer und für Multi-Vektorrechner auch sogenannte automatische Parallelisierer bereits eingesetzt werden, befinden sich entsprechende Werkzeuge für hochparallele Systeme noch in prototypischem Zustand.

Hier werden im wesentlichen zwei Ansätze verfolgt: die (halb-) automatische Partitionierung nach Zima [5] und die Bereitstellung eines virtuellen Shared-Memory-Konzepts. Letztere Lösung erlaubt die Verwendung der vorhandenen automatischen Parallelisierer, dürfte aber weniger effizient sein als die Partitionierung. Ziel ist in jedem Fall die Portabilität der Anwendungssoftware nicht nur innerhalb der einzelnen Architekturklassen, sondern über deren Grenzen hinweg.

Literatur

[1] K. Solchenbach, U. Trottenberg: SUPRENUM: System essentials and grid applications. In [6].

[2] J. Linden, B. Steckel, K. Stüben: Parallel multigrid solution of the Navier-Stokes equations on general 2D domains. In [6].

[3] K. Solchenbach: Grid applications: Implementation and evaluation. In [6].

[4] W.K. Giloi: SUPRENUM: A trendsetter in modern supercomputer development. In [6].

[5] U. Kremer, H.J. Bast, M. Gerndt, H.P. Zima: Advanced tools and techniques for automatic parallelization. In [6].

[6] U. Trottenberg (ed.): Proceedings of the 2nd International SUPRENUM Colloquium "Supercomputing based on parallel computer architectures". PARALLEL COMPUTING, Vol.7, 3, 1988.

Why I like Vector Computers *)

Willi Schönauer

Universität Karlsruhe
Rechenzentrum
Postfach 6980
D-7500 Karlsruhe
Federal Republic of Germany

Abstract

The requirements for supercomputing in technical sciences in an industrial R & D environment or in a versatile job profile university environment are specified: 100 GFLOPS sustained performance, 64 Gwords main memory, flexible data transfer operations (compress, expand, merge, gather, scatter) , portable Fortran 8x, fastest scalar speed. Then the reasons are discussed why the "usual" trend to parallelism via MIMD (message passing systems, shared memory systems, hybrid systems) fail to meet the requirements of the users. The proposition of a Continuous Pipe Vector Computer (CPVC) serves to explain in the form of 10 notes the ideas how parallelism should be organized that it is completely transparent to the user. The proposed CPVC minimizes the lost cycles of a supercomputer so that one gets close to the theoretical peak performance by the most user-friendly architecture.

1. The requirements for supercomputing in technical sciences

This paper deals with large scale scientific computing for the solution of technical problems arising in the environment of a broad scale of applications, e.g. like in a technical university, in automobile or aircraft research and industry. If such an institution selects a new supercomputer, it will compose a benchmark program from its major application problems and submit it to the vendors. It is another problem that this benchmark usually reflects the environment of the old computer and not yet the expected environment of the new computer to be selected. But a careful and detailed discussion of the benchmark results may alleviate this drawback. The leading manufacturer in this area of industrial supercomputers is CRAY, another manufacturer is Control Data Corporation (CDC) with its special subsidiary company ETA, and there are the Japanese manufacturers Fujitsu, Hitachi and NEC. A detailed discussion of the relevant supercomputers which are all vector computers is given by W. Schönauer[1]. An actual survey of the distribution of supercomputers in Europe is presented by I. Duff [3]. A much broader market is attacked by IBM with its "Vector Facility". Each processor of an IBM 3090 general purpose computer can be equipped by a Vector Facility which turns the pro-

---

*) With kind permission of Computing Center, University of Karlsruhe, where this Contribution has been published as Internal Report Nr. 35/89, January 1989, together with an appendix 'Epilog'

cessor into a medium size vector computer such that a 3090/600E with six Vector Facilities is in the range of a supercomputer [1].

The range of computation problems to be solved in an industrial environment or in a research environment directed towards industrial applications is rather manifold. Originally the development of supercomputers was promoted by the needs of the government research establishments for aerodynamics, atomic energy and defence. Gradually from these initializations a whole market has developed and nearly all manufacturers of airplanes and automobiles and the whole oil industry have supercomputers (I. Duff [3] mentions prestige also as a reason to buy a supercomputer) . The purpose of these computers is simulation: all types of technical processes are simulated by their corresponding mathematical models. Typical examples are the fluid flow around airfoils and fuselages or even for whole airplane configurations, flow in ducts and turbomachines, simulation of the turbulent fluctuations which never could be measured. Combined with the flow problems are usually heat conduction problems, e.g. in heat exchangers or in lubrication, or even chemical reactions, like for the flow in the combustion chamber of a gasturbine or in the cylinder of a reciprocating engine. Another important class of problems are those connected to tensile strength, i.e. all problems of structural analysis. Full crash tests for a car can be simulated in a supercomputer. All the types of problems mentioned above are ultimately solutions of (mostly) nonlinear systems of partial differential equations. These equations are "discretized" by a finite difference or a finite element method or by some other discretization method. Thus the problem is reduced to the computation of the unknown function values in a grid and by some linearization process to the solution of a linear system of equations. This solution process has two important steps which determine the overall computation time: the computation of the matrix of the linear system and the direct or iterative solution of the linear system. Usually the matrix is very sparse. It may have a regular or a quite irregular structure for the non-vanishing elements, depending on the discretization method and on the problem to be solved. I would guess that 80% to 90% of the use of supercomputers in a technical environment spend their computation time for these types of problems. Unfortunately, a detailed look at these problems demonstrates that each individual problem class has developed its own type of solution method which is exactly tailored to this problem class, in order to get the best solution from the available computer resources. The fatal thing is, that the power of the available supercomputers is far too small to solve the problems which the engineers would like to solve.

I want to demonstrate this for a typical example of fluid dynamics. In a workshop about the use of supercomputers in computational fluid dynamics [4] it became obvious that on the vector computers available in 1985, namely the CRAY-1, CRAY X-MP and CYBER 205, the size of the main memory and not the speed of the vector pipes limits the size of the problems which can be solved. The reason is that the processing speed or "operand consuming rate" of the vector pipes is by so far larger than the transfer rate of the (even multiple) disk channels, that only problems can be treated which fit entirely into the main memory (see also [1], section 6) . If we want to solve the Navier-Stokes equations, describing steady laminar incompressible viscous flow, in the velocity-vorticity form, we have a system of six nonlinear elliptic partial differential equations for the three components of the velocity vector and the three components of the vorticity vector. We assume a 4th order finite difference method (13 point difference star) and a three-dimensional grid with 50x50x50 grid points, i.e. a resolution of 50 grid points in each space direction x, y, z, respectively. Then we have 750.000 unknowns and equations. The resulting matrix of the linear system has 59 million non-zero elements. It is very sparse, only every 9200th element is nonzero. We assume that 600 matrix-vector multiplications are needed for the iterative solution of the linear systems of equations during the solution process. Now we have to make an assumption about the computation speed of the computer to be used. This is measured for the present generation of supercomputers in

MFLOPS = megaflops = million floating-point operations
per second (we always assume 64 bit-arithmetic)

and for the future generation in

GFLOPS = gigaflops = billion floating-point operations
per second.

But one has to be careful to distinguish between the theoretical peak performance and the real measured performance for a distinct operation. For short vector length the startup time of the vector pipes will reduce the performance. But the performance may be reduced considerably by a narrow memory bandwidth of the computer if the pipes have to wait for the operands. For a detailed discussion of these questions for the available supercomputers see [1]. Let us assume for the solution of the above mentioned Navier-Stokes problem a computer with a **sustained** rate of 100 MFLOPS. Then we need for the solution of this problem nearly one hour CPU time. This is the "reasonable" limit of a problem size for a 100 MFLOPS (sustained) computer. But this corresponds only to an elapsed time of one hour if we can solve the problem incore, i.e. if we have a main memory of 64 Megawords (million words) of 64 bits, or 512 Megabytes. Our analysis of a lot of other discretization problems has demonstrated that this relation holds for the whole class of this problem type, i.e. for the majority of implicit difference methods. So we can note as an experimentally determined rule that we have a well balanced system if we have for a sustained rate of 100 MFLOPS a main memory of 64 Megawords of 64 bits. By the way, the CRAY-2 with 4 Processors and 256 Megawords of main memory has just this relation, because for problems of the type which we are discussing we can assume for well designed programs a sustained rate of about 100 MFLOPS per processor.

It should be mentioned in this context that memory size can be "exchanged" against computation speed. If we use instead of an implicit method a type of "explicit" method, e.g. a pseudo-time marching method with recomputation of the matrix elements instead of storing the elements, we need for the same Navier-Stokes problem only the memory for two profiles of the unknowns, i.e. about 2 Megawords of main memory. But we need much more "iterations" resp. pseudo-time steps. If we assume that the computation of the matrix elements, which includes the computation of derivatives for the nonlinear terms, needs 10 times the number of operations which are needed for one implicit iteration step, and if we assume only twice the number of "iterations" compared to the implicit method, we need 20 hours computation time instead of one hour for the implicit solution. Thus we have paid by a factor of 20 in CPU time for the shortage of main memory. Unfortunately many vector computers are used in this way.

Above we have seen that a three-dimensional grid of 50 grid lines in each space direction is the limit for the solution of the Navier-Stokes problem on a 100 MFLOPS (sustained) computer. But what problem size do engineers need? For a sufficiently detailed modelling, e.g. for the flow around a whole automobile, the engineers need at least a ten-fold resolution in each space direction. This means a three-dimensional grid of 500x500x500 grid points and thus 1000-fold values of the old grid: 750 million unknowns/equations and 59 billion nonzero coefficients in the still more sparse matrix. Note that the length of the diagonals is proportional to the number of unknowns. But this means a supercomputer with at least 1000-fold computation speed and memory for optimal iterative algorithms, namely 100 GFLOPS sustained rate and 64 Gigawords or 512 Gigabytes of main memory. And here we can see the real problem: the size of the main memory. The 512 Gigabytes of main memory are by far more memory than the disks of a large general purpose computer of today. But if such a large memory is not available, we are not able to store the necessary operands in order to keep the extremely fast arithmetic units busy. Such relations become obvious only if one has much experience in the development of software for supercomputers and above all in the use of supercomputers. In our computer center we have a group "Vectorization of Engineering Problems" whose members cooperate with the staff of the engineering departments in order to help them solving their problems on our CYBER 205 vector computer and to develop well vectorized software (they are also trained on all other vector computers) . The experience gained in these cooperations has confirmed our relation of performance and memory size. Thus for engineering problems supercomputers with **100 GFLOPS** sustained rate and **64 Gigawords** main memory are needed for the solution of the challenging technical problems.

In our research group we have developed the FIDISOL (finite difference solver) program package [5], [6], (see also section 17 in [1]) , a "black box" solver for the numerical solution of nonlinear systems of two-dimensional and three-dimensional elliptic and parabolic partial differential equations on a rectangular domain or on a domain which can be transformed analytically to a rectangular domain. A selfadaptive variable order/variable step size finite difference method is used. The user delivers his system of nonlinear partial differential equations and the corresponding Jacobian matrices (for the Newton-Raphson method) into FIDISOL program frames. The solution process selects the optimal consistency order and grid, i.e. the shape of the difference star, for a given relative tolerance. Thus in contrast to "usual" finite difference problems neither the difference star nor the differential operator are fixed. This is the type of software which should be available for present and future supercomputers. During the solution process most of the large amount of data appears and then disappears as intermediate data, e.g. the matrix of the linear system of equations. Compared to this "internal" data the input/output data is fairly small. We wanted to establish by FIDISOL a model example for optimal data structures suitable for all types of vector computers, e.g. data structures which are fully vectorizable independent of a special architecture. FIDISOL has been developed on the CYBER 205 and then has been implemented on the CRAY-1, CRAY X-MP, CRAY-2, Fujitsu VP100 and VP200, IBM Vector Facility and CONVEX C1. Only some subroutines have been adapted for the individual vector computers concerning i/o and the unrolling of loops for the register-to-register machines. Comparative examples for the solution of Navier-Stokes type problems on these computers are presented in Schönauer [1] (section 17) . These examples demonstrate by their high speedup values (scalar execution time divided by vectorized execution time) that the whole solution process is efficiently vectorized. An investigation of the design principles for this exemplary software revealed the rather trivial fact that an optimal algorithm keeps the data continuously "flowing" through the vector pipes which led us to the pragmatic definition of a "data flow algorithm" on a vector computer [1], [7]. The basic rule which holds equally well for vector computers and all type of parallel computers is:

Basic Rule: Separation of the selection and of the processing of the data.

This means that for each task or even subtask at first the optimal data structure must be established by data transfer operations, then the data can be processed. Such data transfer operations on vector computers are pack/unpack/merge operations which are controlled by a mask or logical or bit vector, and gather/scatter operations which are controlled by an index vector and represent indirect addressing, see [1]. If the selection of the data is mixed with the processing of the data, also the processing is retarded and the pipes are waiting for data. If the selection is separated from the processing, only the selection is retarded (this is unavoidable) , but the processing takes place with full speed. An example in FIDISOL is the storing of the large sparse matrices by packed diagonals which reduces the storage requirement for large problems roughly by a factor of 10 (10 million storage locations unpacked, 1 million storage locations packed). Another example is the computation of derivatives: for the computation of x–derivatives the solution must be sorted in planes x=const, then the derivatives can be computed in a whole plane x=const with contiguous storage locations, for details see [1]. Similarly for the computation of y– and z–derivatives the solution must be sorted in planes y=const and z=const, respectively. This sorting corresponds to merging by a mask vector. Presently we are developing a similar type of program frame for finite element programs with optimal data structures for vector computers. The unstructured grids of the finite element mesh lead to indirect addressing, i.e. gather/scatter operations for data transfer during the selection process, but then processing of the data takes place with contiguous vectors. The consequence of these investigations and of the resulting Basic Rule is the necessity and importance of **data transfer operations**. These operations must be seen in the context of the 64 Gigaword main memory: the data must be "concentrated" before it is processed. It is interesting to note that the CYBER 205 has excellent hardware instructions for all types of data transfer operations, but CRAY recognized rather late this necessity. The CRAY–1 and the early CRAY X–MP models had only a masked merge operation. Only the later Cray X–MP models and the CRAY–2 have a still rather poor set of hardware instructions for data transfer, namely gather/scatter and a "compressed index" instruction to create index vectors from a mask vector.

An important question which often is failed to be recognized by theorists is the question of the programming language. Here we discuss the use of supercomputers in industrial and technical research and development environment. And in this environment the history, the available program libraries and the existing user codes have made an unalterable decision for the programming language, namely for Fortran. Now we program in Fortran 77, but the old Fortran IV or Fortran 66 still is "present" as a subset and corresponding codes are still running.

Presently the definition of the new Fortran 8x is being developed [8], [9]. But also in Fortran 8x the preceding standards will survive which is the most difficult problem for the evolution of Fortran to a "modern" programming language. Metcalf [8] writes: "The real strength of the new standard will be its incorporation of powerful array processing features and of derived-data types, allowing users to access vector processor hardware using a convenient notation, and to define and manipulate objects of their own design." Large industrial codes, e.g. for car crash test simulation or for inviscid flow around a complete airplane configuration may contain more than 100 "man years" of highly paid specialists. Usually more than 90% of the computation time is used by less than 10% of the code. The remaining code is pre- and post-processing. Such codes must be written in portable Fortran because for reasons of economy they cannot be changed and adapted to every new computer. For the present generation of vector computers the compute-intensive core of the code (hopefully) has been adapted to the individual vector computer, - an expensive task. In the near future Fortran 8x offers for the first time the possibility to program this core in a portable form for all types of vector computers. The vendors always promise that their autovectorizing compilers would be able to create from any Fortran program a good vector program. But mere code manipulation can never change the wrong data structure, and Fortran 77 had no suitable data manipulation statements to express the algorithms in a form optimally adapted to vector computer architecture. In Fortran 8x at least the compute-intensive core of the large codes can be changed to optimal "data flow" type form according to the Basic Rule in order to use efficiently the vector pipes, and the remaining code may be changed gradually according to its relative part in the overall computation time. If the Fortran 8x compilers are "intelligent" enough, it should be possible to program then in a really portable form. Thus the requirement of the industrial supercomputer users is to be able to use **portable Fortran 8x.**

The final problem which I want discuss in this section on the requirements of supercomputer users is the scalar speed. If we solve a linear system of equations with direct elimination algorithm on a vector computer, the "vector length" shrinks in the last step to 1, but before that we are at a vector length of 4 to 8 already below the break-even length where vectorization no longer pays and scalar execution is faster. For iterative solvers of linear equations, e.g. the conjugate gradient method, most of the computation time is spent in vector or matrix-vector operations, but the computation of some iteration coefficients and control steps are scalar operations. Even if a rather complicated code like the above mentioned FIDISOL program package is extremely carefully designed for "data flow", there remains a certain number of operations which cannot be vectorized (or parallelized in a more general sense) . The larger the problem size is, the less important is the relative part of the scalar operations. Note that we must count the operations dynamically, i.e. at execution time, not statically in the code. If we have for the above mentioned Navier-Stokes problem on a 50x50x50 grid a relative part of 1% scalar operations, which is fairly large for such a large problem if it has an optimal data structure, then on a 500x500x500 grid theoretically a relative part of 0.001% scalar operations would result. Unfortunately for register-to-register vector computers the vectors are strip-mined with the length of the vector registers which causes by the additional restarts for longer vectors an effect like the execution of scalar code. So the ideal value of 0.001% for such computers would not be obtained. But independent of the architecture, the absolute number of (really) scalar operations remains constant, whatever the size of the problem. Therefore also this part of the solution process must be accelerated as far as possible. This can be obtained only by the reduction of the cycle time. We assume that all other possibilities like instruction pipelining already have been exhausted. A scalar operation with off-the-shelf technology of 100 nsec (nanosec = 10^{-9} sec) cycle time needs 25 times more time than a scalar operation with 4 nsec, the present technological limit (the CRAY-2 has 4. 1 nsec cycle time) . The consequence of these considerations is that the fastest technology available must be used in order to obtain **the fastest scalar speed.**

Up to now we have discussed the requirements for supercomputing in technical sciences. These requirements are characterized by a broad spectrum of applications and large amount of available complicated Fortran codes. The compute-intensive kernels of the codes are mostly discretization methods for partial differential equations. The requirements for this area of supercomputing can be summarized as follows: 100 GFLOPS sustained computation rate, 64 Gigawords main memory, sophisticated data transfer operations, programability in portable Fortran and fastest available scalar speed. Future supercomputers which meet these requirements will meet the requirements of the largest commercial market. If they have also an architecture which allows a flexible use, these supercomputers will also meet the requirements of other areas with large computational needs, e.g. high energy physics (whose ultimate needs will never be met by whatever future supercomputers or accelerators) .

2 Against the trend

The broad breakthrough in supercomputing has been achieved by the CRAY-l, CRAY X-MP, CRAY-2 line and the STAR100, CYBER 205, ETA10 line, i.e. more precisely by vector computers. These computers have "opened" the market thus that supercomputing was no longer exotic but became a key tool in research and development also in industry. We want to make supercomputers arbitrarily fast. But this is limited by the attainable switching time of the basic technology. The fastest cycle time (which is much larger than the elementary switching time) presently is 4.1 nsec for the CRAY-2. In this time a 64-bit result is produced if the startup time of the vector pipe has passed. This means 243.9 MFLOPS for a single pipe and 487.8 MFLOPS if in a compound operation the add and the multiply pipe are working in parallel. The CRAY-3 is expected in 1990 with 2 nsec cycle time which means that the performance for a single pipe is roughly twice that of the CRAY-2. Until 1995 we can expect 1 nsec cycle time if the continuous development goes on and if there will not be a completely new technology available at that time. Therefore higher MFLOPS rates can only be obtained by parallel pipes. The question is "only", how to organize this parallelism, i.e. what architecture is to be used. The architecture will decide, how many of the above mentioned theoretical peak MFLOPS can really be expected as a sustained MFLOPS rate for a distinct program. The other problem is that of the memory size. According to an empirical marketing rule of the manufacturers the price of a supercomputer should not exceed 20 million $. What size of the memory can be obtained for this price depends on the available packaging density of the VLSI memory chips and also on the architecture, namely how many memory banks are used and how long is the bank busy time (time after which a new request is accepted by the bank) . The concept of banking allows a correspondingly slower technology for the expensive memory, e.g. a bank busy time of 100 nsec for a machine with 10 nsec cycle time allows a ten times slower technology for the memory, but then requires a correspondingly higher number of memory banks, above all if multiple processors share this memory. The recent 4-processor CRAY-2 model with 256 Megawords of main memory has 128 banks with 160 nsec (39 cycles) bank busy time, but for contiguous vectors these banks behave like 256 banks with approximately the same bank busy time (odd/even banks) . This is the approach by the large commercial vector computers.

At the other hand there is the off-the-shelf technology in the region of 100 nsec cycle time which is by far less expensive. If we have at any case to use parallelism of the pipes, why not combine many slow but inexpensive pipes in the form of small processors to form a supercomputer? In order to illustrate the situation let us discuss the following event: When the German branch of Floating Point Systems (FPS) announced its T-series [11] they reported that a combination of 64 nodes (T-processors) combined to a 6-dimensional hypercube would deliver 1 GFLOPS and that the (present) maximal configuration of 16000 nodes (14-dimensional hypercube) would deliver a peak rate of 262 GFLOPS. This would be the most powerful supercomputer of the world, and all at a price of 1/7 of "conventional" supercomputer hardware. A corresponding press report is given by E. Schmitt [12]. For a desired performance of 100 GFLOPS we would need "only" 6400 nodes, although it would be very debatable how many nodes we would really need for a sustained rate of 100 GFLOPS for an engineering problem. But we would also need 64 Gigawords of memory for the operands in order to be able to solve the desired problems. The T-Series has only a distributed memory, each node has 1 MB of memory. For 8-byte operands (64-bit words) we thus would need 512000 nodes for a memory of 64 Gigawords, which is not possible. The maximal configuration of 16000 nodes offers only 16 GB or 2 Gigawords of memory. Only if every node would have 80 MB (instead of 1 MB) of memory, we would have a well balanced relation between computation speed and memory size. Note that we need the **memory size** for the solution of the desired problem classes which have been discussed above. But if we would install such a memory, would the T-series still be cheaper than "conventional" supercomputer hardware? I do not want to discuss at this point of the paper the "useability" of the T-series computer which is another important question. I only wanted to demonstrate that mere GFLOPS which are gained by merely adding up parallelized pipes may not be the desired solution, even if the GFLOPS seem to be "cheap". The real problem is the memory, not the GFLOPS.

So, what choice do we have to select the appropriate parallelism in order to obtain a future supercomputer with the desired properties? Let us discuss more seriously the basic ideas of the different architectural concepts. I estimate that presently more than 50 projects for different parallel processors are investigated worldwide. I never could present a survey with sufficient details in a paper like this one. J. Dongarra has compiled an interesting survey book [13], there are numerous conference proceedings [2], [10], [14] and special issues of Journals dedicated to confernces [2], [15], [16]. An especially rich source concerning hypercube multiprocessors is the book edited by M. Heath [17]. We can distinguish the three main trends in architecture aiming at supercomputing: dataflow computers, parallel computers which themselves have the two subcategories of distributed memory (or message passing) computers and shared memory computers, and finally the large multiprocessor vector computers. Before I give a raw characterization of the different types of architectures I have to recall that we want to discuss here supercomputers which reach much farther than any existing computer. Thus we exclude such computers which only aim at obtaining the same performance, say, as a CRAY-1, at a much lower price. This means that the performance can be obtained only by parallelizing **pipelined** arithmetic units (with 64 bit arithmetic) . Combining only scalar arithmetic units, e.g. microprocessors, where vectors are processed element by element in a scalar loop, will have no chance to compete with pipelined units, neither in speed, nor in the price/performance relation [18]. But using pipelined arithmetic units means that in a parallel processor environment of any architecture we have to use data structures and algorithms which are fully **vectorizable** in the innermost computational kernel. This is not even a consequence of vector computing. If we look more carefully we recognize that this is rather a property of the problem size. The large general purpose computer IBM 3090/600 can have a user-transparent real memory, including the expanded storage, of 1280 MB. if a program deals with real storage of this size and does not apply the Basic Rule mentioned above, it may cause with each memory reference a cache miss or even a page fault, e.g. by accessing a very large matrix by row elements.

The first and obviously the most elegant choice of the future supercomputer might be a **dataflow computer**, a recent comparison of design features has been presented by V. Srini [19]. The basic idea of the dataflow computer is to keep the data continuously flowing. Each data has a token which indicates its destination processing unit and if all input tokens are available the unit "fires", i.e. it processes the data and sends it with a new token on the way. It is interesting to note that the Manchester group has built a first model without a memory, but then the second model had a memory, see J. Gurd et al. [20]. This memory is the "hardware demonstration" that the basic idea did not work in reality, because a memory contradicts the original dataflow concept. Behr et al. [21] write: "However, it should not be overlooked that such measures (added: the introduction of a structure memory) in effect constitute a deviation from the pure dataflow scheme by introducing beneath the dataflow control level an SIMD control level for handling data structure objects." Srini [19] writes: "However, developing a practical system that will outperform CRAY-2 or similar machines is several years away." And finally there is the language problem: dataflow machines (up to now) must be programmed in a special single-assignment language (e.g. SISAL for the Manchester dataflow computer) and automatic conversion of Fortran to such a language is an open problem. I consider the most serious problem for dataflow supercomputers to be the memory problem. If we need to store data of 64 Gigawords (of 64 bits) and we have a whole set of independently working dataflow processors to deliver the 100 GFLOPS, then we run into exactly the same problems as we shall find it below for the shared memory computers. So I exclude dataflow computers as competitors for the future supercomputers. Nevertheless we can learn much from the ideas of the dataflow community: if we succeed, whatever computer we are designing, in keeping the pipes continuously busy by a continuous data flow, we have at any case an optimal use of our computer.

The next proposition for the future supercomputer is the wide range of **parallel computers**, present models ranging from an 8 processor Alliant FX/8 [22] to a 65000 processor Connection

Machine [23]. But this field of machines is not at all homogeneous. The two main categories are the **message passing** (distributed memory) machines and the **shared memory** machines. If we now paint in extreme black and white, we can characterize these two types of architecture, modifying two questions posed by G.F. Pfister et al. [24] (p. 134) , by saying:

Message passing systems can easily be built, but they cannot be programmed.

Shared memory systems can easily be programmed, but they cannot be built.

This is surely exaggerated, but there is a lot of truth in these statements.

In **message passing systems** we have individual processors, each with its own memory, there is no global or shared memory. Thus it is easy to build message passing machines with arbitrary many processors. Nevertheless these processors must be able to communicate with each other by an interconnection network, for a corresponding discussion see e.g. [21]. The mostly used network is the d-dimensional hypercube with $N=2^d$ processors, where each processor is connected by d connections to its "neighbors", namely those processors which differ only in one bit from its own binary number or address. Examples of hypercubes are the Caltech Mark II and Mark III [25], the Intel IPSC [26], or the above mentioned FPS T-series [11]. An example for a hierarchical cluster bus architecture is the German SUPRENUM project [18], [21]. However, the real problem for message passing systems is the **software**. In order to use efficiently a message passing system of N processors a problem must be broken up into N pieces of (nearly) equal amount of computation **and data**. Such a message passing system is optimally used if no message has to be passed between the individual processors, i.e. if the problem breaks up into disjoint parts. (We have a room with 80 loosely connected Macintosh II personal computers with 80 students working independently on their exercises. In a general sense this is a perfect parallel computer.) The present parallel computers are single user computers. There must be a node operating system for each processor, usually there is also a host computer with a host operating system, and lastly there is the user with his application software who is finally responsible for an efficient use of such a parallel computer. Let me cite some statements from Heath's book [17]. M. Chen [27]: "One of the most critical problems in parallel processing today is that of programming parallel machines. The difficulty lies in task decomposition: "how to partition a given task into pieces, one for each processor, so that it can be accomplished by the cooperation of many processors in parallel." and "A critical research question raised here is: can a parallel program be written in a highly abstract form such that the detailed interaction among processes in space and time are suppressed, and yet it is still possible to generate efficient code for an assemblage of communicating processors?" W. Williams [28]: "Load balancing is an issue of fundamental importance to multiprocessor concurrent systems. For certain types of problems, such as inhomogeneous numeric problems and symbolic problems, without load balancing a parallel system gains little over traditional Von Neumann machines. Moreover, appropriate data decomposition for load balance is not always obvious or consistent. The ability to determine load distribution and to redistribute it is essential for an efficient parallel system." J. Saltz et. al. [29]: These architectures may be quite cost effective from the hardware point of view, but unattractive due to the difficulty of providing software able to exploit the potential of the machines. " and:

"The effective utilization of multiprocessors, particularly those with architectures that cannot support shared memory in an efficient way, is currently dependent on the ability of the user to map the problem onto the multiprocessor." K. Schwan et al. [30]: "Two issues must be addressed when mapping parallel programs to a hypercube architecture (1) determination of the mapping using application-specific and architectural information and (2) efficient runtime support for the mapped application." D. Walker et al. [31]: "When porting a sequential program, or a program from a shared memory machine to a hypercube, algorithmic changes are usually necessary. " J. Francioni et al. [32]: "For any numerical problem, even very simple ones, efficient parallel programs are highly dependent on effective communication. It is also the case that an algorithm's communication structure can be efficient for one kind of computer architecture but not for another.'' R. Chamberlain [33]: "The solution of linear equations is a fundamental tool on any general-purpose computer. The choice on a sequential or vector machine is usually a simple one between a direct or an iterative method. If a direct method is chosen, then a library subroutine is usually available and this subroutine has often been optimised. However on parallel machines it is not so clear-cut. The "best" method depends on the number of processors, the number of equations, the communication time and computational speed of the processors. " V. Maik et al. [34]: "We have considered the performance issues involved in implementing the multigrid methods on a hypercube multiprocessor system. It is shown that both algorithm dependent as well as implementation dependent parameters affect the performance considerably and the selection of an algorithm or of a partioning scheme must be based on the combined effect of these parameters."

These quotations which are specific to hypercubes but also to other message passing systems illustrate the (exaggerated) statement "cannot be programmed." Naturally all the cited papers try to alleviate the discussed difficulties, but they will not be able to eliminate them completely because these difficulties are inherent in this type of architecture. In the exploding literature about message passing systems we find many examples where on an N processor computer a nearly N-fold speedup (time to solve the problem on one processor divided by time to solve the problem on N processors) is obtained. But it would be wrong to conclude from these examples that a message passing parallel computer is a candidate for the future supercomputer in an industrial research and development environment. We come back to this question later.

The other parallel computer alternative would be the **shared memory system**. If we have many processors with arithmetic pipelines and only a shared memory, all these processors with their high operand consuming and result producing rate must access the shared memory. Here the statement made above "cannot be built" is really true. Therefore in reality "shared memory" systems are hybrid systems with a combination of local (distributed) and global (shared) memory. But this immediately introduces the problem of data coherence which must be solved by some type of synchronization. From the point of view of a user the shared memory system is much more attractive than the message passing system. For a pure shared memory system only the amount of computation must be distributed onto the different processors whereas for a message passing system computation and data must be distributed. However, as the "shared memory" systems in reality are hybrid systems, the situation is not so easy. Obviously such a shared memory machine is optimally used if it is not necessary to share the memory. It is quite interesting to see that people who are engaged also in software and compiler design and who want to offer to the user immediately a computer which is "useable" in a sense as close as possible to a "usual" computer, are shared-memory-oriented. Examples of shared memory machines are the Alliant FX/8 [22], the CEDAR of D. Kuck's group [35] which uses the FX/8 as a cluster, the NYU Ultracomputer of A. Gottlieb's group [36], and the IBM RP3 [24]. The RP3 extends the Ultracomputer architecture by a memory which can be defined between a purely distributed local memory, a purely global shared memory and all stages in between. So this is a really flexible research tool for software and hardware design. The main problem of the shared memory computer is ultimately the memory bandwidth of the shared memory, combined with the necessity of synchronization. When extremely high processing rates must be obtained by a large number of processors, and if the size of the memory in order to store the operands becomes extremely large, then the only possibility is to shift more and more data to the local memories of the processors - and immediately one runs into the software problems of the message passing systems. The essential advantage of the shared memory system, however, is its possibility to use a global operating system with a global resource scheduling of the whole computer.

The next alternative for the future supercomputer are multiprocessor systems of the large vector computers. The CRAY X-MP/4 and the CRAY-2/4 have 4 processors sharing a single main memory, the IBM 3090/600 may have up to 6 Vector Facilities accessing the main memory, the ETA 10 may have up to 8 processors with local memories and there is also a shared memory. Each of these processors is a powerful SIMD (single instruction stream/multiple data stream) computer in the taxonomy of Flynn [37]. This holds still, if we execute independent jobs on the different processors in the usual multiprogramming style. But if we want to use some or all the processors in a multitasking style for the same job, the computer becomes an MIMD (multiple instruction stream/multiple data stream) computer. Quite naturally for a special application the computation can be distributed by the user (not automatically) to the different processors and there may result for N processors a speedup of nearly N, see e.g. [38], [39], [40]. For the vector computers one observes carefully all the sources of performance degradation. Hockney defines the half performance length $n_{1/2}$ in [39], [41], see also in [1], which is (for a certain type of operation) a measure for the wasted operations by the startup time of the pipes. If we use in one processor N parallel pipes, the $n_{1/2,N}$ for the cluster of N pipes is N times the $n_{1/2}$ of a single pipe, see [1], [41]. If we use N processors as "parallel pipes", e.g. to process N segments of the same loop, we also have to use $n_{1/2,N} = N * n_{1/2}$. But now we also have lost operations because of the lost cycles for the synchronization of the processors. Hockney [39] characterizes these lost operations by $s_{1/2}$ for the synchronization of two processors. If we must synchronize N processors, the lost operations are characterized by $s_{1/2,N}$ which is between $s_{1/2}$ and $(N-1) * s_{1/2}$ depending on the synchronization mechanism. A further essential source of lost operations is load balancing. If in an N processor system in a certain phase of the calculation only one processor is busy and N-1 processors would be idling, there is the question if it is better to use the free processors for another job by a program switch or to let them idle until the original job will reuse them in a later phase of the computation. For certain types of jobs load balancing will be the most important source of performance degradation. This is the reason why computer center managers do not like multitasking on multiprocessor systems, see e.g. Myers [42]. Multitasking introduces all the above mentioned synchronization problems into the user program. Automatic use of several processors could be made only on the do-loop level which is called microtasking, this has only limited range of application. But there is a case where the manager of a computing center must force the user to change his program to a multitasking program, namely if a single user wants to use in an N processor computer the whole (shared) memory. If he would run his job in monotasking, N–1 processors would idle, even in a multiprogramming environment, because there is no space for other jobs in the memory. Again we see that not the speedup of a single job but the throughput of the whole computer is the scale for an economic rating of a supercomputer.

Up to now we have predominantly presented the different architectures for parallel computers in a more or less descriptive way. Now I want to discuss these architectures from the point of view of the **user**. As mentioned above candidates for the future supercomputer must use pipelined arithmetic units. This means that the innermost kernel of the programs must be **vectorized**. If we now use the notion of "parallelization" this means the next higher level **above** the vectorization, which naturally includes also the splitting of a do–loop into N parts and distributing them onto N processors. In an excellent paper A. Karp [43] discusses the programming for the use of parallel computers in scientific computing environment. But he restricts to "moderately parallel systems: No more than tens of processors." And he writes: " Massively parallel systems of the order of a thousand or more processors are quite different. At this time there are no general–purpose, MIMD machines in this class that are widely available, so no one has experience programming them." He also restricts to explicitly declared parallelism where the programmer is responsible for parallelization and writes: "However, the programmer must be aware of the details of the hardware implementation in order to produce efficient code. Even a factor of two delay in getting data can seriously degrade performance." Karp gives a survey of programming style and of necessary tools for the programming of message passing systems, shared memory systems and hybrid systems. The basic problem of parallel processing of any kind is the additional factor of **time** which is introduced into the program: one has to know which data is where at what time. It is not the place here to repeat the methods presented by Karp. I only want to quote some statements from the summary: "Algorithms are easy to design for shared memory systems. One simply puts the data in memory as if running on a uniprocessor. On the other hand, programs are hard to debug" and "Message passing systems are different. Algorithm design is hard because the data must be distributed so that communications traffic is minimized. Debugging is easier than in shared memory systems because errors normally cause the system to stop at the point of the errors." If we now think that hybrid systems would alleviate these problems we can read in Karp's paper: "Hybrid systems are the worst of both worlds. Errors are hard to find because they are the same ones made on shared memory systems." So we can conclude from this excellent investigation that seen from the point of view of a user of a parallel computer, the organization of the program parallelism for any of the above mentioned architectures is a serious retrogression compared to uniprocessor systems. The unsolved problems in hardware and software of parallel processing are shifted to the poor user. He is burdened with the responsibility of an efficient use of such a computer and he must pay the increased speed by a corresponding redesign of his program, one redesign for each parallel computer.

Now I want to mention some further critical points concerning parallel processors. If the user has to design his program for the individual parallel processor, in reality the parallel processor comes close to a special purpose computer. Such examples are e.g. Clementi's lCAP–1 or lCAP–2 computers [44], loosely coupled systems of IBM host computers, Floating Point Systems array processors and bulk shared memories. If such a computer is used for a high energy physics problem it may be an excellent instrument for that purpose. This holds for all parallel processors which are used for a single purpose, and I consider just this useage as a real chance for parallel processors. But this is not the problem which we want to discuss in this paper. Here we want to discuss the useability of a parallel processor for large industrial or research codes. And in this case there are two essential points. Firstly, the user should not have to do more in his code than he has to do nevertheless for an excellent vectorization. It is quite unnatural to break up a matrix into submatrices and to distribute them onto different processors and memories. This is still a regular structure. But in real problems much more complicated data structures will be present which cannot be treated by a simple library routine like that for a matrix. Secondly, the computer must be able to organize himself, i.e. it must be able to manage for a continuously varying job profile an optimal use of all its main components, namely CPU, memory and i/o. This results in a high throughput which finally decides if the supercomputer is used efficiently. Both requirements mean that the computer has to serve to the user and not the user to the computer. When a customer submits a benchmark of his job profile to a vendor he expresses by this procedure that the large investments in his software cannot be ignored when selecting the new computer. The system price of the new computer must be considered in the context of the past and of the future software cost. A special architecture which requires special software adaptation for the next computer means that this software probably will no longer be suited for the overnext computer. The large multiprocessor vector computers like CRAY X-MP or CRAY-2 can process such benchmarks only because they process them as independent jobs on different processors. If we would try to use them in an MIMD style and ask for automatic multitasking, we could not run the benchmark. For the experimental parallel processors we are far from that point where we can deliver an industrial benchmark to such a computer. My conclusion of these considerations is, that I consider multiprocessor systems **not** to be candidates for the future supercomputers in an industrial research and development environment. .

This conclusion does not mean that I consider **research** in the area of multiprocessor systems to be unnecessary. Quite on the contrary. Only the detailed investigations will really make visible the difficulties and help to clear up the situation. In his paper about parallel processing in USA-1984, Hockney [45] writes: "It will be most interesting to review the situation in five years time, to see which of these varied computer architectures have proved the most successful in practice." So he applies Darwin's principle to computers. The HEP of Denelcor is the first of the commercially available parallel processor systems of Hockney's paper which did no longer survive. The pure research processors cannot be considered in the same way because here other factors than market factors are decisive. I think that researchers in parallel processing should recognize that a speedup of N for N processors for a special application has not much to do with the throughput measurement for a benchmark.

3. A proposition for a Continuous Pipe Vector Computer (CPVC)

It is easy to give a negative criticism. But it is much more difficult to present a positive criticism by developing the ideas for an architecture which avoids as far as possible the drawbacks pointed out for multiprocessor systems. I am not a computer architect. But I am developing software for supercomputers of different manufacturers and I am using supercomputers for the solution of engineering problems. Seen from this point of view a large monoprocessor is the ideal tool to be used and to preserve the large investments in software development. But if we need a sustained rate of 100 GFLOPS we need parallelism because the present and near-future technology cannot deliver this speed by a single pipe. So the problem is "only", **how** the parallel pipes should be organized. This parallelism must be completely transparent to the user of the computer. Examples of such a parallelism are the CYBER 205 with 2 or 4 pipes, the Fujitsu VP 200 and VP 400 with 2 and 4 pipes, the NEC SX/1 and SX/2 with 2 and 4 pipes, see the discussion of the different architectures in [1]. But neither of these large monoprocessors has a sufficient bandwidth to keep the add and multiply pipes continuously busy for a vector triad. Thus real MFLOPS rates are far below the theoretical peak rates for these computers, except for special problems, e.g. matrix multiplication.

In the following I want to develop the ideas for a Continuous Pipe Vector Computer (CPVC) which is my proposition for the architecture of a future supercomputer. As this development needs some accompanying explanations to which I have to refer in later parts, I present the ideas in the form of the following notes:

Note 1: The most important operation in vector computing is the general **vector triad**

$$d_i = a_i + b_i * c_i \ .$$

One should not consider this as "an addition plus a multiplication", but as a new operation, namely the vector triad. The reason is that in vector computers and all types of pipelined architectures there are either separate pipes for addition and multiplication or compound addition/multiplication pipes (e.g. CYBER 205) . In the triadic operation the result of one pipe can be delivered immediately into the other pipe. Then the add and multiply pipes operate in parallel as a single pipe group and deliver two results per cycle, which is called supervector speed. The theoretical peak performances which are announced by the manufacturers are usally these supervector speeds of the pipes. In practical formula evaluation one usually has an equidistribution of + and * which then can be executed as vector triads. The statement

$$x_i = a_i + b_i * (c_i + d_i * e_i)$$

can be executed as two vector triads. If we have the simultaneous solution of many linear systems of equations with full or with tridiagonal or some other type of matrix, the vector triad is the basic operation [1]. The iterative solution of linear equations usually is based on the matrix-vector multiplication. If the matrix results from a finite difference or finite element method, it is stored by its diagonals to allow full vectorization. Then the basic operation is also the vector triad [1]. U. Haas [46] has made a detailed investigation of the operations in such a type of problem and she has demonstrated the drastic predominance of the vector triad.

The linked triad with one scalar operand,

$$d_i = a_i + s * c_i \quad ,$$

is a special case of the vector triad. This is the basic operation for the matrix multiplication and the solution of linear systems of equations if we have full matrices.

If a vector computer (or any pipelined computer) should come as close as possible to the theoretical peak performance it should be able to execute the vector triad with full speed, which needs 3 loads for the operands and 1 store for the result per cycle and pipe group. This is the **necessary bandwidth** between main memory and CPU. None of the existing large commercial vector computers has this bandwidth. The CYBER 205 and ETA 10 have 2 loads and 1 store per cycle and pipe group from which follows that the only chance of supervector speed for these computers is for the linked triad. For the CYBER 205 (2 pipes) for the vectorlength n = 100/1000/10000 we obtain [1] for the vector triad 50/91/99 MFLOPS, but for the linked triad 78/171/194 MFLOPS. Thus the missing load reduces the performance by a factor of two for the vector triad. The CRAY-2 has a memory bandwidth of only one word per cycle and pipe group. For one processor we have measured [1] for n = 100/1000/10000 for the vector triad 49/51/51 MFLOPS and for the linked triad 60/63/63 MFLOPS. These are mean values of 10 measurements because of the influence of the competing three other processors on the CRAY-2/4. The measured values are far from the theoretical peak rate of 488 MFLOPS because of the narrow memory bandwidth. The conclusion of these investigations is, that a future supercomputer should have a memory bandwidth of 3 loads and 1 store per cycle and pipe. Else the real performance might be far below the theoretical peak performance and additional pipes must be used in order to balance the degradation caused by the narrow memory bandwidth.

Note 2: The size of the **main memory** ultimately determines the price of a large supercomputer. If we discuss a future supercomputer with a main memory of 64 Gigawords of 64 bits we have to ask if we could afford such a large memory with the necessary bandwidth requested in the above Note 1. The investigation of many large engineering problems has demonstrated that it is not necessary to have all the data available with random access. The situation is mostly that only about 10% of the data must be directly accessible and the remaining 90% can be accessible sequentially like a file. For example for the iterative solution of extremely large linear systems, which is usually the most time consuming part of the overall solution process, 90% of the active data is represented by the matrix of the linear system which is scanned once per iteration step. Therefore we could subdivide the "main memory" into a **local memory** and an **extended memory** in the relation 1:9. In the case of the desired 64 Gigawords this would mean that 6.4 Gigawords could be local memory and 57.6 Gigawords extended memory. This would be the only way to obtain such large main memories at an acceptable price. Only the local memory must have the bandwidth of 3 loads and 1 store to the CPU. But the essential requirement for the bandwidth between local memory and extended memory is that one word per cycle and pipe group can be transferred. The transfer can be in blocks and is organized like that for a buffered file. This gives the possibility to use far less expensive hardware technique for the extended memory and also offers readily available software tools. The (blocked) transfer rate of one word per cycle and pipe group means that in the vector triad one operand can be obtained via the buffer from the extended memory. Thus for the iterative solution of large linear systems the matrix can be stored in the extended memory and can be shifted, e.g. diagonal by diagonal or column by column, through the local memory for each iteration step. Examples of such extended memories are the SSD (solid-state storage devise) of CRAY which delivers with 1000 MB/sec just one word per cycle and pipe group for one processor of the CRAY X-MP, or the shared memory of the ETA 10 which delivers 1/2 word per cycle and pipe group. But as a vector triad needs two cycles, it is just sufficient to obtain one operand from the shared memory for this "slow" vector triad, for details see [1]. The existence of the extended memory means, that the local memory must have, in addition to the bandwidth to the CPU, also the blocked bandwidth to the extended memory.

Note 3: The desired speed of a sustained rate of 100 GFLOPS can be obtained only by **parallel pipes.** If we assume the memory bandwidth which has been requested in Notes 1 and 2, we have a real chance to come with well designed programs for large problems close to the theoretical supervector speed of two operations (one vector triad) per cycle. So let us take this as the measure of the performance. How many pipes we need for the 100 GFLOPS peak performance supervector speed depends on the cycle time, i.e. on the basic technology which is used. Presently we have 4 nsec, for 1990 we can expect 2 nsec (CRAY-3?) , for 1995 we may obtain 1 nsec cycle time. At 1995 we can also expect a technology for memory chips which permits a main memory as proposed in Note 2 at a price of 20 million Dollars. If we assume 1 nsec cycle time we would need 50 parallel pipes. Because usually powers of two are used, we can assume 64 parallel pipe groups (add and multiply pipe) which means a cycle time of 1.28 nsec. (In principle we could also discuss the following with 128 parallel pipes at a cycle time of 2.56 nsec which will be obtained in the near future.) These 64 pipes are arranged as a single "bundle" of pipes.

Note 4: If we now assume 64 parallel pipe groups as a bundle and if we consider the required memory bandwidth of Notes 1 and 2, we see the real problem: the necessary total bandwidth of the local and of the extended memory. Each separate data path must have the capacity to transfer 64 words of 64 bits (plus control bits) simultaneously, i.e. we need a type of "**data highay**". Here we encounter a similar problem as in the shared memory multiprocessor (this is the reason for the "cannot be built") . But in the multiprocessor system there is an arbitrary asynchronous access of each processor to the shared memory. Here in the Continuous Pipe Vector Computer (CPVC) we need a special synchronous access which can be controlled easily. The parallelism of the 64 pipes has the only consequence that also the data path, which predominantly will be of bus type, must have the same parallelism. Let us assume that the memory is subdivided as usually into banks which can be accessed after a preceding access only if the so called bank busy time is over. For each access a bank delivers one word to the bus. If we have 64 parallel pipes we must have a synchronous request for 64 consecutive banks which then deliver 64 words to the highway bus which will transport them to the pipe. This means that vector operations must be executed with contiguous memory locations. All non-contiguous operands must be treated by gather/scatter operations which will be discussed below. The data highways for 64 parallel word transfer are surely a difficult problem for the hardware designer because of the physical dimension. But at the same time it is the simplest access method and I think the only chance to reduce the difficulties of the hardware design of a future supercomputer to an acceptable minimum. As we need for the local memory 3 loads and 1 store per cycle and pipe and the block transfer to the shared memory, it may happen that a bank is accessed before the bank busy time is over, i.e. we have a bank conflict. But we need the operand to arrive at a certain cycle together with the other operand at the entry of the pipe. Therefore we must have delay registers which "synchronize" the arrival of the operands in unfortunate situations. The larger the number of memory banks and the shorter the bank busy time, the lower is the probability for bank conflicts of this kind.

Note 5: Not every customer wants (or can afford directly) such a large supercomputer. Therefore such a supercomputer should be composed of **"building blocks"**. For example such a block could be composed itself of 4 parallel pipes which would deliver 6.25 GFLOPS, and a main memory of 4 Gigawords, subdivided into 0.4 Gigawords (400 Megawords) of local memory and 3.6 Gigawords of extended memory. If the supercomputer is upgraded by further blocks, automatically the memory and the data highways are correspondingly increased. The composition by building blocks gives at the same time the possibility of a mass production of the basic units, thus allowing for an economic manufacturing, and above all a wide spectrum of performance for the different types of customers. The composition of the supercomputer as a monoprocessor with many parallel pipes is the main difference to the multiprocessor concept of the present large supercomputers.

Note 6: The hardware organization of the Continuous Pipe Vector Computer (CPVC) should be made in such a way that for **maintenance** single modules or blocks can be devoted to the maintenance control unit and the remaining computer continues production. In a similar way "ill" modules could be taken automatically out of the system, eventually combined with an error recovery feature. Thus the CPVC is rather fail-soft and a reliable tool for time-critical calculations, e.g. weather forecast. This will be still more important if in the years to come such supercomputers will be tightly integrated into computer integrated manufacturing (CIM) and computer aided design (CAD) .

Note 7: Above we have mentioned that the **half performance length** $n_{1/2}$ is a measure for the wasted operations caused by the startup time of a single pipe and that for the half performance length of a cluster of N pipes holds $n_{1/2,N} = N * n_{1/2}$. If we have 64 pipes and single pipe has an $n_{1/2} = 20$, then each startup of a cluster of 64 pipes would waste $n_{1/2,64} = 1280$ operations. This means that at a vector length of $n = 1280$ we have only half the peak performance of this supercomputer. This cannot be avoided for a first startup. But in large scientific computing problems we have mostly nested loops. This means that we have large sequences of consecutive vector operations. The ETA 10 can already reduce the $n_{1/2}$ for consecutive vector operations of the same vector length [1]. The question is now, if we could avoid the $n_{1/2,N}$ completely for sequences of arbitrary vector operations, i.e. in such sequences we would have no wasted operations at all, except for the first startup of the sequence. This would be another essential means to come with the sustained GFLOPS rate closer to the peak rate of the supercomputer.

My proposition is depicted in Fig. 1. The "classical" vector computer is

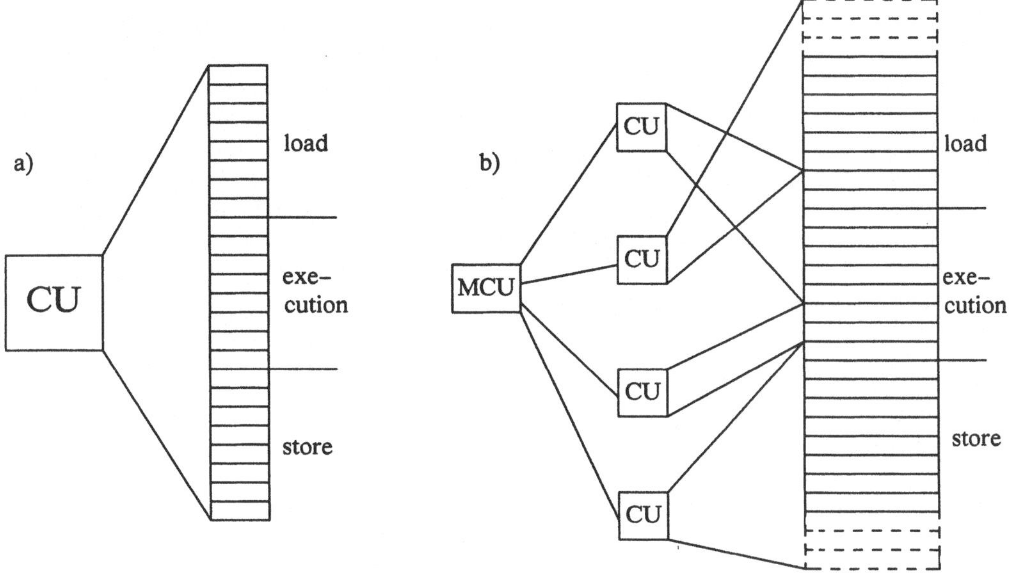

Fig. 1. a) "classical" vector computer, b) Continuous Pipe Vector Computer (CPVC) . CU = control unit, MCU = master control unit, sketched in Fig. 1 b).

The pipe, which may be subdivided into load, execution and store part, is controlled by a single control unit (CU) . Before the next vector operation can produce results the pipe must be cleared, new information loaded into the control unit and the pipe must be refilled. This results in the $n_{1/2}$ for a single pipe and in $n_{1/2} = N * n_{1/2}$ for a bundle of N pipes. In Fig. 1b there is presented what I call the Continuous Pipe Vector Computer (CPVC) . There are several control units (CU's) which themselves are controlled by a master control unit (MCU) . (In a limited sense by instruction overlapping also existing (vector) computers have such a principle.) The "pipe" now is the bundle of N pipes, e.g. of N = 64 pipes for the computer discussed in this Note. Each control unit is responsible for one vector operation and "guides" this operation on its way from the memory through the pipes back to the memory. In the ideal case there should be as many control units as there are lost cycles of one pipe, i.e. 20 control units for $n_{1/2} = 20$. Thus the CPVC is a combination of ideas from a vector computer, from a hierarchical computer and from a dataflow computer. The control unit contains the "tokens" (in the terminology of dataflow computers) for the vector operation to which it is dedicated. For dyadic operations the part "execution" of Fig. 1b means the add or the multiply part, for triadic operations the coupled add and multiply part of the pipe bundle (there is no simple add and simple multiply in parallel because of simplicity of control and of lacking memory bandwidth) . The purpose of the individual control units is to prepare all the necessary steps of their operations that they can be executed in the stages of the pipe without a single gap between independent vector operations.

Thus for a sequence of independent and/or sufficiently long vector operations we have the data continuously flowing through the pipes which is the optimal use which can be obtained. Therefore we call this a CPVC. There are lost operations only for the startup of the whole sequence of vector operations and quite naturally for each of the individual vector operations for the "unused" operations in the last "section". Because of the N = 64 pipes a long vector is processed in "sections" of 64 elements and a remainder. If in the last (remainder) section there is only one element, then in this worst case 63 operations are lost, which is nevertheless much smaller than the 1280 lost operations for a single control unit. Thus for such sequences of vector operations we have for N pipes a range for $n_{1/2,N}$ between zero and N–1, from which results a mean value of $n_{1/2,N,mean} = (N-1)/2$. This is the best we can do for N parallel pipes. All other strategies will loose more operations. The cooperation of the different control units is controlled by the master control unit which is also responsible for detecting data dependencies and ambiguities at runtime. This is discussed in the following note.

Note 8: If we have $n_{1/2} = 20$ for a single pipe and we have 64 pipes, we have 20 * 64 = 1280 vector elements in the bundle of pipes in different stages of processing, i.e. we have a "volume" of the pipes of 1280 elements. Therefore we have a "critical vector length" $n_c = 1280$. If we have for the vectors which are processed $n > n_c$ we have to make no special precautions. But for $n < n_c$ there may be **data dependencies** which must be detected by the master control unit and for which we have to care if we have dependent vector operations. As an example take the matrix-vector multiplication formulated by diagonals [1]. There we have a type of operation

$$c_i^{(s)} = c_i^{(s)} + d_i * r_i^{(s)}$$

where the upper index s denotes a shifted part of that vector. Here the "old" $c_i^{(s)}$ on the right hand side cannot be used before it has left the add pipe. Or, if we have complicated operations like

$$a_i = b_i + c_i / d_i - (e_i * f_i + g_i) * h_i \quad ,$$

there are automatically produced intermediate vectors and the computation would be executed as the following sequence: $p_i = e_i * f_i + g_i$ (vector triad) $a_i + b_i$, $a_i = a_i - p_i * h_i$ (vector triad) . If such dependent vectors are long enough,i.e. $n > n_{c'}$, the elements are back in the memory before they are reused for the next operation and there is no problem because then from the memory the correct actual value will be obtained. But if $n < n_{c'}$, the correct value would not yet be back in the memory when it is requested for the next operation. So we have to take special precautions for short dependent vectors. The best which we can do in this case is to avoid to go back to the (local) memory with such intermediate results and in order to shorten the delay to deliver them to a type of "register file" where they are immediately available as input for the next operation. Then less stages of the execution part are lost while the pipes are waiting for the availability of the next operand. The size of the register file must be four times the "volume" of the execution part for coupled add and multiply (for 3 operands and 1 result) . If other independent vector operations could be inserted between the dependent vectors (a challenge for the compiler designer) , the dependencies could be reduced or completely eliminated. Remember that this is needed only for $n < n_c$. For the special case of the $c_i^{(s)}$ expression from above we have still another possibility for $n < n_c$. This expression appears in a nested loop, i.e. there is still another k–loop around the i–loop. Thus we have in reality

$$c_i^{(s)} = c_i^{(s)} + d_{i,k} * r_i^{(s)}$$

i.e. in $c_i^{(s)}$ a sum is built up with as many terms as we have cycles of the k–loop. In this case we can use as many "copies" of the $c_i^{(s)}$ vector as there are stages in the "short" turnaround cycle over the register file. In these now independent copies partial sums of $c_i^{(s)}$ are built up in a similar way as in the "wheel method" (see [1]) for the summation of the elements of a vector, the only difference is that we have now a "vector wheel method. " The final sum then is built up by a "vector cascade sum. " In Fig. 2 is presented the "data flow graph" for the CPVC.

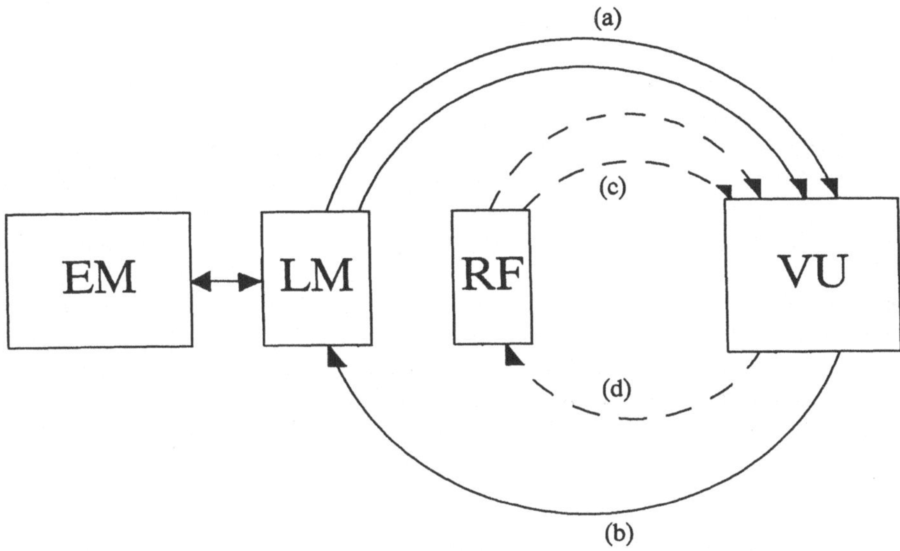

Fig. 2. "Data flow graph" of the CPVC. (a) , (b) is for initial/long/final vectors, (c) , (d) is for short intermediate vectors. EM = extended memory, LM = local memory, RF = register file, VU = vector unit.

The dashed paths are for short intermediate vectors. The decision for "long" and "short" path should be made by the hardware, i.e. by the master control unit at runtime. Depending on the instruction set of microcode and of normal instructions, eventually the compiler must generate code for long and short path and the decision is made by the actual value of n. It is quite natural that for a vector length n below 64 the performance of such a supercomputer with N = 64 pipes will drop drastically. But this is still much more pronounced for all types of parallel processors which have to overcome for short vectors the same type of problem and they have in addition the lost operations for synchronization and for load balancing. For really large problems which are designed for optimal dataflow with long vectors (how to design algorithms with such properties can be seen in [1]) , there are relatively few operations with short vectors or with scalar operations. Then the CPVC is that type of architecture which comes with its sustained rate for a given technology as close as possible to the theoretical peak rate. But if short vectors should be dominant in a certain type of problem, then the CPVC would be wasted money because of the wasted operations for short vectors. Then it would be better to solve such problems on an IBM Vector Facility which is more close to a general purpose computer.

In the context of the register file we also could discuss the question, if it is better to have a memory-to-memory computer like CYBER 205 or its follower ETA 10, or to have a register-to-register computer with vector registers like the CRAY's or Fujitsu VP's. It is interesting to note that the IBM Vector Facility can obtain one operand directly from the cache and thus needs no vector register for this operand. The answer is clear: if we have sufficient memory bandwidth we do not need vector registers. The vector registers have the only purpose to "uncouple" the operations from the main memory and thus to "bridge" the narrow memory bandwidth. For such types of computers the performance for large problems is rather determined by the memory bandwidth and not by the speed of the pipes. But memories are by their bank structure much slower than the CPU cycle time. Therefore I have proposed a "register file" for short intermediate vectors. Such a register file can have an access time comparable to the cycle time of the pipes and thus can considerably shorten the delay compared to a memory-to-memory operation. This advantage can be used for the dashed paths in Fig. 2 and helps to increase considerably the performance for short dependent vectors. But for long/independent vectors a vector register would be not only wasted money (provided we have the necessary memory bandwidth proposed in Notes 1 and 2) , but it would also increase considerably the problem of an optimal dataflow because the "administration" of the vector registers must be included into the overall control process executed by the control units and the master control unit. The very restricted use of the register file for the short dependent vectors is just "manageable".

Note 9: I have discussed above the necessity of **data transfer operations**, which is illustrated by the Basic Rule of the separation of the selection and of the processing of the data. Therefore for the CPVC the data transfer operations are as important as the arithmetic operations. There are basically two types of data transfer operations [1]. The first type are those operations which are controlled by a bit or logical or **mask vector**. These are operations of the type of masked assignment, masked simple arithmetic operations, masked merge and pack/unpack under the control of a mask. These operations pose no problem at all if the pipes are designed to operate under the control of a mask vector. They need as many cycles as the mask has (bit) elements and they profit in the same way from the "dataflow" type architecture of the CPVC as the arithmetic
operations. For the dataflow through the pipes there is no difference between an arithmetic operation and e.g. a pack under mask operation: one element is processed per cycle if the pipe is "filled". The second type of data transfer operations are those controlled by an **index vector** i(k),

namely

gather: b(k) = a(i(k)) and
scatter: a(i(k)) = b(k) .

These are indirect addressing operations which are amply used e.g. in the finite element method and in all types of unstructured data sets. These operations pose a new and serious problem and a challenge, too. For contiguous data we have the "data highways". There is the great danger that indirect addressing results in a significant decrease in speed, compared to contiguous data. I want to explain my proposition for the solution of this problem for the **gather** operation. The basic principle is illustrated in Fig. 3 for a bandwidth of 4, i.e. for a computer

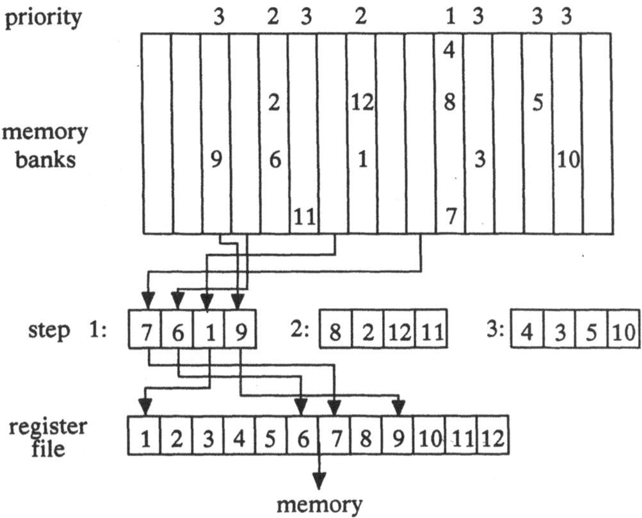

Fig. 3. Illustration for the principle of a two-stage gather operation for a bandwidth of 4.

with N = 4 parallel pipes where all data paths are designed for the parallel transfer of 4 words. In Fig. 3 we have a memory subdivided into memory banks and in this memory we have operands which are to be selected and then stored into contiguous storage locations according to their number. There are up to three operands in one bank, but a memory bank can be accessed only if the bank busy time of the previous access is over. Now I want to present what I call a priority-controlled two-stage gather. It is known from the addresses of the operands to be selected, how many operands are in each bank. The banks with the highest number of elements get the highest priority, the banks with the next lower number of operands get the next lower priority and so on. In Fig. 3 we have one bank with 3 operands and highest priority 1, two banks with 2 operands and priority 2 and 5 banks with 1 operand and priority 3. The selection is made by the control units. Every cycle a free control unit selects N operands with the highest (remaining) priority. In the usual vector processing the memory bus gets contiguous bank addresses. In the gather operation the memory bus gets different bank addresses, but nevertheless N operands are transferred. These operands are stored in the control unit. In the next possible cycle the next free control unit selects another N operands and the preceding control unit stores the selected but unordered operands in the register file. If selections can be inserted before the bank busy time of a previous higher priority bank is over, it is preferred to select these operands first. Thus the priority and the still running bank busy time together determine the selection of the next operands. The selection and storing of the first 4 operands is illustrated with the data arrows in detail in Fig. 3, the selection of the remaining 8 operands is sketched. When the register file is filled up or the operation is terminated, the register file is stored into the memory where we now have contiguous memory locations (and thus consecutive bank addresses) . This final process is controlled by the master control unit. It is clear that the more banks are in the memory and the shorter the bank busy time, the less bank conflicts will arise. At least one needs m times the bank busy time for the gather operation if in one bank are m operands. In the ideal case that there is only one operand in one bank or the bank busy time is always over if a bank with several operands is addressed, we get for the gather operation the same speed of N operands per cycle as for contiguous storage locations. The worst case is if all the elements to be selected are in the same bank. But this is again a regular structure which usually can be avoided by a better algorithm, e.g. columnwise processing instead of rowwise processing for matrices in Fortran.

In a similar way a priority-controlled two-stage **scatter** operation can be devised. In this case we have to distribute operands which are stored in contiguous memory locations onto scattered memory banks. Then in principle there holds again Fig. 3, but the direction of the arrows must be inverted. From the preceding explanation of the gather operation it should be clear how the scatter is executed. Thus for the CPVC with N parallel pipes efficient mask-controlled or index-controlled data transfer operations are available as an essential tool to come with the real performance close to the peak performance.

Note 10: I want to conclude the discussion of the CPVC with some remarks to the **software**. The hardware architecture has been developed that we obtain the highest possible sustained GFLOPS rate from the available bundle of pipes. It might be astonishing but if we think a little more we see that it is in fact trivial, that the CPVC offers all the advantages also for the software. As a monoprocessor (where the number of pipes is transparent to the user except that he gets catastrophic performance for very short vectors) the CPVC has an operating system like any existing vector computer, i.e. the problem of resource scheduling is solved. We can use multiprogramming with program switch (this is a reason to keep the register file as small as possible because it must be dumped for a switch) , i.e. we can process short test programs in the foreground and long running large problems in the background. I do not consider timesharing to be a reasonable use of such a supercomputer, this should be done on host workstations which may interact with the supercomputer more or less in a high priority batch mode. Thus from the point of view of operating system the CPVC is the ideal tool to obtain a high throughput. All special organization problems of the hardware are solved where they should be solved, namely by the hardware organization itself.

The greatest advantage of the CPVC is that it offers to the user a tool which requires only an excellent vectorization and nothing more. It preserves the large investments in software which are being made and which will be made to solve extremely large problems and to integrate the supercomputer into the whole design and manufacturing process. There is no fear that for the next generation of supercomputers the data and the algorithms must again be changed. And above all the CPVC frees the user from the frustation that he gets sustained rates far below the theoretical peak rates even for well designed programs. The key for the easy use of the CPVC is that the whole parallelization is made completely user-transparent. And as mentioned above the solution of large problems on any type of computer, including the general purpose computer, needs optimal "dataflow type" data structures and algorithms.

4 Concluding remarks

In order to solve the challenging engineering problems of the future we must use parallelism in the supercomputers, combined with extremely large memories which ultimately dictate the price of the computer. The present trend of multiprocessor systems introduces extreme difficulties for the software if we consider throughput as a measure of performance. Such computers may be the ideal tool for a distinct application as a special purpose computer. But if they are used in the domain of engineering research and development and manufacturing the problem of an efficient use of such a computer is shifted to the user. I have presented a way out of these problems by a Continuous Pipe Vector Computer (CPVC) , where the pipes are bundled and organized in principle like a single pipe. Thus the parallelism is completely transparent to the user. He has to care only for an excellent vectorization of his program which he has nevertheless to do for any type of computer if he wants to solve extremely large problems. In the CPVC the architecture and the hardware organize the parallelism themselves and thus free the software and the user from all further difficulties, therefore preserving the large investments of the software. By its architecture the CPVC is able to produce sustained GFLOPS rates as close as possible to the peak rate. And this is the reason why I like (Continuous Pipe) Vector Computers.

Acknowledgement:
I want to thank seven (!) anonymous referees for their positive and negative criticism and for valuable suggestions.

5 References

[1] W. Schönauer, Scientific Computing on Vector Computers, North-Holland, Amsterdam, New York, 1987

[2] Proceedings of the "2nd International SUPRENUM Colloquium 1987",Bonn, Sept. 30 to Oct. 2, 1987, to appear as special issue of "Parallel Computing"

[3] I.S. Duff, A survey of Supercomputing in Europe, to appear in [2]

[4] W. Schönauer, W. Gentzsch, The Efficient Use of Vector Computers with Emphasis to Computational Fluid Dynamics, Vieweg, Braunschweig/Wiesbaden, 1986

[5] W. Schönauer, E. Schnepf, FIDISOL, a "black box" solver for partial differential equations, to appear in Parallel Computing

[6] W. Schönauer, E. Schnepf, H. Müller, The FIDISOL Program Package, Interner Bericht Nr. 27/85 des Rechenzentrums der Universität Karlsruhe, 1985. This internal report is the documentation for the customers of FIDISOL.

[7] W. Schönauer, E. Schnepf, H. Müller, Designing PDE software for vector computers as a "data flow Algorithm", Computer Physics Communications 37 (1985) , pp. 233–237 and I.S. Duff, J.K. Reid (Eds) , Vector and Parallel Processors in Computational Science, North-Holland, Amsterdam, New York 1985, pp. 233–237

[8] M. Metcalf, Fortran 8x – the emerging standard, Computer Physics Communications 45 (1987) , pp. 259–268

[9] Fortran, X3J3/S8.104, June 1987, American National Standards Institute. This is the actual draft under discussion for Fortran 8x.

[10] K. Hwang, S.M. Jacobs, E.E. Swartzlander (Eds) , Proceedings of the 1986 Internat. Conf. on Parallel Processing, IEEE, Washington D.C. , 1986

[11] J.L. Gustafson, S. Hawkinson, K. Scott, The architecture of a homogeneous vector supercomputer, in [10], pp. 649–652

[12] E. Schmidt, Rechnergiganten aus dem Baukasten, VDI nachrichten 16, 18. April 1986, p. 17

[13] J.J. Dongarra (Ed) , Experimental Parallel Computing Architectures, North-Holland, Amsterdam, New York 1987

[14] D. Degroot (Ed) , Proceedings of the 1985 Internat. Conf. on Parallel Processing, IEEE, Washington, D.C. , 1985 .

[15] Proceedings of the Int. Conf. on Vector and Parallel Computing, Loen, Norway, Parallel Computing 5 (1987) pp. 1–263

[16] Proceedings of the 1984 IBM Europe Institute course on Highly Parallel Processing, Parallel Computing 2 (1985) , pp. 185–288

[17] M.T. Heath (Ed) , Hypercube Multiprocessors 1987, SIAM, Philadelphia, 1987

[18] W. Giloi, The SUPRENUM architecture, to appear in [2]

[19] V.P. Srini, Anarchitectural comparison of dataflow systems, Computer, vol 19, No. 3 (1986) pp. 68–88

[20] J. Gurd, C. Kirkham, W. Böhm, The Manchester dataflow computing system, in [13], pp. 177–219

[21] P.M. Behr, W.K. Giloi, H. Mühlenbein, SUPRENUM: The German supercomputer architecture - rationale and concepts, in [10], pp. 567–575

[22] Alliant Computer Systems Corporation, Acton, Mass. , FX/ Series Product Summary, 1985

[23] W.D. Hillis, The Connection Machine, MIT press, Cambridge, Mass. 1985

[24] G.F. Pfister, W.C. Brantley, D.A. George, L.S. Harvey, W.J. Kleinfelder, K.P. McAuliffe, E.A. Melton, V.A. Norton, J. Weiss, An introduction to the IBM Research Parallel Processor Prototype (RP3) , in [13], pp. 123–140

[25] G.C. Fox, Questions and unexpected answers in concurrent computation, in [13], pp. 97–121

[26] Intel, iPSC User,s Guide, Intel, Portland, Oregon, 1985

[27] M.C. Chen, Very-high-level parallel programming in Crystal, in [17], pp. 39–47

[28] W. Williams, Load balancing and Hypercubes: A preliminary look, in [17], pp. 108–113

[29] J.H. Sultz, M.C. Chen: Automated problem mapping: The Crystal runtime system, in [17], pp. 130–140

[30] K. Schwan, W. Bo, N. Bauman, P. Sadayappan, F. Ercal, Mapping parallel applications to a hypercube, in [17], pp.141–151

[31] D.W. Walker, G.C. Fox, A. Ho, G.R. Montry, A comparision of the performance of the Caltech Mark II hypercube and the Elxsi 6400, in [17], pp. 210–219

[32] J.M. Francioni, J.A. Jackson, An implementation of a 2^d-section root finding method for the FPS T-series hypercube, in [17], pp. 495–500

[33] R.M. Chamberlain, An alternative view of LU factorization with partial pivoting on a hypercube multiprocessor, in [17], pp. 569–575

[34] V.K. Naik, S. Taasan, Performance studies of the multigrid algorithms implemented on hypercube multiprocessor systems, in [17], pp. 720–729

[35] D.J. Kuck, E.S. Davidson, D.H. Lawrie, A.H. Sameh, Parallel supercomputing today and the CEDAR approach, in [13], pp. 1–23

[36] A. Gottlieb, An overview of the NYU Ultracomputer project, in [13], pp. 25–95

[37] M.J. Flynn, Some computer organizations and their effectiveness, IEEE Trans. Comput. C–21 (1972) , pp. 948–960

[38] B.L. Buzbee, Applications of MIMD machines, Computer Physics Communications 37 (1985) , pp. 1–5, or I.S. Duff, J.K. Reid (Eds) , Vector and Parallel Processors in Computational Science, North-Holland, Amsterdam, New York, Oxford, Tokyo 1985, pp. 1–5

[39] R.W. Hockney, $(r, n_{1/2}, s_{1/2})$measurements on the 2–CPU CRAY X–MP, Parallel Computing, vol 2, Nr. 1, March 1985, pp.1–14

[40] A.K. Dave, The efficient use of the CRAY X–MP multiprocessor vector computer in computational fluid dynamics, in [4], pp. 209–220

[41] R.W. Hockney, C.R. Jesshope, Parallel Computers, Adam Hilger, Bristol, 1981

[42] W. Myers, Getting the cycles out of a supercomputer, Computer, vol 19 (1986) , pp. 89–92

[43] A.H. Karp, Programming for Parallelism, Computer, vol 20 (1987) , pp. 43–57

[44] E. Clementi, J. Detrich, Large scale parallel computation on a loosely coupled array of processors, in [13], pp. 141–176

[45] R.W. Hockney, MIMD computing in the USA–1984, Parallel Computing, vol 2 (1985) , pp. 119–136

[46] U. Haas, Modelling of a program by an artificial benchmark program for vector computers, with discussion of the efficiency of the vectorization, Interner Berich Nr. 31/87 des Rechenzentrums der Universität Karlsruhe, 1987. Free copies of this internal report can be obtained on request.

Durch die Berechnung von Moleküleigenschaften zum gezielten Entwurf von neuen Wirkstoffen

Gerhard Klebe

Hauptlaboratorium der BASF-AG,
Carl-Bosch-Straße,
D-6700 Ludwigshafen/Rhein

Zusammenfassung

Die Entwicklung von selektiven, zuverlässigen und sicheren Wirkstoffen ist mittlerweile eine extrem zeit- und kostenintensive Aufgabe geworden. Die Strukturchemie ermöglicht es, unter Einsatz der Computergraphik, die Vorgänge bei der Wechselwirkung eines Wirkstoffmoleküls mit seinem Rezeptorprotein auf molekularer Ebene zu verstehen und rechnerisch zu simulieren.

Voraussetzung dazu ist die Strukturaufklärung bzw. Strukturberechnung beider Komponenten, des Wirkstoffmoleküls und seines biochemischen Rezeptors. Bedingt durch ihre Flexibilität können Moleküle unterschiedliche Gestalten annehmen. Diese konformellen Umwandlungen lassen sich auf leistungsfähigen Computern simulieren. Die Kenntnis der energetisch günstigen Konformationen eines Moleküls ist entscheidend, da unter diesen sich auch die biochemisch relevanten Anordnungen befinden. Beim gezielten Design neuer Wirkstoffe mit Hilfe des Computers wird dann versucht, die dreidimensionale Gestalt eines Wirkstoffmoleküls unter Berücksichtigung seiner konformellen Flexibilität so zu modifizieren, daß zum einen eine optimale Wechselwirkung, zum anderen eine hohe Selektivität zur Bindestelle des Rezeptors erzielt wird.

Einleitung

Trotz intensiver Pharma- und Pflanzenschutzforschung ist das Spektrum an bekannten Wirkstoffen zur Behandlung von Krankheiten bzw. zum Einsatz als Fungizide, Insektizide oder Herbizide noch keineswegs ausreichend oder befriedigend[1]. An neue Wirkstoffe wird ein stetig wachsendes Anforderungsprofil gerichtet. So muß ihre Wirkung möglichst selektiv sein, es sollten keine Nebenwirkungen auftreten und ihr Metabolismus muß in allen Einzelheiten aufgeklärt werden. Für die gesamte Verweilzeit dieser Substanzen und den aus ihnen gebildeten Abbauprodukten muß die toxikologische Unbedenklichkeit für Menschen, Tiere und Nutzpflanzen und deren Umwelt gewährleistet sein. Durch die ständige Veränderung und Anpassungsfähigkeit der belebten Natur ist es schon häufig zu Resistenzen bestimmter Organismen (z. B. Unkräuter, Bakterien) gegen potente Wirkstoffe gekommen. Schon aus diesem Grunde ist keine Sättigung bei der Suche nach neuen Wirkstoffen abzusehen.

Aus den genannten Gründen ist die Entwicklung von neuen, zuverlässigen Wirkstoffen inzwischen extrem zeit- und kostenaufwendig geworden. Um einen Wirkstoff zur Marktreife zu bringen, sind heutzutage ca. 10.000 - 20.000 Substanzen neu zu synthetisieren und biologisch zu testen.

Durch den stürmisch wachsenden Erkenntnisstand über die Mechanismen, nach denen Wirkstoffe in den unterschiedlichen Organismen ihre Wirkung erreichen, bieten sich Wege zum gezielten Entwurf dieser Substanzen auf dem Computer an.

Wie können Wirkstoffe in biochemische Reaktionspfade eingreifen?

Exemplarisch sollen an dem Beispiel der Hemmung eines Enzyms ein paar grundlegende Vorstellungen über die biochemischen Vorgänge erläutert werden, die auf molekularer Ebene bei der Wechselwirkung eines Wirkstoffmoleküls mit einem Rezeptormolekül auftreten.

In höherentwickelten Organismen laufen eine Vielzahl von chemischen Prozessen ab. Beispielsweise werden die molekularen Bausteine hergestellt, die zur Synthese des Moleküls benötigt werden, das die Erbinformation eines sich reduplizierenden Organismus trägt.

Bei diesem Molekül handelt es sich um die Desoxyribonucleinsäure (kurz: DNA, s. Abb. 1). Es besitzt die Struktur einer treppenförmigen Doppelstranghelix, wobei sich außen, den Polymerstrang aufbauend, Zucker- und Phosphatgruppen befinden. Im Zentrum stehen sich auf jeder "Treppenstufe" jeweils zwei Basen gegenüber. Insgesamt werden für den Aufbau nur vier verschiedene Basen verwendet (Guanin, Adenin, Cytosin und Thymin), die aber, wenn man eine Treppenstufe betrachtet, zueinander komplementär eingesetzt werden, d.h. ein Guanin hat immer ein Cytosin als gegenüberliegenden Partner, ein Adenin immer ein Thymin. Die Natur codiert in der Abfolge dieser Basenpaare entlang des Doppelstrangs ihre Erbinformation.

Will eine Zelle ihre Erbinformation über dieses DNA-Molekül vermitteln, muß sie zuerst einmal dieses Molekül aus seinen Primäreinheiten aufbauen. Wie schon erwähnt, zu diesen Bausteinen gehört das Thymin.

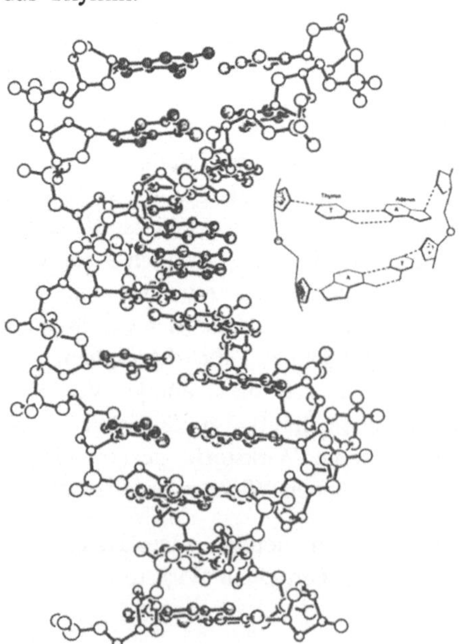

Abb. 1:

Molekülstruktur der Desoxyribonucleinsäure (Ausschnitt Dekanucleotid). Das Molekül besitzt einen helikalen Aufbau mit "treppenförmig" zueinander orientierten Basenpaaren im Zentrum (schraffiert) und außenliegenden Polymersträngen, die aus Phosphatgruppen und Zuckerringen zusammengesetzt sind.

Die Base Thymin wird nun in einem anderen Prozess in der Zelle synthetisiert. Die Vorstufe, aus der Thymin hergestellt wird, ist Uracil (Abb. 2). Während dieses Reaktionsschrittes wird eine Methylgruppe an den Heterocyclus übertragen[2].

Stellen wir uns ein Reaktionsgefäß vor, in dem eine chemische Reaktion abläuft. In dem Gefäß stoßen die Moleküle, die eine Umsetzung miteinander eingehen können, zusammen. Wenn sie in der richtigen Orientierung aufeinander zufliegen, und die Teilchen beim Stoß eine ausreichende Energie besitzen, kann eine neue Verbindung gebildet werden. Die Natur bedient sich für die gleichen Vorgänge ausgefeilter Katalysatoren. Damit die Reaktionspartner in eindeutiger Weise miteinander reagieren, werden sie in ein ganz spezifisch passendes Gerüst "eingespannt", in dem die reagierenden Gruppen optimal zueinander orientiert werden. Gleichzeitig wird durch dieses "Einspannen" die Aktivierungsbarriere für die Reaktion stark erniedrigt. Diese "biochemischen Katalysatoren" werden vom Chemiker als Enzyme bezeichnet, und es handelt sich um Biopolymere, sogenannte Proteine.

Bei der betrachteten Umwandlung von Uracil in Thymin wird eine Substanz benötigt, die die Methylgruppe "liefert". Diese Aufgabe übernimmt Methyltetrahydrofolsäure (Me-THF, Abb. 2). Aus der Methylierungsreaktion mit Uracil in dem Enzymkatalysator Thymidylat-Synthetase tritt das Molekül als Dihydrofolsäure (DHF) heraus, die nun wiederum zurück zu Tetrahydrofolsäure hydriert werden muß. Auch dieser Prozess erfolgt in einem Enzym, der Dihydrofolatreduktase (DHFR), und als wasserstoffliefernder Agenz kommt Nicotinsäureamid in seiner hydrierten Form zum Einsatz.

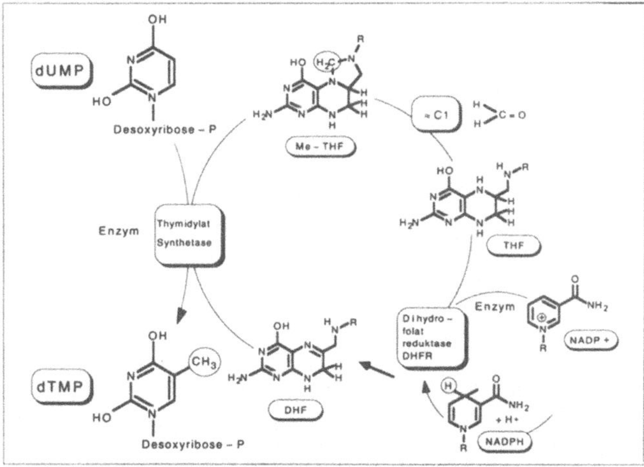

Abb. 2:

Biochemischer Reaktionspfad eines Schrittes bei der Thymin-Synthese. Die Methylierung von Uracil zu Thymin wird durch das Enzym Thymidylat-Synthetase katalysiert, Methyltetrahydrofolsäure (Me-THF) wird dabei in Dihydrofolsäure (DHF) überführt. Die anschließende Hydrierung der Dihydrofolsäure erfolgt in dem Enzym Dihydrofolatreduktase (DHFR), wobei Nicotinsäureamid (NADPH) in seiner hydrierten Form als Coenzym wirkt. Die hierbei resultierende Tetrahydrofolsäure (THF) wird mit einem C1-Baustein wieder in ihre methylierte Form überführt.

Wie man sieht, werden die Reagentien in einem Kreisprozess geführt. Wenn es nun gelingt, auf irgendeine Weise in diesen Kreisprozess einzugreifen, so können wir die Produktion an Thymin beeinflussen. Dies hätte dann einen drosselnden Einfluß auf die Syntheserate des die Erbinformation tragenden Moleküls DNA zur Folge. Doch gerade dieses Molekül wird von Zellen, die eine hohe Vermehrungsrate besitzen, in großem Umfang benötigt. Ein schnelles Wachstum weisen z. B. Krebszellen auf, d.h. will man ihr Wachstum reduzieren, so könnte dies über die Drosselung der Thyminsynthese gelingen, möglicherweise indem das Enzym Dihydrofolatreduktase "außer Funktion gesetzt" oder besser inhibiert wird. Dazu wird ein Molekül benötigt, das dem natürlichen Substrat Dihydrofolsäure strukturell verwandt ist, aber fester bzw. möglichst irreversibel an das Enzym bindet. Verbindungen dieses Typs, zum Beispiel das Methotrexat (s. Abb. 3), stellen potente Chemotherapeutika dar.

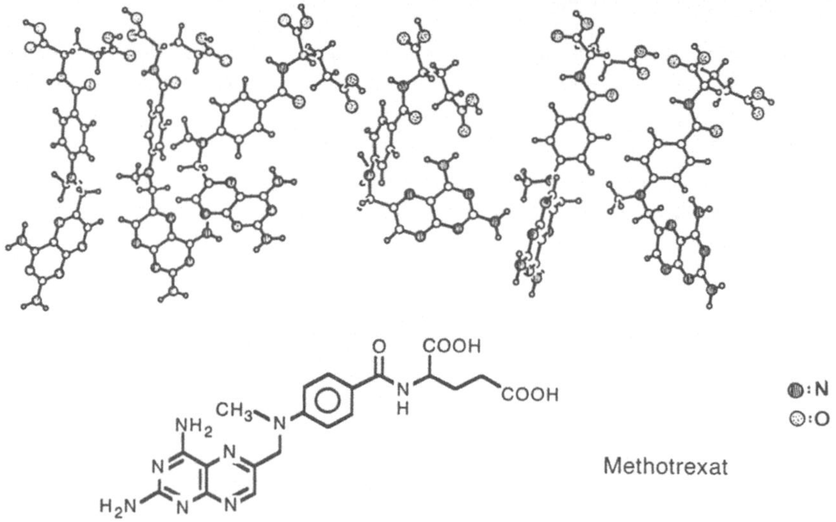

Abb. 3:

Strukturformel und sechs energiegünstige Konformationen des Chemotherapeutikums Methotrexat. Je nach Konformation kann die räumliche Ausdehnung und die Oberfläche eines solchen Moleküls deutlich variieren.

Experimentelle Verfahren zur Bestimmung von Molekülstrukturen

Stellen wir uns das Problem, neue Inhibitoren für dieses Enzym zu entwickeln. Wie können computerunterstützte Methoden bei dieser Aufgabe helfen?

Um sich strukturelle Vorstellungen über die Inhibierung dieses Enzyms auf molekularer Ebene zu verschaffen, wird die dreidimensionale Geometrie der beteiligten Moleküle benötigt. Als experimentelle Methode zur Bestimmung der dreidimensionalen Gestalt von Molekülen ist die Röntgenstrukturanalyse zu nennen. Dieses Verfahren setzt voraus, daß die zu untersuchende

Verbindung in kristalliner Form vorliegt. In einem Kristall ordnen sich die Moleküle in einem sich periodisch wiederholenden Packungsmuster an. Dabei wird der Raum zwischen den Molekülen möglichst vollständig ausgefüllt, und gleichzeitig orientieren sie sich so, daß die intermolekularen Wechselwirkungen ein Optimum erreichen. Betrachtet man das Molekül (oder genauer die asymmetrische Einheit der Elementarzelle) als ein sich in allen Raumrichtungen wiederholendes Motiv, so kann man den Kristall als ein dreidimensionales Gitter auffassen. An einem solchen Gitter lassen sich mit Röntgenstrahlen Beugungsexperimente durchführen. Aus der abgebeugten Strahlung, die experimentell registriert werden muß, läßt sich dann über ein recht aufwendiges Rechenverfahren die Struktur des zur Beugung verwendeten Gitters, und damit die Struktur der Moleküle zurückrechnen. Wogegen diese Rechnungen bei kleinen Wirkstoffmolekülen (30 - 80 Atome) in akzeptabler Zeit heute (Stand Frühjahr 1989) auf Mikrorechnern (z. B. Micro VAX II) möglich sind, erfordern die mehrere tausend Atome umfassenden Proteinstrukturen für ein effektives Arbeiten einen (Mini-) bzw. Supercomputer (z.B. Convex, Cray etc.). Als "akzeptabel" wird ein Arbeiten bezeichnet, daß Intervalle, die ein Eingreifen und Beurteilen der Rechenergebnisse durch den Experten erfordern, nicht mehr als einige Stunden auseinander liegen.

Neben der Röntgenstrukturanalyse sind weiterhin spektroskopische Verfahren, vor allem die 2d-NMR-Spektroskopie sehr wichtige Hilfsmittel zur Strukturbestimmung. Auch diese Methoden sind zur Datenauswertung auf sehr leistungsfähige Rechner zum Aufstellen eines Strukturmodells angewiesen.

Darstellung von Molekülmodellen mit Hilfe der Computergraphik

Der wohl wichtigste Aspekt, der in den letzten Jahren den Strukturuntersuchungen mit Hilfe des Rechners (auch in der Industrie) zum Durchbruch verholfen hat, besteht in der computergraphischen Darstellung bzw. Auswertung der Rechenergebnisse. Die Anforderungen an die Graphik sind dabei teilweise so groß, daß die Graphikprozessoren in den Leistungsbereich heutiger Supercomputer vorstoßen. Um beispielsweise ein raumerfüllendes Kugelmodell eines Proteins auf dem Graphikschirm in Echtzeit drehen zu können, müssen pro Sekunde ca. 100 Millionen Rechenoperationen durchgeführt werden. Sicherlich klaffen an dieser Stelle die Ansprüche an die Computergraphik (Auflösung, Schattierung, Objekttransparenz) und die zur Zeit erreichte Leistung noch weit auseinander, aber in der Zukunft ist mit deutlich verbesserten Hilfsmitteln für den Chemiker zu rechnen.

Von dem oben diskutierten Enzym Dihydrofolatreduktase ist die Geometrie röntgenstrukturanalytisch bestimmt worden[3]. Es gelang das Protein zusammen mit dem Coenzym NADPH und dem Inhibitor Methotrexat auszukristallisieren. Im oberen Teil der Abb. 4 ist das Enzym (dunkle Kugeln) mit dem Wirkstoff und dem Coenzym (helle Kugeln) mit seiner van der Waals-Oberfläche dargestellt. Der Inhibitor bindet das Enzym in einer Spalte, die sich in vertikaler Richtung an der Oberfläche des Proteins abzeichnet. In der unteren Hälfte der Abb. 4 ist das Protein zusammen mit dem Wirkstoff und dem Coenzym NADPH gezeigt. Diese Abbildung illustriert, wie die beiden Moleküle (mit Oberfläche) durch das Protein in eine für die Reaktion günstige Position gebracht werden, die hier am Methotrexat - im Gegensatz zum natürlichen Substrat Dihydrofolsäure - allerdings nicht ablaufen kann.

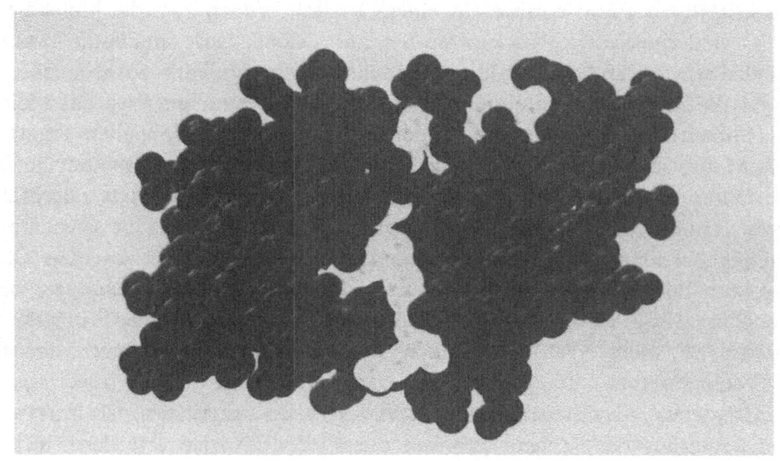

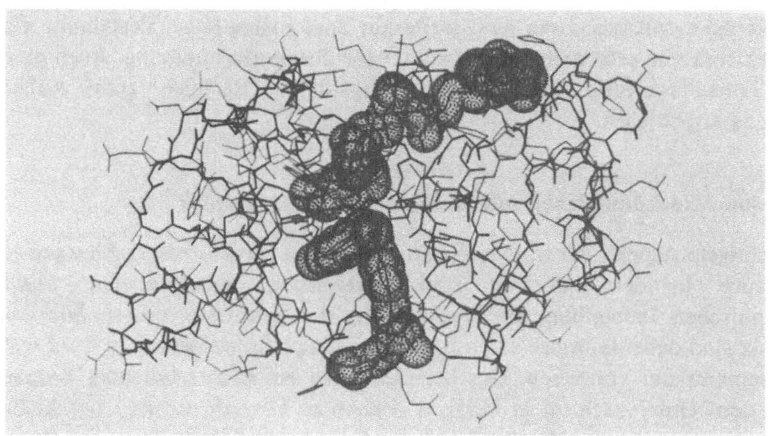

Abb. 4:

Im oberen Teil ist die Molekülstruktur des Enzyms Dihydrofolatreduktase (dunkle Kugeln) mit dem Inhibitor Methotrexat (helle Kugeln, Mitte vertikal) und dem Coenzym NADPH (helle Kugeln, horizontal an der oberen Seite) mit seiner van der Waals Oberfläche gezeigt. Im unteren Teil ist das Enzym als Stäbchen-Modell mit dem Inhibitor und dem Coenzym (beide mit Oberfläche) dargestellt.

Da die Geometrie der Substratbindestelle genau bekannt ist, kann mit Hilfe der Computergraphik und Strukturberechnungen versucht werden, neue Inhibitoren für diese Bindetasche zu konzipieren. Dabei ist zu beachten, daß die Wechselwirkung zwischen dem Wirkstoff und den Aminosäureresten in der Bindetasche des Proteins optimiert wird.

Vorherberechnung von Molekülmodellen mit dem Computer

Doch wie geht man bei diesen Berechnungen vor? Welche Verfahren gibt es, neben den experimentellen Strukturbestimmungsmethoden, um Vorstellungen über die Geometrie von Molekülen zu bekommen?

Liegen als Datenmaterial die Kristallstrukturen vieler tausend Verbindungen vor, so lassen sich daraus Gesetzmäßigkeiten und Standardwerte über den Aufbau und die intermolekularen Verknüpfungen von Molekülen ableiten. Dieses Material kann man, zusammen mit einem physikalischen Kraftfeldmodell, in ein Rechenprogramm einbauen und so energiegünstige Gleichgewichtsstrukturen von Molekülen vorherberechnen. Andere Ansätze versuchen über die Lösung der Schrödinger-Gleichung für die Elektronenstruktur eines Moleküls, dessen Geometrie und Energieinhalt zu bestimmen. Im Vergleich zu den erwähnten Kraftfeldmethoden erfordern die quantenchemischen Verfahren (je nach verlangtem Genauigkeitsgrad) einen deutlich größeren Rechenaufwand (s. unten, Tab. 1).

Legt man einen heute als Supercomputer bezeichneten Rechner zugrunde, so lassen sich die Moleküle mit mehreren tausend Atomen nur nach der Kraftfeldmethode berechnen. Die quantenchemischen Methoden (semiempirische Rechnungen) lassen sich heute bis hin zu einigen hundert Atomen anwenden. Die genauesten Verfahren, die sogenannten ab-initio Verfahren, die nicht, wie die anderen Methoden, an experimentellen Daten parametrisiert werden, sind immer noch auf Moleküle bis z.Z. etwa 50 Atome beschränkt. Die alleinige Steigerung der Rechenleistung der Hardware wird hier nicht ausreichen, beispielsweise wächst bei den zuletztgenannten ab-initio Verfahren der Rechenaufwand mit der 4-5 Potenz der Atomzahl (besser: Zahl der Basisfunktionen) im Molekül. Neben gesteigerter Rechenleistung ist auch eine deutliche Verbesserung der Algorithmen gefordert, und eine Ausnutzung neuerer Rechnerarchitekturen muß geprüft werden.

Aber eine weitere Eigenschaft der Moleküle erschwert die Vorausberechnung von Strukturen und macht gerade hier den Rechner zu einem Werkzeug unschätzbaren Wertes.

Konformelle Flexibilität und Dynamik von Molekülen

Moleküle besitzen keinen starren Aufbau, vielmehr können sie durch Drehungen um Einfachbindungen ihre Gestalt verändern. Der Chemiker spricht hier von konformellen Umwandlungen. Jede dieser Formänderungen ist mit einer Änderung des Energieinhaltes des Moleküls verbunden. Betrachten wir die Drehung um die zentrale Einfachbindung im Butan (Abb. 5). Dieser Drehung unterliegt ein Potential, sodaß nur drei Anordnungen (besser: Konformationen) energetisch günstig erscheinen. Ob nun ein Molekül, z.B. bei Raumtemperatur oder unter physiologischen Bedingungen in allen diesen Konformationen vorliegen kann, hängt von den Energiebarrieren zwischen den Minima und den relativen Energielagen dieser Minima zueinander ab (vergl. Butan, von den drei Minima liegen zwei auf gleichem Niveau, das weitere energetisch etwas tiefer).

Rein aus kombinatorischen Gründen läßt sich vorstellen, daß bei Molekülen mit mehreren drehbaren Bindungen die Zahl der möglichen Konformationen beträchtlich ansteigt. Um mit einem Rezeptor (vergleiche Beispiel Methotrexat/Dihydrofolatreduktase) in Wechselwirkung treten zu können, muß ein Molekül in einer ganz bestimmten Konformation vorliegen. Dies kann, muß aber nicht die energetisch günstigste Form sein, denn durch die Bindung an den Rezeptor kann es zu einem Energiegewinn kommen, der den Übergang in eine etwas weniger günstige Konformation überkompensiert.

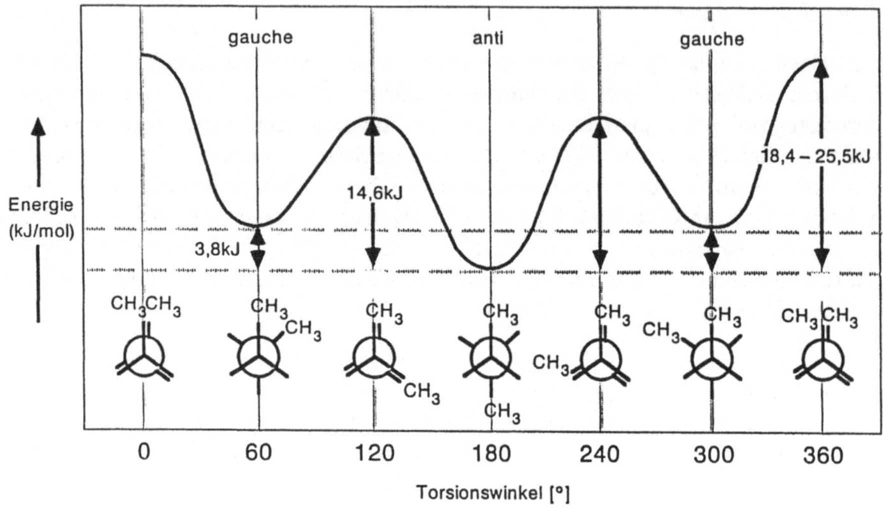

Abb. 5:

Potentialverlauf für die Drehung um die mittlere Einfachbindung im Butan (CH_3-CH_2-CH_2-CH_3). Bei einer Drehung um 360 Grad treten drei Energieminima auf, zwei lokale Minima, die etwas ungünstiger liegen (gauche-Konformation) und ein globales Minimum (anti-trans-Konformation).

Betrachten wir den oben vorgestellten Inhibitor Methotrexat. Zählt man die frei drehbaren Bindungen in diesem Molekül, so ergeben sich dreizehn Bindungen. Wie lassen sich alle energetisch günstigen Konformationen eines solchen Moleküls bestimmen?

Prinzipiell könnte man systematisch in z.B. 30 Grad Schritten um alle Bindungen[4] drehen und jede so generierte Anordnung an eine Kraftfeldrechnung übergeben, die dann durch Energieoptimierung das nächstliegende, lokale Minimum auffindet. Dieses Verfahren hat den Vorteil, umfassend zu sein, ist aber, wegen seines immensen Rechenaufwandes kaum praktikabel . Günstiger gestaltet sich die Suche, wenn man als Torsionen um die einzelnen Bindungen nur die energetisch favorisierten Erfahrungswerte zuläßt, z.B. für die Peptidbindung 0 und 180 Grad. Dennoch verbleiben auch so noch fast 42.000 Startkonformationen für Methotrexat, die kraftfeldoptimiert werden müßten[4]. Sicherlich würden viele dieser Startstrukturen ins gleiche Minimum konvergieren, aber auf diesem Weg lassen sich das globale Minimum und die energetisch günstigen Konformationen auffinden. Es ist zu hoffen, daß die biologisch relevanten Konformationen sich unter diesen, in einem Energieband von ca. 10 kcal/mol oberhalb des globalen Minimums, befinden. In Abb. 3 sind z.B. sechs energiegünstige Konformationen von Methotrexat gezeigt, die alle eine deutlich verschiedene Ausdehnung im Raum besitzen.

Berechnung energiegünstiger Konformationen

An einem anderen Beispiel soll erläutert werden, welche Wege es zur Durchführung einer Konformationsanalyse gibt, und welcher Rechenaufwand mit den einzelnen Verfahren verbunden ist. Das Testbeispiel, ein neungliedriges Cyclolactam, kann als einfache Modellverbindung für cyclische Peptide (hier Tripeptid) gelten.

Für diese ringförmigen Verbindungen existieren mehrere energetisch bevorzugte Konformationen. Betrachtet man z.B. die temperaturabhängig vermessenen NMR-Spektren des cyclischen Tripeptids Tri-N-Benzylglycin in Lösung[5] (Abb. 6), so ändert sich deren Aussehen mit der Temperatur. Für den Chemiker ist dies ein Hinweis auf konformelle Umwandlungen des untersuchten Moleküls. Aus derartigen Spektren läßt sich entnehmen, zwischen welchen Formen sich ein Molekül umlagert, ob mehrere stabile Konformere auftreten und wie deren relative Energielage zueinander ist. Weiterhin lassen sich die relativen Umwandlungsbarrieren und die Geschwindigkeitskonstanten des Umwandlungsprozesses abschätzen. Im geschilderten Fall wird dem Tripeptid eine "kronenförmige" Struktur als stabile Konformation zugeordnet (Abb. 7). Die Ringinversion dieser Krone verläuft vermutlich im geschwindigkeitsbestimmenden Schritt über eine cis/trans Isomerisierung (Drehung um 180 Grad) einer der Peptidbindungen, wobei intermediär eine bootförmige Konformation auftreten sollte[6].

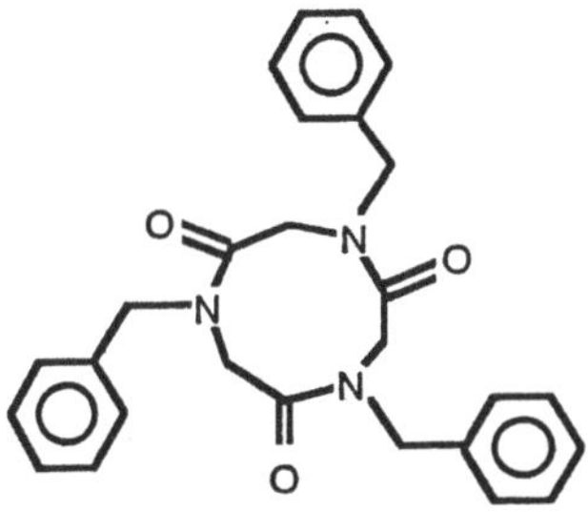

Abb. 6:
In Abhängigkeit von der Temperatur vermessene 1H-NMR-Spektren des symmetrischen Tripeptids Tri-N-benzylglycin. Der Spektrenverlauf weist auf konformelle Umlagerungen des Neunrings hin.

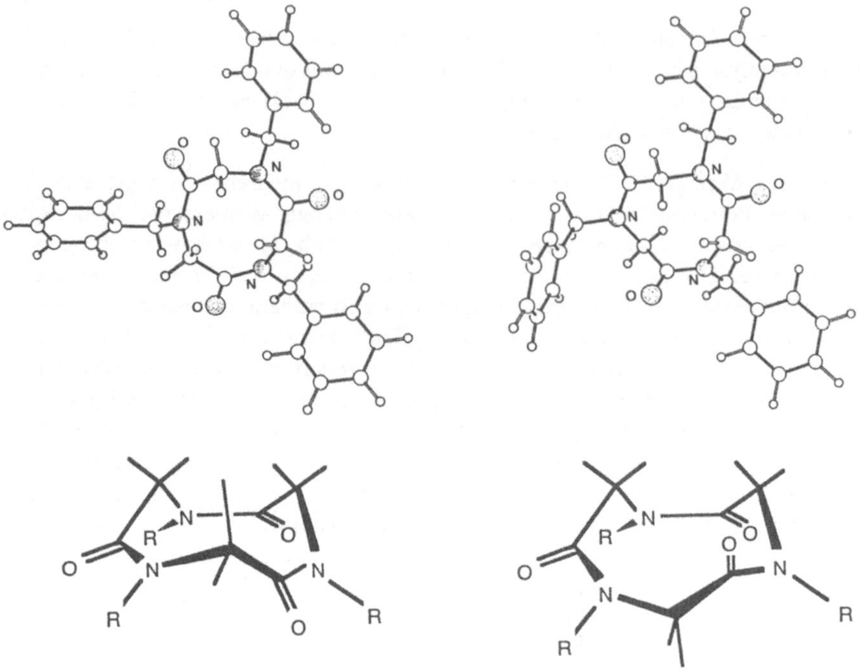

Abb. 7:

"Kronenförmige" Konformation (links) des Tri-N-benzylglycins. Durch cis/trans-Isomerisierung einer Peptidbindung läßt sich das Molekül in eine weniger stabile, "bootförmige" Konformation (rechts) überführen.

Diese beschriebene Umwandlung läßt sich auf dem Rechner simulieren. Dazu muß die Bewegungsgleichung der Atome eines Moleküls gelöst werden. Unter Wirkung der Kräfte, die sich aus dem Wechselwirkungspotential der Atome berechnet, wird eine Bewegung durch das zufällige "Anheften" von Geschwindigkeitsvektoren an die Atome simuliert, die aus einer Boltzmann-Verteilung stammen. Diese Rechenverfahren ermöglichen es, über ein bestimmtes Zeitfenster, die dynamischen Eigenschaften von Molekülen zu studieren. Die damit verbundenen Rechnungen sind aber recht rechenintensiv. Für das beschriebene Tripeptid erfordert ein Zeitschritt, der eine Femtosekunde (10^{-15} sec) umfaßt, auf einer Convex C210 ca. 0,06 sec Rechenzeit. Aus den vermessenen Spektren läßt sich abschätzen, daß bei Raumtemperatur etwa im Millisekunden-Bereich mit einem Umklappvorgang zu rechnen ist[7].

Daher wäre eine Simulationszeit von ca. > 10^7 sec auf dem Rechner notwendig, um mit Sicherheit eine Umwandlung zu beobachten. Da aber Prozesse auf molekularer Ebene mit steigender Temperatur beschleunigt ablaufen, versucht man durch eine fiktive Simulation bei z.B. einer Temperatur von 1000 K das Beobachtungszeitfenster zu verkürzen.

Diese moleküldynamischen Rechnungen lassen sich aber auch einsetzen, um Startstrukturen für eine Konformationsanalyse zu generieren. Man führt eine Simulation z.B. bei 1000 K durch, speichert die Molekülgeometrie z.B. nach jedem 100. Zeitschritt ab und optimiert anschließend deren Geometrie. Im Falle des cyclischen Neunringlactams werden auf diesem Weg aus 2000 generierten Startstrukturen 32 günstige Konformationen gefunden[7],[8].

In einer systematischen Suche[4] wird eine Bindung im Lactamring formal gebrochen, anschließend um die verbleibenden Bindungen in 10 Grad-Schritten gedreht und abgeprüft, ob die so erzeugten Geometrien eine Distanz zwischen den Ringatomen an der Öffnungsstelle zwischen 1.2 und 1.8 A besitzen. Alle akzeptierten Startstrukturen werden einer Kraftfeldoptimierung zugeführt.

In einem Ansatz von Gerber et. al[9] wird angenommen, daß sich die Atome in einem Ring genähert auf einem geschlossenen Kurvenzug befinden, der sich durch eine Fourierreihe mit einem Radial- und Axialanteil beschreiben läßt. Man kann nun umgekehrt durch unterschiedliche Kombinationen der einzelnen Fourierkoeffizienten ringförmige Gebilde erzeugen, auf denen dann die Atome der betrachteten Ringe verteilt werden. Dieses Verfahren stellt eine effiziente Methode zum Generieren von Startstrukturen für eine Konformationsanalyse dar, da bereits 450 Startstrukturen ausreichen, die oben erwähnte Zahl von Konformationen zu generieren.

Will man nun die einzelnen Konformationen miteinander vergleichen (s. Abb. 8) bzw. zwischen ihnen bezüglich ihrer biologischen Relevanz diskriminieren, ist ihr relativer Energieinhalt von zentraler Bedeutung. Die berechneten Energieunterschiede zwischen den verschiedenen Konformeren schwanken mit dem verwendeten Rechenverfahren. Eine höhere Genauigkeit erfordert einen deutlich anwachsenden Rechenaufwand (s. Tab. 1, Vergleich der Geometrieoptimierungen bzw. Energieberechnungen mit Kraftfeldmethoden, semiempirischen Verfahren und ab-initio Rechnungen). Darüber hinaus hängt die relative Energieabstufung noch stark davon ab, ob bei den Rechnungen eine Umgebung (z.B. Lösungsmittel) berücksichtigt wurde, oder ob die Rechnungen praktisch im Vakuum durchgeführt wurden.

Kraftfeldmethode	$C_8H_{15}NO$	6- 15 sec
Semiempirische Methode	$C_8H_{15}NO$	120-800 sec
ab-initio Methode	$C_8H_{15}NO$	3600 sec

Tab. 1:
Vergleich der Rechenzeiten auf einer CONVEX 210 für die Energie- bzw. Geomtrieoptimierung mit verschiedenen Methoden. Die Kraftfeldrechnungen (MOMO, Lit. 12). beziehen sich auf unterschiedliche, teilweise stark verzerrte Startgeometrien eines Neuringlactams ($C_8H_{15}NO$). Der angegebene Zeitbereich schwankt wegen der unterschiedlich schnellen Konvergenz der Strukturen. Für die semiempirischen Rechnungen (VAMP, Lit. 13) wurden die kraftfeldoptimierten Geometrien als Startstrukturen eingesetzt (mit "precise-option"). Mit

ab-initio Methoden ("TURBOMOLE", Lit. 14) wurden für eine 3-21 G Basis die Energien der semiempirisch optimierten Geometrien berechnet. Die dabei bestimmten Gradienten erwiesen sich als sehr klein. Für eine Energieoptimierung müßten ca. 500 dieser Energieberechnungen durchgeführt werden.

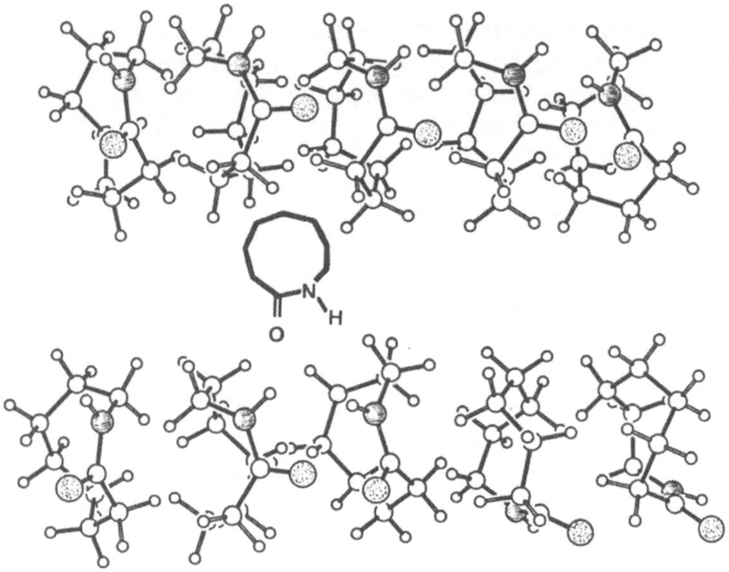

Abb. 8:

Zehn strukturell verschiedene, energetisch nahe beieinander liegende Konformationen des Neunringlactams, in denen die Peptidbindung cis-konfiguriert vorliegt. Entsprechend existieren weitere Konformere, in denen diese Verknüpfung trans-orientiert auftritt.

Einpassung von neuen Wirkstoffmolekülen auf eine bekannte Enzymstruktur

Nachdem an einem vergleichsweise einfachen Beispiel die Durchführung einer Konformationsanalyse gezeigt wurde, wollen wir zu der vorgestellten Enzymstruktur zurückkehren, für die nach neuen Inhibitoren gesucht werden soll. Wie oben beschrieben, spielt die Dihydrofolatreduktase eine wichtige Rolle im Synthesecyclus von Bausteinen für das Molekül, das die Erbinformation von Zelle zu Zelle weitergibt. Um eine antibakteriell wirkende Substanz zu erhalten, müßte es gelingen, spezifisch dieses Enzym in Bakterien zu inhibieren. Die Proteine mit gleicher Funktion sind in den unterschiedlichen Organismen miteinander strukturell verwandt, doch können Unterschiede auftreten, die auch den Aufbau der Bindetasche betreffen. Diese Geometrieunterschiede lassen sich für die Entwicklung selektiver Wirkstoffe ausnutzen.

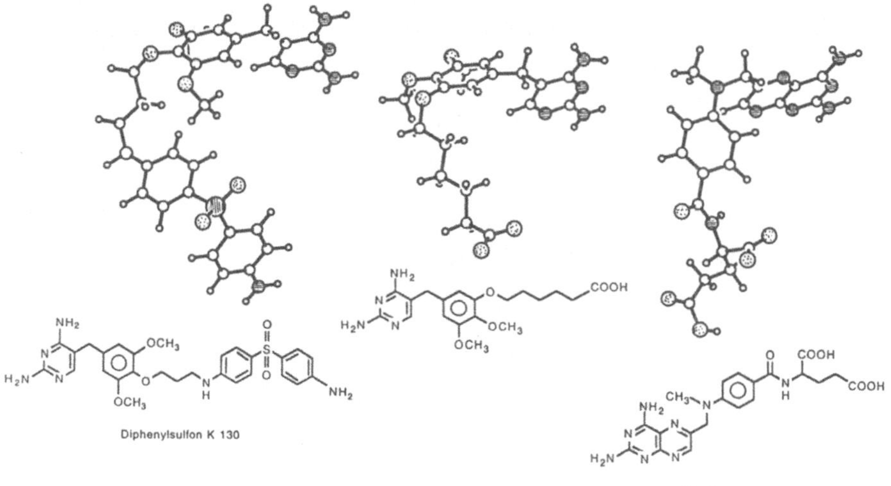

Diphenylsulfon K 130

Methotrexat

Abb. 9:

Molekülstrukturen von drei Inhibitoren der Dihydrofolatreduktase: Methotrexat (rechts), einem Trimethoprim-Analogon mit $(CH_2)_5COOH$-Rest (Mitte) und dem Diphenylsulfon K130. Die Moleküle sind in einer Konformation gezeigt, in der sie sich in die Enzymstruktur einpassen lassen.

Trimethoprim ist ein bekanntes Bakterizid (Abb. 9). Läßt sich diese Verbindung so modifizieren, daß ihre Affinität zum Rezeptor gesteigert wird? Betrachtet man die Bindungstasche des Enzyms genauer, so fällt eine polare Aminosäure (Arginin) an der gegenüberliegenden Seite auf. Das Methotrexat knüpft eine Bindung zu diesem Rest über eine Carboxylatgruppe. Ersetzt man im Trimethoprim eine der Methoxygruppen durch einen Carboxyalkylrest ($(CH_2)_nCOOH$), so wird auch in diesem neuen Trimethoprim-Analogen eine Bindung zu dieser polaren Aminosäure möglich. Modelleinpassungen auf dem Computer sagen eine $(CH_2)_5COOH$-Kette als optimales Verbindungsglied voraus. Tatsächlich wird diese Verbindung etwa 16 mal fester an das Enzym gebunden als Trimethoprim[10].

Doch leider fehlt diesen Verbindungen eine bakterienspezifische Selektivität, und sie erweisen sich, vermutlich durch die zusätzliche Säurefunktion, als so polar, daß sie Probleme beim Transport durch die Zellwände hin zum Zielort aufweisen. Dieses Phänomen verdeutlicht, daß ein optimales "Passen" eines Wirkstoffes auf sein Enzym zwar eine notwendige Voraussetzung für die Wirkung ist, aber noch viele andere Faktoren, die den Weg einer Substanz hin zu ihrem Wirkort beeinflussen, entscheidend sind. In Abb. 9 ist eine andere Verbindung aufgeführt, die deutlich lipophiler ist und daher ein günstigeres Transportverhalten aufweist[11]. Ihre strukturelle Übereinstimmung mit den anderen Inhibitoren ließ sich auf dem Rechner überprüfen und optimieren (s. Abb. 9).

Die ständig anwachsende Kenntnis über Strukturen von Wirkstoffen und ihren Rezeptoren versetzen den Wirkstoffchemiker zunehmend in die Lage, seine Wirkstoffe strukturell maßzuschneidern ("designen"). Voraussetzung dazu sind schnelle Rechner, zuverlässige Rechenalgorithmen und hochauflösende Computergraphik, die ihn in seiner Kreativität beim Entwickeln zuverlässiger Wirkmodelle unterstützen.

Literatur

[1] W.G.J. Hol, Angew. Chemie, **98**, 765 (1986)

[2] A.L. Lehninger, "Biochemistry", Worth Publ. Inc., New York (1975)

[3] J.T. Bolin, J.D. Filman, D.A. Matthews, R.C. Hamlin, J.J. Kraut, J. Biol. Chem., **257**, 13650 (1982)

[4] "Sybyl", Programmsystem von Tripos, Ass., St. Louis, USA

[5] P. Krämer, Dissertation, Univ. Frankfurt (1976)

[6] J. Schaug, Acta Chem. Scand., **25**, 2771 (1971)

[7] "Discover", Programmsystem von Biosym Tech., San Diego, USA

[8] H. J. Böhm, G. Klebe, T. Lorenz, T. Mietzner, L. Siggel (in Vorbereitung)

[9] P.R. Gerber, K. Gubernator, K. Müller, Helv. Chim. Acta, **71**, 1429 (1988)

[10] L.F. Kuyper, B. Roth, D.P. Baccanari, R. Ferone, C.R. Beddell, J.N. Champness, D.K. Stammers, J.G. Dann, F.E. Norrington, D.J. Baker, P. J. Goodford, J. Med. Chem., **28**, 303 (1985)

[11] K.H. Czaplinsky, M. Kansy, J.K. Seydel, Quant. Struct.-Act. Relat., **6**, 70 (1987)

[12] H. J. Lindner, Tetrahed., **30**, 1127 (1974)
Programmversion "MOMO", H. Beck, E. Egert, Univ. Göttingen (1988)

[13] M.J.S. Dewar, W. Thiel, J. Am. Chem. Soc., **99**, 4899 (1977)
Programmversion "VAMP", T. Clark, Univ. Erlangen (1988)

[14] M. Häser, R. Ahlrichs, J. Comp. Chem., **10**, 104 (1989)
Programmversion "Turbomole", Univ. Karlsruhe (1989)

Supercomputer in der Produktions- und Ablaufplanung

Dieter B. Preßmar

Universität Hamburg
Betriebswirtschaftliche Datenverarbeitung
von-Melle-Park 5
2000 Hamburg 13

1. Betriebswirtschaftliche Problemstellung der dynamischen Produktionsplanung

Aufgabe der dynamischen Produktionsplanung ist es, sowohl die Verteilung der Produktions aufgaben auf die verfügbaren Produktionskapazitäten anzugeben, als auch die zeitliche Reihenfolge der Produktionsdurchführung in den einzelnen Produktionsanlagen zu bestimmen. Bei einer Anwendung betriebswirtschaftlicher Optimierungskriterien zur Lösung dieser Planungsaufgabe ergeben sich daraus zugleich Hinweise auf die Losgrößenpolitik, die Kapitalbindung und Lagerraumbeanspruchung im Produktionsprozeß, auf die günstigste Auslastung der Produktionskapazitäten oder auf die geeignete Zusammensetzung des Produktionsprogramms [1].

Diese typische Aufgabe der Produktionsplanung und -steuerung wird in den traditionellen PPS-Systemen (PPS = Produktionsplanung und -steuerung) der CIM-Anwendungen mit Hilfe von heuristischen Methoden gelöst. Die hohe Komplexität der Optimierungsaufgabe hat es bisher verhindert, daß exakte und optimierende Verfahren eingesetzt wurden. Geeignete mathematische Ansätze für das Planungsmodell sind gleichermaßen wesentlich für die Beherrschung dieses Planungsproblems wie die Verfügbarkeit über höchste Rechenleistungen und effiziente numerische Verfahren. Das hohe Leistungsniveau der heute verfügbaren Supercomputer läßt erwarten, daß im Bereich der PPS-Systeme eine neue Entwicklung in Richtung auf mathematische Verfahren eröffnet werden kann.

2. Modellierung eines dynamischen Produktionssystems auf der Grundlage von diskreten Zustandsfunktionen

Im Unterschied zu dynamischen Systemen in den Naturwissenschaften, deren Zustandsänderungen mit Hilfe von Differentialgleichungen beschrieben werden können, zeichnen sich betriebswirtschaftliche Fertigungssysteme im allgemeinen durch diskrete Zustandswechsel aus. Die Änderung des Produktionszustands einer Produktionsanlage von einem Produkt zum nächsten erfolgt nach Durchführung einer Umrüstungszeit. Der Zustandswechsel bedeutet für die Produktionsplanung den Übergang von einem Zustand 1 in einen anderen Zustand 2. Daher muß die Zustandsfunktion einer Produktionsanlage den Übergang von einem Zustand in den anderen durch eine diskrete Änderung des Funktionswerts darstellen können.

In der folgenden Abb. 1 ist das Bild einer zweidimensionalen diskreten Zustandsfunktion über der Zeit wiedergegeben. Der Funktionswert nimmt jeweils den Wert 1 an, wenn ein Zustand realisiert ist. Da zum gleichen Zeitpunkt jeweils nur ein Zustand definiert sein kann, müssen mit Ausnahme des betrachteten Zustands alle anderen Zustände den Wert 0 aufweisen. Die Dauer der Zustände wird auf der Zeitachse angegeben, wobei die Intervalle zwischen zwei Zustandswechseln durch die Variable T_t gemessen werden. Das Vorliegen eines Zustands z kann mit Hilfe einer Binärvariablen u_z beschrieben werden [2].

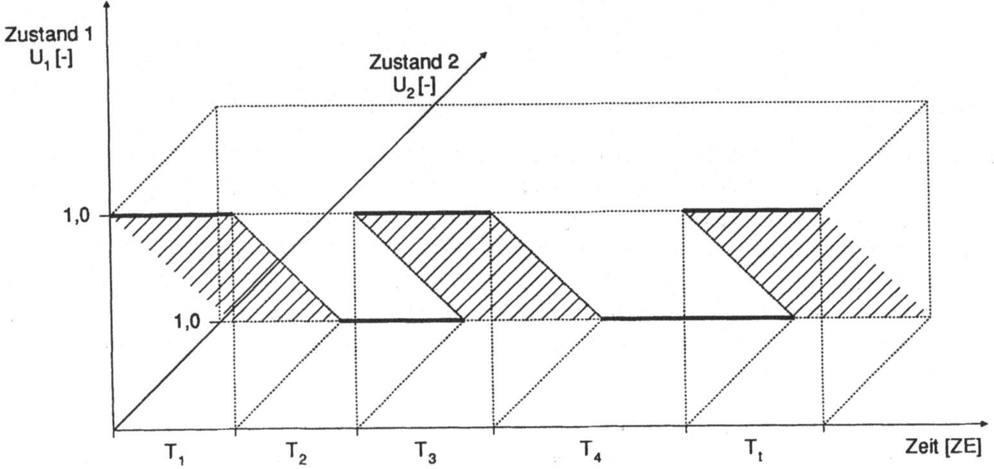

Abb. 1: Zweidimensionale diskrete Zustandsfunktion

Ein betriebliches Fertigungssystem besteht aus einer Anzahl von einzelnen Produktionsanlagen. Diese können als die Elemente des zu beschreibenden Systems betrachtet werden. Das Zustandsverhalten des Gesamtsystems ergibt sich aus dem Verhalten der einzelnen Elemente im Zeitablauf. Da das Verhalten der einzelnen Systemelemente durch die bereits dargestellte diskrete Zustandsfunktion definiert ist, kann das Verhalten des Systems im Zeitablauf mathematisch beschrieben werden, wobei die Interaktionen der Systemelemente zu berücksichtigen sind.

In Abb. 2 ist ein entsprechendes Modell für ein Produktionssystem, bestehend aus 5 Fertigungsanlagen, dargestellt. Die Interaktionen der Systemelemente (Fertigungsanlagen) werden beispielsweise durch die Produktionsverhältnisse und die dadurch festgelegte Führung des Güterstroms innerhalb des Systems festgelegt. Zugleich kann die Interaktion der Elemente im Güterstrom noch zusätzlich durch eine Verflechtung der Geldströme im System überlagert werden. Auch diese Wirkungen des Geldstroms können ebenso wie die Wirkungen des Güterstroms mit Hilfe der Zustandsfunktionen einzelner Elemente quantitativ erfaßt und modelliert werden. Dabei entsteht ein dynamisches Modell des Produktionssystems, das in der Lage ist, dessen Zustandsverlauf innerhalb der betrachteten Planungsperiode zu beschreiben.

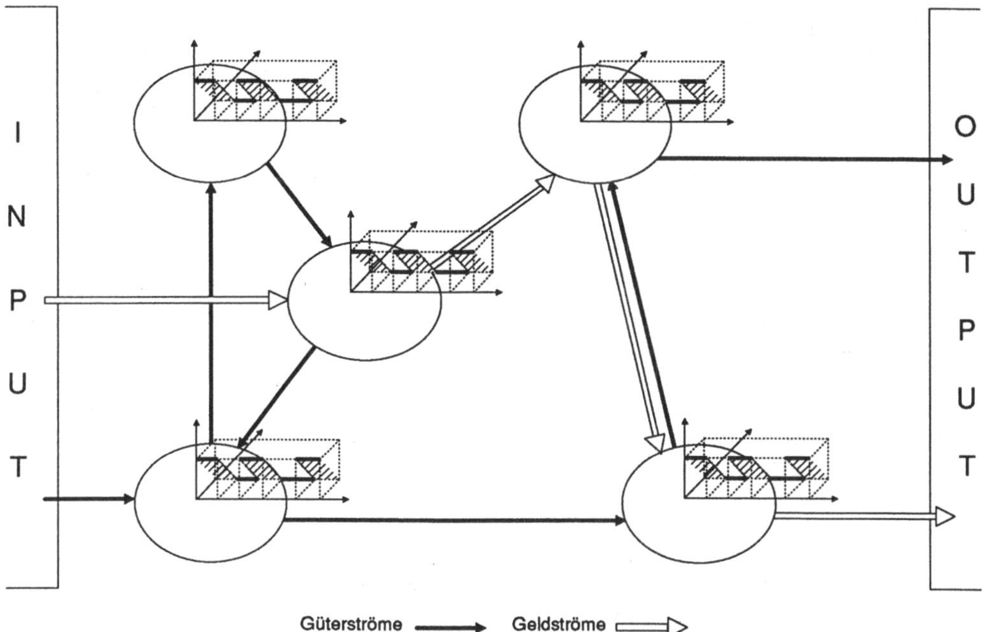

Abb. 2: Modell für ein Produktionssystem mit 5 Anlagen

3. Probleme der Optimierung des Modells für ein Produktionssystem

Aufgrund der betriebswirtschaftlichen und technischen Randbedingungen weisen derartige Fertigungssysteme hinsichtlich des Flusses der Güterströme und insbesondere im Hinblick auf die zeitliche Reihenfolge der Fertigungsvorgänge eine große Zahl von Freiheitsgraden auf. Diese können genutzt werden, um das Zustandsverhalten eines Systems entsprechend einer vorgegebenen Zielfunktion zu optimieren. Unter betriebswirtschaftlichem Aspekt können als Zielkriterien beispielsweise Kostenminimierung, Durchlaufzeitminimierung oder auch Gewinnmaximierung in Frage kommen.

Zur mathematischen Lösung dieses Optimierungsproblems hat sich vor allem das Verfahren der "Linearen Programmierung" bewährt, wobei sowohl die Zielfunktion als auch die das Systemverhalten beschreibenden Gleichungen und Ungleichungen lineare Funktionen sein müssen. Bei einer Analyse der zur mathematischen Systembeschreibung erforderlichen Beziehungen zeigt sich, daß nahezu ausnahmslos Linearität gewährleistet ist. In Abhängigkeit bestimmter Formen des Kostenverlaufs, z.B. bei Lagerkosten, Finanzierungskosten oder Produktionskosten, können Polynome zweiten Grades oder bilineare Funktionen auftreten; diese können jedoch mit bekannten Verfahren linear approximiert werden [3]. Somit besteht die Optimierung eines Produktionssystems im Zeitablauf grundsätzlich aus der Lösung einer Aufgabe der "Linearen Programmierung".

Allerdings kommt als zusätzliches Problem noch die Forderung hinzu, daß einige Variable dieser Optimierungsaufgabe nur ganzzahlige Werte annehmen dürfen. Dies gilt insbesondere für die binären Variablen u_z der diskreten Zustandsfunktion der einzelnen Fertigungsanlagen. Diese Variablen sind jeweils nur für die Werte 0 oder 1 definiert. Aus dieser Eigenschaft ergibt sich ein Optimierungsproblem der gemischt-ganzzahligen linearen Programmierung. Damit entsteht jedoch zugleich ein kombinatorisches Optimierungsproblem hoher Komplexität, zu dessen Lösung ein erheblicher numerischer Rechenaufwand erforderlich ist.

Die Lösung kombinatorischer Optimierungsprobleme wird traditionell mit Hilfe von Branch-und-Bound-Verfahren berechnet [4]. Für das vorliegende Problem bedeutet dies die Evaluation eines binären bzw. mehrwertigen Entscheidungsbaumes, an dessen Knoten jeweils ein Problem der linearen Optimierung zu lösen ist. Ein derartiger Entscheidungsbaum kann für die Dimensionen eines praktischen Planungsproblems der Industrie 10^9 bis 10^{12} Knoten aufweisen. Mit Hilfe des Branch-und-Bound-Verfahrens können größere Teile des Entscheidungsbaumes abgeschnitten werden, so daß sich die Zahl der zu berechnenden Knoten um den Fakter 10^3 bis 10^4 kürzen läßt. Als Berechnungsaufwand verbleibt dann prinzipiell noch die Aufgabe, 10^5 bis 10^8 LP-Modelle zu lösen.

Es liegt nahe, hier zu vermuten, daß vektorisierte und parallelisierte Verfahren in der Lage sind, diese gewaltige numerische Rechenaufgabe in vertretbarer Zeit zu lösen. Obwohl für Skalarrechner bereits leistungsfähige Optimierungsverfahren entwickelt wurden [5], steht die Forschung auf dem Gebiet der vektoriellen linearen Optimierung am Anfang, da die für den Skalarrechner entwickelten Verfahren im Hinblich auf Effizienzsteigerung nicht auf den Vektorrechner übertragen werden können. Im folgenden Abschnitt soll daher auf technische Probleme bei der Entwicklung vektorieller Algorithmen zur linearen Optimierung kurz eingegangen werden.

4. Vektorisierungsmöglichkeiten eines Verfahrens zur linearen Optimierung

Die erste mathematische Formulierung eines Verfahrens zur Optimierung einer linearen Zielfunktion unter der Berücksichtigung von linearen Nebenbedingungen wurde in den Jahren 1939 bis 1941 von dem sowjetischen Mathematiker Kantorowich vorgenommen. Nach 1945 hat der amerikanische Mathematiker Dantzig das heute noch benutzte Simplexverfahren entwickelt und auf einer Rechenanlage erstmals implementiert. Seit dieser Zeit wurden viele Verbesserungen insbesondere auf dem Gebiet der numerischen Verfahren erreicht, um einerseits die Verarbeitungseffizienz auf Skalarrechnern zu steigern und andererseits das Entstehen und die Fortpflanzung von Rundungsfehlern zu vermindern.

Am Beispiel eines einfachen Verfahrens, der sogenannten "Revidierten Simplexmethode" [6] soll gezeigt werden, welche Möglichkeiten und Probleme bei der Vektorisierung dieser Methode gegeben sind.
Eine Aufgabe der linearen Optimierung für ein Modell mit ausschließlich kontinuierlichen Variablen wird durch folgende Ausdrücke beschrieben:

Maximiere die Zielfunktion: $c^T x$
unter den Nebenbedingungen: $Ax = b$
$x \geq 0.$

In den Nebenbedingungen sind Ungleichungen durch Einfügen von Schlupfvariablen in Gleichungen überführt worden.

Der Vektor c enthält die Koeffizienten der Zielfunktion, während der Vektor x die zu optimierenden Variablen des Modells repräsentiert. Das Gleichungssystem mit der Koeffizientenmatrix A und dem Vektor der rechten Seite b beschreibt in Verbindung mit der Nichtnegativitätsbedingung den zulässigen Lösungsraum für das Optimierungsproblem. Da das Gleichungssystem erheblich mehr Variablen als Gleichungen enthält, besteht eine Lösungsmannigfaltigkeit, die mit Hilfe des Kriteriums der Zielfunktion derart beseitigt wird, daß schließlich der verbleibende Lösungsvektor zugleich den Wert z der Zielfunktion maximiert (siehe dazu Abb. 3).

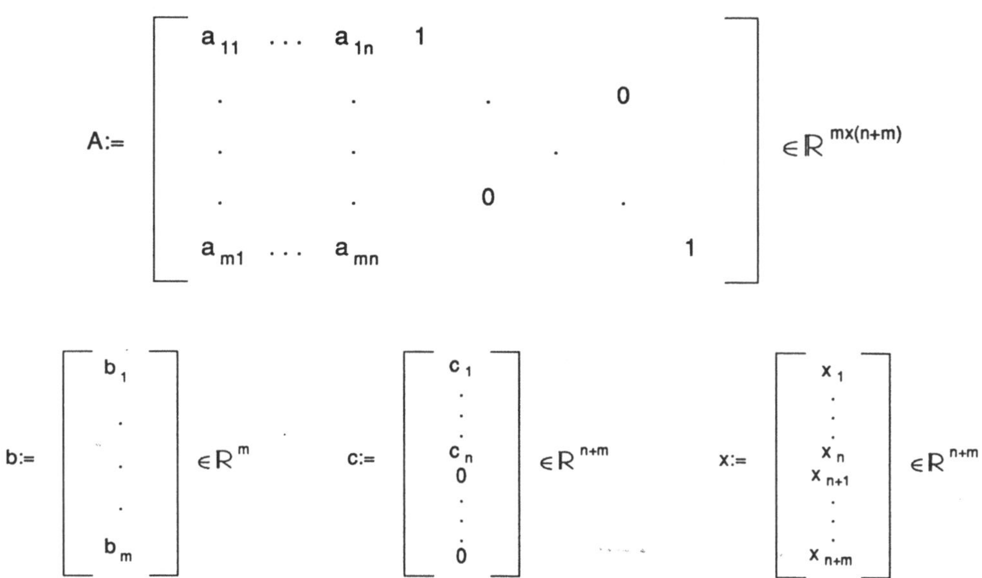

$$A := \begin{bmatrix} a_{11} & \cdots & a_{1n} & 1 & & & \\ \cdot & & \cdot & & \cdot & 0 & \\ \cdot & & \cdot & & & \cdot & \\ \cdot & & \cdot & & 0 & & \cdot \\ a_{m1} & \cdots & a_{mn} & & & & 1 \end{bmatrix} \in \mathbb{R}^{m \times (n+m)}$$

$$b := \begin{bmatrix} b_1 \\ \cdot \\ \cdot \\ \cdot \\ b_m \end{bmatrix} \in \mathbb{R}^{m} \qquad c := \begin{bmatrix} c_1 \\ \cdot \\ \cdot \\ c_n \\ 0 \\ \cdot \\ \cdot \\ 0 \end{bmatrix} \in \mathbb{R}^{n+m} \qquad x := \begin{bmatrix} x_1 \\ \cdot \\ \cdot \\ x_n \\ x_{n+1} \\ \cdot \\ \cdot \\ x_{n+m} \end{bmatrix} \in \mathbb{R}^{n+m}$$

Abb. 3: Definition der Modellgrößen

Zur Beseitigung der Lösungsmannigfaltigkeit wird die Koeffizientenmatrix A in eine Basis und eine Nichtbasis unterteilt. Entsprechend besteht der Vektor x aus Basis- und Nichtbasisvariablen. Durch wiederholten Austausch der Basisvariablen gegen die Nichtbasisvariablen läßt sich schrittweise eine Basis erzeugen, die schließlich jene Variablen enthält, die den Zielfunktionswert maximieren.

Das numerische Verfahren umfaßt daher im wesentlichen zwei Phasen. Zunächst findet ein Auswahlprozeß statt, mit dessen Hilfe eine geeignete Nichtbasisvariable gesucht wird, die gegen eine entsprechende Basisvariable ausgetauscht wird. Anschließend wird die Basisinverse so transformiert, daß wieder eine zulässige Lösung für den Vektor x der Entscheidungsvariablen entsteht.

Die numerischen Operationen bauen auf der Matrix D auf, die dadurch entsteht, daß zur Matrix A der Vektor b, der transponierte Vektor c und das Skalarelement z hinzugefügt werden. Das Skalarelement gibt den aktuellen Wert der Zielfunktion an. Die Basis B ist eine quadratische Teilmatrix der Matrix D. Während D und somit auch B im allgemeinen dünn besetzte Matrizen mit weniger als 0.1% Nichtnullelementen sind, entwickelt sich B^{-1} im Laufe des iterativen Austausch- und Transformationsprozesses zu einer relativ dicht besetzten Marix. Zur Speicherung von D kann deshalb ein Pointer-Verfahren angewandt werden, das nur die Nichtnullelemente berücksichtigt. Dagegen kann für B^{-1} eine Speicherung der vollen Matrix vorgesehen werden (zur Definition vgl. Abb. 4).

$$
D := \begin{bmatrix}
c_1 & & c_n & 0 & & \cdots & 0 & z \\
a_{11} & \cdots & a_{1n} & 1 & & & & b_1 \\
\cdot & & \cdot & & \cdot & 0 & & \cdot \\
\cdot & & \cdot & & & \cdot & & \cdot \\
\cdot & & \cdot & & 0 & & \cdot & \cdot \\
a_{m1} & \cdots & a_{mn} & & & & 1 & b_m
\end{bmatrix}
=
\begin{bmatrix}
d_{01} & \cdots & d_{0n+m+1} \\
\cdot & & \cdot \\
\cdot & & \cdot \\
\cdot & & \cdot \\
d_{m1} & \cdots & d_{mn+m+1}
\end{bmatrix}
\in \mathbb{R}^{(m+1)x(n+m+1)}
$$

$$
B := \begin{bmatrix}
d_{0i_0} & \cdots & d_{0i_m} \\
\cdot & & \cdot \\
\cdot & & \cdot \\
\cdot & & \cdot \\
d_{mi_0} & \cdots & d_{mi_m}
\end{bmatrix}
\in \mathbb{R}^{(m+1)x(m+1)} \qquad i_j \in I_B,\ j=0,m
$$

Abb. 4a: Dünn besetzte Matrizen

Das Auswahlverfahren für den Basistausch der Variablen beruht auf der Bestimmung einer Pivotzeile und einer Pivotspalte. Die Pivotzeile markiert eine Variable, die aus der Basis entfernt werden soll, während die Pivotspalte eine Nichtbasisvariable anzeigt, die in die Basis eingefügt wird.

$$B^{-1} := \begin{bmatrix} \bar{b}_{00} & \cdots & \bar{b}_{0m} \\ \cdot & & \cdot \\ \cdot & & \cdot \\ \cdot & & \cdot \\ \bar{b}_{m0} & \cdots & \bar{b}_{mm} \end{bmatrix} \in \mathbb{R}^{(m+1)x(m+1)}$$

Abb. 4b: Dicht besetzte Matrix

In Abb. 5a ist die Vektor-Matrixoperation angedeutet, die zur Auswahl der Pivotspalte erforderlich ist. Dabei ist jeweils die zur Zielfunktions- und zur Pivotzeile gehörende Zeile der Basisinversen mit der Nichtbasis zu multiplizieren. Da die Nichtbasis eine Teilmatrix der Matrix D ist, muß diese Rechenoperation auf die indizierte Speicherungsorganisation der Nichtnullelemente von D abgebildet werden, wodurch der Vektorisierungsgrad dieser Rechenschritte erheblich beeinträchtigt wird.

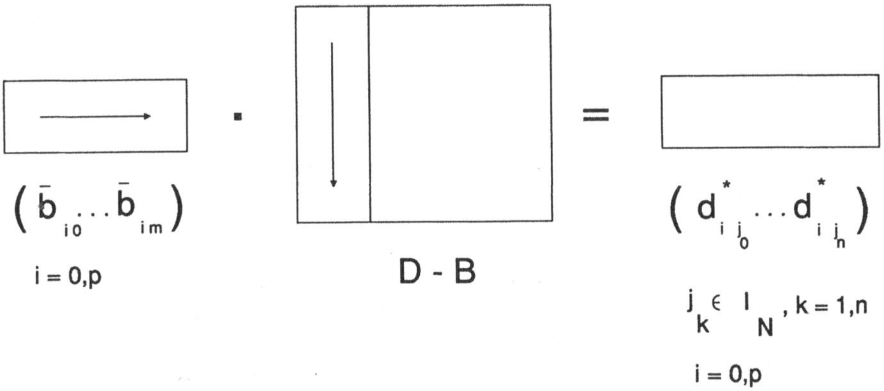

Abb. 5a: Auswahl Pivotspalte q

Zur Auswahl der Pivotzeile ist die Matrix der Basisinversen mit der letzten Spalte von D zu multiplizieren (vgl. Abb. 5b). Hier ist eine dicht besetzte Matrix bei voller Speicherung mit einem dünn besetzten Vektor mit indizierter Speicherung der Koeffizienten zu multiplizieren. Zur effizienten Ausführung dieser Operation sind in Abb. 6 zwei mögliche Varianten angegeben. Einerseits kann das "dot-product" gebildet werden, wenn die Basisinverse zeilenweise verarbeitet wird. Andererseits kann eine vektorisierte Multiplikation und Addition ausgeführt werden, wenn diese Operation bezüglich der Basisinversen spaltenweise durchgeführt wird. Das letztere Verfahren ergibt wegen des höheren Vektorisierungsgrades eine erheblich größere Verarbeitungsleistung.

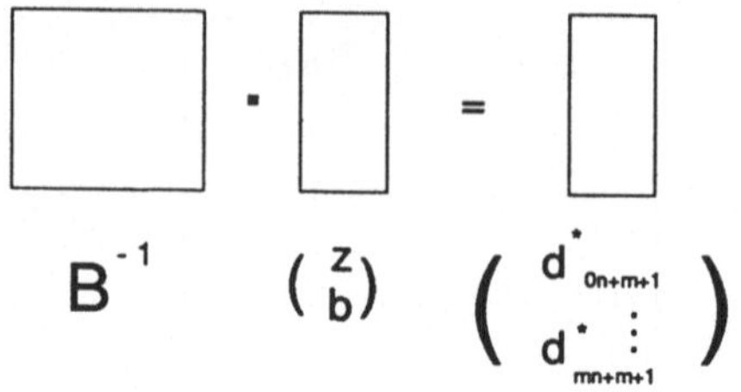

$$B^{-1} \cdot \binom{z}{b} = \begin{pmatrix} d^{*}_{0n+m+1} \\ \vdots \\ d^{*}_{mn+m+1} \end{pmatrix}$$

Abb. 5b: Auswahl Pivotzeile p

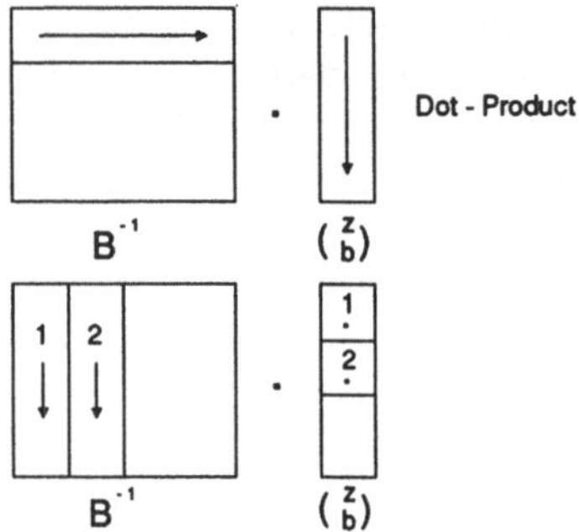

Abb. 6: Vektorisierungsmöglichkeiten

Nach Abschluß der Auswahlprozedur erfolgt die Transformation der Basisinversen entsprechend den in Abb. 7 angegebenen Transformationsvorschriften. Daraus läßt sich erkennen, daß als Folge der Quotientenbildung mit anschließender Subtraktion die latente Gefahr der Entstehung von Rundungsfehlern gegeben ist. Im Zusammenhang mit der iterativen Transformation der Koeffizienten der Basisinversen pflanzen sich diese Rundungsfehler systematisch fort. Daher muß regelmäßig eine Reinversion der Basis durchgeführt werden, um die Basisinverse neu zu konditionieren. Hierfür bieten sich für den Vektorrechner die bereits in den Standardbibliotheken verfügbaren schnellen Gleichungslöser für dichtbesetzte Matrizen an [6]. In Abb. 8 sind die beiden Wege angedeutet, um zu einer neuen Basisinversen zu gelangen. Die mit wenig Aufwand verbundene Transformation läßt sich solange anwenden wie die Koeffizienten der Basisinversen noch keine relevanten Rundungsfehler aufweisen. Das Inversionsverfahren muß dann eingesetzt werden, wenn eine Konditionierung der Basisinversen erforderlich ist.

Diese kurz skizzierten wesentlichen Verarbeitungsschritte der revidierten Simplexmethode mögen zeigen, daß eine weitgehende Vektorisierung des Verfahrens der "linearen Programmierung" nicht ohne weiteres erreicht werden kann. Das entscheidende Gewicht muß daher bei der Implementation auf die Vektorisierung des Programmcodes gelegt werden. Hier lassen sich aufgrund der ersten praktischen Erfahrungen Vektorisierungsgrade von mehr als 60% erreichen.

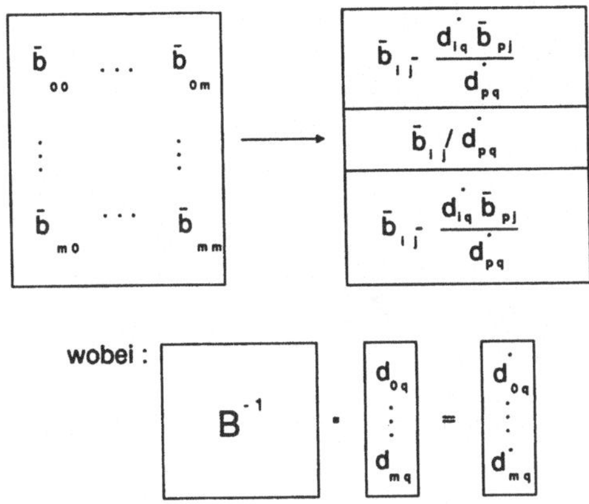

Abb. 7: Transformationsvorschriften Basisinverse B^{-1}

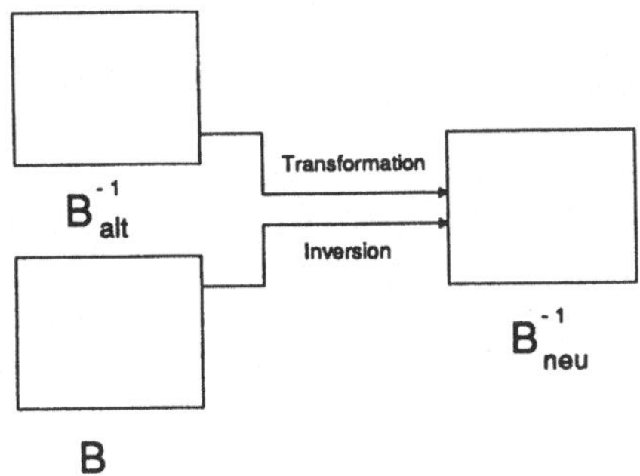

Abb. 8: Möglichkeiten zur Berechnung der neuen Basisinversen

5. Hinweise zur Lösung des kombinatorischen Problems der gemischt-ganzzahligen Optimierung

Da die Aufgabe der dynamischen Produktionsplanung auf ein gemischt-ganzzahliges Optimierungsproblem führt, muß die Lösung der LP-Aufgabe mit kontinuierlichen Variablen mit der Branch-und-Bound-Methode verbunden werden, um die Ganzahligkeit einzelner Variablen zu erzwingen.

Die mathematische Formulierung der diskreten Zustandsfunktionen eines Produktionsplanungsmodells führt auf die Verwendung von binär-ganzzahligen Variablen, die zu Teilmengen zusammengefaßt jeweils einen special ordered set vom Typ 1 (SOS1) bilden. Dies bedeutet, daß jeweils eine Binärvariable aus einem special ordered set den Wert 1 animmt, während die übrigen Binärvariablen den Wert 0 aufweisen müssen. Eine derartige multiple-choice-Situation kann z.B. mit Hilfe eines mehrwertigen Entscheidungsbaums (vgl. Abb. 9) abgebildet werden.

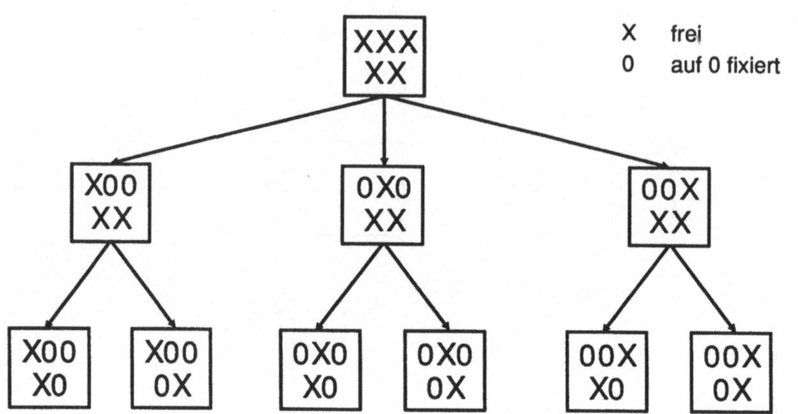

Abb. 9: Mehrwertiger Entscheidungsbaum

Das Optimierungsverfahren muß nun so gestaltet werden, daß für einzelne Knoten des Baums LP-Aufgaben gelöst und in Abhängigkeit von dem erzielten Ergebnis im Baum weiterverzweigt oder die Rechnung z.B. im Falle der Unzulässigkeit an einem anderen Ast des Baums fortgesetzt werden kann. Der Aufwand für das Optimierungsverfahren hängt somit einmal davon ab, inwieweit es gelingt, möglichst große Teile des Baums wegen erkennbarer Nichtoptimalität bzw. Unzulässigkeit im Verlauf des Verzweigungsprozesses abzuschneiden. Zum anderen ist es notwendig, daß viele tausend LP-Probleme bzw. Pivotierungsschritte mit größter Geschwindigkeit berechnet werden; hier kommt dem Hochleistungsrechner eine herausragende Bedeutung für das Optimierungsverfahren zu.

6. Erfahrungen und Ausblick

Unter Leitung des Verfassers wurde das Programmsystem VLP (Vektorisierte Lineare Programmierung) in der Sprache FORTRAN entwickelt, um die gemischt-ganzzahligen Modelle der dynamischen Produktionsplanung zu optimieren. Erste Erfahrungen in der Implementation des Verfahrens liegen mit verschiedenen Vektorrechnern vor (ETA10, VP400 und CONVEX). Es zeigt sich, daß eine volle Leistungsfähigkeit des Verfahrens nur dann erzielt werden kann, wenn die Implementation an die Eigenschaften der Hardwarearchitektur weitgehend angepaßt wird. Gegenüber der skalaren Version des Verfahrens ergibt die vektorielle Implementation einen Leistungsgewinn um den Faktor 5 bis 15. Wird dabei noch die hohe Verarbeitungsleistung eines Supercomputers berücksichtigt, so sind Leistungssteigerungen in der Größenordnung von 100 gegenüber den skalaren Mainframes zu erzielen. Allerdings wird die Optimierungsleistung ebenso entscheidend von der Qualität der verwendeten Algorithmen beeinflußt. Es kann jedoch davon ausgegangen werden, daß mathematisch optimierende Produktionsplanungssysteme im Hinblick auf die erforderliche Rechenleistung nunmehr auch in jenen Dimensionen eingesetzt werden können, die im praktischen Einsatz gefordert werden.

Literaturhinweise

[1] Zäpfel, G.: Produktionswirtschaft - Operatives Produktions-Management, Berlin New York 1982, S. 30 ff. und S. 290 ff.

[2] Preßmar, D.B.: Modelling of Dynamic Systems by Linear Programming and its Application to the Optimization of Production Processes, in: J.P. Brans (Hrsg.): Operational Research '84, Amsterdam-New York-Oxford 1984, S. 519-530

[3] Preßmar, D.B. und B. Jahnke: Efficient Approximations of Univariate Nonlinearities for Linear Planning Models, in: EJOR (European Journal of Operational Research), Amsterdam, Bd.1, Nr. 3, 1977, S. 185-203

[4] Neumann, K.: Operations Research Verfahren, Bd. 1, München-Wien 1975, S. 333 ff.

[5] IBM (Hrsg.): Mathematical Programming System Extended/370 (MPSX/370), Program Product 5740-XM3, o. J. und
SCICON (Hrsg.): SCICONIC/VM Mathematical Programming System, London 1984

[6] Neumann, K.: Operations Research Verfahren, Bd. 1, München-Wien 1975, S. 107 ff.

[7] Corona, A., Martini, C., Morando, S., Ridella, S. and C. Rolando: Solving linear equation systems on vector computers with maximum efficiency, in: Parallel Computing (1988), Vol. 8, Nr. 1-3, S. 133-139 und
Radicati, G.; Robert, Y. and P. Sguazzero: Dense linear systems FORTRAN solvers on the IBM 3090 vector multiprocessor, in: Parallel Computing (1988), Vol. 8, Nr. 1-3, S.377-384